Fostering Creativity in Children, K–8

Theory and Practice

EDITED BY

Mervin D. Lynch
Northeastern University

Carole Ruth Harris
*G.A.T.E.S. Research & Evaluation
and Northeastern University*

Allyn and Bacon
Boston • London • Toronto • Sydney • Tokyo • Singapore

T 66042

Senior Editor: Virginia Lanigan
Series Editorial Assistant: Jennifer Connors
Marketing Manager: Stephen Smith
Manufacturing Buyer: Suzanne Lareau

Copyright © 2001 by Allyn & Bacon
A Pearson Education Company
Needham Heights, MA 02494

Internet: www.abacon.com

Library of Congress Cataloging-in-Publication Data

Fostering creativity in children, K–8: theory and practice /
edited by Mervin D. Lynch, Carol Ruth Harris.
    p. cm.
    Includes bibliographical references and index.
    ISBN 0-205-30600-4
    1. Creative thinking—Study and teaching—United States. 2. Creative ability in
children—United States. I. Lynch, Mervin D. (date)   . II. Harris, Carole Ruth.
LB1590.5C73 2001
370.15′7—dc21

          99-052536

Printed in the United States of America
10   9   8   7   6   5   4   3   2   1   04   03   02   01   00

Contents

*This book is dedicated to
the contributing authors,
all of whom were a pleasure to work with*

*and to
Daphid, Maryl, and Eric Lynch
children of Mervin Lynch*

*and to
Laura, Heidi, Chuck, and Gary
children of Carole Ruth Harris and John N. Harris*

*and especially to
John N. Harris
who disentangled us from the computer traps*

Preface

Although aspects of the research on creativity complement each other, there has been little consensus on its definition. Creativity is a human characteristic, albeit an elusive one, frequently difficult to capture. Like the human mind, it has no boundaries. Attempts to develop creativity fully continue to challenge and even to confound the educator who must address it within the context of school time and be able to create objectives dedicated to the cognitive domain, and to the achievement of academic skills.

All too often the development of creativity remains beyond the reach of the confines of the classroom, as it hovers on its perimeters. When realized, creativity provides the impetus for connecting individuals to their own human uniqueness. Researchers weave snares to capture it for analysis, and educators continue to pursue it, for it is a rare and intriguing treasure, well worth the effort or you would not be reading this book.

The research focus of the last fifty years may be divided roughly into two 25-year time periods. From 1950 to 1975, the main focus was on the identification of personality traits or characteristics associated with creativity in adults. From 1975 to date the focus has been more on methods of developing talent in children.

The primary focus of this book is the identification of strategies that may be utilized by classroom teachers and other specialists who work with children in grades K–8 to nurture the development of creativity. Written in four sections, the book encompasses theory and practice, with a view to optimization of creative thinking along a continuum from the discovery of the presence of creativity to encouraging its growth, enhancing its attributes and characteristics, and strengthening creative productivity.

The four chapters in Section I are devoted to the delineation of general strategies that teachers may use to stimulate the growth of productive thinking in children grades K–8. Methods of presenting children with multiple options are suggested by Feldhusen, who in his chapter offers an array of methods to incorporate modeling and teaching creative behavior. The schoolwide enrichment program proposed by Reis and Renzulli offers a flexible approach to developing creativity utilizing alternative planning and strategies for the incorporating creative thinking through alternative structuring. The presentation of refutational strategies for the development of error detection rules is delineated by Lynch, Harris, and Williams in their chapter on utilizing refutation as an approach to creative thinking. Jane Piirto in her pyramid of talent development offers the development of precepts for parents and teachers, with focus on domains as the foundation for concrete application to successful nurturance of creative behavior.

The two chapters in Section II treat personality correlates of creative thinking with respect to selection and strategies for development of productive thinking capability and application. The chapter by Levin and Greenwald focuses on the rebelliousness and anti-conformity of children who develop their creative thinking talents late. In his chapter Farley associates risk-taking with individuals who have "Big T" personalities and proposes that there may be some genetic predisposition to the development of creativity through thrill-seeking behaviors.

Section III is dedicated to special populations, with two chapters on culturally different students and one chapter on learning disabilities. Baldwin's chapter suggests ways for educators to understand and recognize creative behaviors in students of African descent and utilize unique cultural aspects as a catalyst for unlocking creativity through classroom activities. In the chapter on fostering creativity in the Asian-Pacific child, Harris analyzes the complex factors associated with identification and offers culturally appropriate strategies for aiding creative development with respect to diversity within the Asian community. Phillips provides a research base for her chapter on creative development in children with learning disabilities, illuminated by case studies and field-based strategies for enhancement of innate and unrecognized attributes in this special population.

The seven chapters in Section IV are dedicated to the content areas. Creativity in science is treated as problem-based in the chapter by Plucker and Nowak, who illustrate how to encourage critical thinking coupled with technology directed to real-life multiple problems without an easily identifiable solution. The chapter on reading by Robinson illustrates ways in which teachers can intertwine various approaches to stimulating creativity within the teaching of reading, utilizing understanding, auditory and visual discrimination, and goal-directed exercises in sequencing and directionality to provide challenge. The multi-faceted nature of poetic expression, with its power to stimulate creative productivity, to reach inner thoughts and feelings, and to communicate with meaningful verbal articulation and artistry is presented by Harris in the chapter on poetry, with attention to sense-training as a vehicle for connecting poetry with the disciplines. In the chapter on the performing arts, Harris builds a framework for reaching aesthetic excellence through structured, interactive process, establishment of standards, responsibility, and control. Schulkind's chapter provides flexible scaffolding for all learning by stimulating creativity through establishment of the sound-symbol relationship and integration of music into the content areas. Clark and Zimmerman focus on frameworks for creative development in art, with emphasis on procedures for developing art talent and creativity through educational intervention.

The final chapter in this section, and in this book, is provided by Kaplan, who introduces the reader to the Math Circle, a program dedicated to creative inspiration through mathematics or, as Kaplan explains it, *rigor without mortis*.

Creativity is change because it reflects originality, and originality, by definition, is always new. Like the children in our charge who grow day by day, reaching for new things, discovering new powers, creativity shifts and changes. A mysterious source present in all human beings, creativity in the growing child attains new depths and reaches greater heights with each nurturing touch. In gathering this collection of experts in creativity, it is our hope that teachers and parents will find it a rich resource for all of the rewarding work that lies ahead of them in helping each child to find fulfillment in the realization of creative potential.

Mervin D. Lynch
Carole Ruth Harris

Acknowledgments

We wish to acknowledge the work of Mary Martin and Nicole Korodi in preparing the manuscripts and computer disks.

We also wish to acknowledge the especially helpful recommendations and comments made on the manuscript by Gary Davis. His comments and suggestions were right on target.

Our appreciation goes to the following reviewers for their comments on the manuscript: Amy P. Dietrich, The University of Memphis; Gary A. Davis, University of Wisconsin–Madison; and James H. Borland, Teachers College, Columbia University.

About the Editors

Mervin D. Lynch is Professor of Education and Director of Graduate Programs, Department of Education, Northeastern University, Boston, Massachusetts. He holds a Ph.D. in Mass Communications Research from the University of Wisconsin. He is founder, Executive Director, and President of the Association for Advancement of Educational Research, and President Elect of the National Academy of Educational Research. He was the founder and President of the Eastern Educational Research Association and President and Vice President of the New England Educational Research Organization. He has authored two books: *Elements of Statistical Inference in Education and Psychology* and *Self-Concept: Advances in Theory and Research.* He has authored four book chapters, more than 100 journal articles, and more than 300 conference papers. His distinguished awards include Social Science Research Council Fellow in Mathematical Statistics, Harvard University; Fellow of the Center for Innovation in Urban Education at Northeastern University; Founder of the Eastern Educational Research Association; and a national award with a colleague from the American Counseling Association for research on group processes. He has published extensively on the topic of creativity, inclusive of papers reporting on the development and validation of a creativity test for elementary grade level children and measures of affective reactions of children differing in levels of creativity on measures of anxiety, self-esteem, rigidity, and mathematics ability. He has published judgmental and correlate measures of creativeness in reading and writing, and has studied effects of creativity, task distribution, priming and incubation, and freedom of choice on stylistic and content measures of writing performance. He has taught at the Schools of Journalism at Indiana University and the University of Missouri and in the Department and School of Education at Northeastern University.

Carole Ruth Harris is Adjunct Professor of Education at Northeastern University, Boston, Massachusetts, and Director of G.A.T.E.S. Research & Evaluation, an independent consulting firm specializing in evaluation, educational counseling, and individualized curriculum design for gifted and talented children. She holds the Doctorate from Columbia University, where she studied with A. Harry Passow, Abraham Tannenbaum, and F. A. J. Ianni. Formerly Associate in Education at Harvard University and researcher on the Hollingworth Longitudinal Study at Teachers College, Columbia University, she has taught education of the gifted at the University of Hawaii and education of the gifted, creativity, and qualitative research methods at University of Massachusetts–Lowell. Founder of the Ebeye Center for Gifted and Talented in the Marshall Islands under the auspices of the Research Corporation of the University of Hawaii, she lived and worked in Micronesia for several years. She was Master Teacher of Creative Writing and Humanities at the BOCES Institute for Talented Youth and taught English in the New York City Public Schools. The author of more than 40 articles and book chapters, she has presented more than 115 conference papers and appeared as an invited speaker at national and international conferences. An active member of the National Association for Gifted Children and recipient of the Gowan award, she serves on the Asian Pacific section of the Special Populations Division. She has served as co-vice chair of the International Children's Network of World Council for Gifted and Talented Children, and is a member of The Association of the Gifted/CEC, CIES, MA/AIP, APA, AAER, KDP, and the Hollingworth Center for the highly gifted. Dr. Harris was recently named as a Fellow of NAER and director of symposiums at AAER and SIG chair of Gifted, Talented and Creative at EERA. Her special focus is the disadvantaged and culturally different, immigrant and refugee populations, international studies, ethnography, qualitative research, and interdisciplinary curriculum design for asynchronous highly and profoundly gifted. Her poems have been published in various literary journals. The student anthology, *Catch Me a Poem*, and other student anthologies written under her direction, have received wide attention in magazines and journals directed to creativity and teaching creative children. She was also a poet-in-the-schools in Long Island, New York.

CEC = Council for Exceptional Children
CIES = Comparative and International Education Society
NAER = National Academy of Educational Research
AAER = Association for the Advancement of Educational Research
SIG = Special Interest Group
EERA = Eastern Educational Research Association
MA/AIP = Massachusetts Association for the Advancement of Individual Potential
APA = American Psychological Association
AERA = American Educational Research Association
KDP = Kappa Delta Pi

About the Contributors

Alexinia Young Baldwin, Ph.D., Professor, Department of Curriculum and Instruction, University of Connecticut, Storrs, Connecticut, is an elected member of Board of Directors of the National Association for the Gifted (NAGC). She is a former president of The Association of the Gifted (TAG) and is one of three elected U.S. delegates to the World Council for the Gifted and Talented (WCGT). She has served as Associate Editor and member of the Editorial Board of *Exceptional Children*. She is a member of the Advisory Board of the journal *Understanding Our Gifted*. Her university teaching and research have been centered around the identification of the gifted and designing curriculum with special emphasis on the gifted minority child. The Baldwin Identification Matrix was designed to help identify children of minority groups. Recent publications include but are not limited to *Gifted Black Adolescents: Beyond Racism to Pride and Accomplishments*; *Ethnic and Cultural Issues*; *Teachers of the Gifted*; *Affective Concerns for Gifted Minority Students*; and *The Many Faces of the Gifted: Lifting the Masks*.

Dr. Gilbert A. Clark investigates art curriculum theory and development, child development in art, test development, and assessment of learning and programs in art and gifted education. He has helped develop several major curriculum projects in art and is author of more than sixty articles in professional and popular journals, five books, and a number of monographs in art education and gifted/talented education. His books include *Art/Design: Communicating Visually* (with E. Zimmerman), *Educating Artistically Talented Students* (with E. Zimmerman and M. Zurmuehlen), and *Understanding Art Testing* (with E. Zimmerman and M. Zurmuehlen). His articles and monographs include "Discipline Based Art Education: Becoming Students of Art" (with M. Day and D. W. Greer) (in *Journal of Aesthetic Education Examining Discipline Based Art Education as a Curriculum Construct* (ERIC/ART) and "The Influence of Theoretical Frameworks on Clark and Zimmerman's Research About Art Education" in *Journal of Aesthetic Education*. He has been an invited speaker or workshop director in more than fourteen countries and has served as a World Councilor for the International Society for Education Through Art (INSEA). Clark is a Professor Emeritus of art education and Gifted/ Talented Education, Indiana University, School of Education.

Frank Farley is the Laura Cannell Professor at Temple University, Philadelphia. Prior to this, he was on the faculty at the University of Wisconsin–Madison from 1966 to 1994. He received a Ph.D. in psychology in 1966 from the Institute of Psychiatry, University of London, England. He is a past President of the American Psychological Association (APA) and the American Educational Research Association (AERA). He is currently President of the National Academy of Educational Research and APA's Division of General Psychology, President-elect of APA's Division of Media Psychology, and Vice President of the Federation of Behavioral, Psychological and Cognitive Sciences. He holds the E. L. Thorndike Award for Distinguished Contributions of Psychology in Education. He is a Fellow of the American Association for the Advancement of Science, New York Academy of Sciences, APA. His bibliography exceeds 200 publications, including six books. His work has been reported by *Time Magazine, U.S. News and World Report, The New York Times, The Wall Street Journal, USA Today*, and *20/20*.

John F. Feldhusen is Robert B. Kane Distinguished Professor of Education at Purdue University and director of the Purdue Gifted Education Resource Institute. He has authored books and articles on gifted education and talent development, is a former editor of *Gifted Child Quarterly*, and a former editor of *Gifted and Talented International*, the journal of the World Council for Gifted and Talented Children. He is a fellow of the American Psychological Association and, among many other awards, received a Distinguished Scholar award from the National Association for Gifted Children.

Nina L. Greenwald, Ph.D., is an educational psychologist in the Graduate Program of Critical and Creative Thinking at the University of Massachusetts, Boston, who specializes in creativity, teaching thinking, gifted education, multiple intelligences, humor, and problem-based learning. A national teacher trainer, workshop leader, and keynote speaker, she has also appeared on radio and television. Greenwald has published articles on creativity and gifted education, and problem-solving curricula for The National Institutes of Health, American Medical Association, Massachusetts Society for Medical Research, New England Aquarium, and public television (*NOVA*). She is an adviser for the Museum of Science, Boston, helping to develop interactive exhibits that engage visitors in active problem solving. Her thinking about this has been reviewed in the AAAS journal, *Science*. Greenwald is a member of the Danforth Associates of New England (distinguished higher-education teachers), was director of critical thinking programs for a major educational collaborative, and is a co-founder and former president of The Massachusetts Association for Advancement of Individual Potential (MA/AIP), an advocacy/ educational organization on behalf of gifted students. Currently she is writing a problem-based learning textbook for high school students created from interviews with leading biomedical researchers and physicians from Boston hospitals.

Robert Kaplan, although his work is centered in mathematics and philosophy, has also taught German, Greek, and Sanskrit and courses on Aspects of Psychology, Theories of Mind, and Inspired Guessing. These courses have been not only within the context of Harvard, but at various primary and secondary schools in the Greater Boston Area. In 1994, along with his wife, Ellen, he founded The Math Circle, of which he is the President. Both have given presentations on it in Zürich, Barcelona, Edinburgh, and at the 1997 Convention of the American Mathematical Society, in whose *Notices* his article on The Math Circle appeared (September 1995). He is on the Advisory Board of the Mathematical Foundation of America, has been the yearly keynote speaker at the Center for Talented Youth's Boston meeting since 1995, and has lectured at the Hollingworth Center. He was in the first group of Distinguished Teaching Fellows at Harvard in 1996, and is a member of the Leverett House Senior Common Room. Awards include excellence in teaching at Harvard, 1994 through 1997. His book, *The Nothing That Is: A Natural History of Zero*, was published by Oxford University Press in 1999.

Jack Levin, Ph.D., is the Irving and Betty Brudnick Professor of Sociology and Criminology at Northeastern University, where he directs its Program for the Study of Violence and Conflict. He has written nineteen books, including *Hate Crimes: The Rising Tide of Bigotry and Bloodshed* (1993, with J. McDevitt), *Overkill: Mass Murder and Serial Killing Exposed* (1996, with J. Fox), *Killer on Campus* (1996, with J. Fox), *Elementary Statistics in Social Research* (1996, with J. Fox), and *Sociological Snapshots,* 3d edition (1999). He has also written numerous articles in professional journals and major newspapers. Levin is past president of the New England Sociological Association and past vice president of the Eastern Sociological Society. He appears frequently on national television programs including *Today, Good Morning America, Unsolved Mysteries*, *48 Hours, 20/20, Oprah*, and *Larry King Live*. He has served as an expert witness or consultant in a number of trials, and has given hundreds of addresses to community, university, and professional groups, including the recently held White House Conference on Hate Crimes.

Jeffrey A. Nowak, M.S., is a doctoral student in science education at Indiana University. He is an experienced geologist and high school science teacher, and he is active in the Hoosier Association of Science Teachers, Inc. He is currently concerned with the effectiveness of applying principles of problem-based learning to geology and earth sciences education.

Amy L. Phillips, Ph.D., is assistant professor of early childhood and special education at Wheelock College. She co-develops, teaches, and supervises in the early childhood certification program, now combining regular and special education and a new interprofessional program across education, social work, and child life (a health profession) in which students work in partnership with citizens, schools, health, and community-based organizations in Roxbury, Massachusetts. She edited *Playing for Keeps: Supporting Children's Play* for Redleaf Press in 1996 and co-wrote the City of Boston's Blue Ribbon Commission for Community Learning Center's Elementary Education Report, which situates integrated education, health, and social services within a ten-year master plan for rebuilding the Boston public school infrastructure. She was the architects' educational consultant for the prototype document for three new early education centers recommended by the Blue Ribbon Commission, focusing on the physical realization of the community-based model. She is writing a book featuring insights of youngsters with autism at League School of Boston with whom she taught art, did play, art, cognitive, behavioral, and psychodynamic therapies, and for whom she developed schoolwide curriculum to support visuo-spatial and creative strengths and served on inter-professional/family support teams.

Jane Piirto is a Trustees Professor at Ashland University, Ashland, Ohio. She teaches in the Department of Graduate Education and is the Director of Talent Development Education. She has been a high school and college teacher of English and French, a counselor, a coordinator, and the principal of the Hunter College Elementary School in New York City. She has taught and spoken throughout the United States and internationally, in southern Asia, South America, and Finland. An award-winning novelist and poet, she has written eight books, among them *Understanding Those Who Create* (Gifted Psychology Press), *Talented Children and Adults: Their Development and Education* (Prentice-Hall/Merrill), and *A Location in the Upper Peninsula: Collected Poems, Essays, and Stories* (Sampo Publishing). Her most recent is *My Teeming Brain: Creativity in Creative Writers* (Hampton Press). She has two grown children.

Jonathan A. Plucker, Ph.D., is an assistant professor of learning, cognition, and instruction at Indiana University. A former elementary and high school science teacher, he is interested in the study and enhancement of creativity, especially as manifest in science and technology. He is active in the National Association for Gifted Children and Division 10 (Arts and Psychology) of the American Psychological Association and serves on the editorial boards of *Journal of Research on Science Teaching* and *Gifted Child Quarterly*.

Sally M. Reis is a Professor of Educational Psychology at the University of Connecticut, where she serves as Principal Investigator of the National Research Center on the Gifted and Talented. She was a teacher for fifteen years, eleven of which were spent working with gifted students at the elementary, junior high, and high school levels. She has authored more than seventy articles, five books, twenty-three book chapters, and numerous monographs and technical reports. She has traveled extensively across the country conducting workshops and providing in-service training for school districts designing gifted programs based on the Enrichment Triad Model and the Revolving Door Identification Model. She is co-author of *The Revolving Door Identification Model, The Schoolwide Enrichment Model, The Secondary Triad Model, The Triad Reader,* and a new book published in 1998 about gifted females entitled *Work Left Undone.* Sally serves on the editorial board of the *Gifted Child Quarterly* and is the president-elect of the National Association for Gifted Children.

Joseph S. Renzulli is the Neag Professor of Gifted Education and Talent Development at the University of Connecticut, where he serves as the Director of the National Research Center on the Gifted and Talented. He has served on numerous editorial boards in the fields of gifted education, educational psychology, research, law, and education; and he also served as a Senior Research Associate for the White House Task Force on Education for the Gifted and Talented. His major research interests are in identification and programming models for both gifted education and general school improvement. His Enrichment Triad Model has been cited as the most widely used approach for special programs for the gifted and talented. The Three Ring Conception of Giftedness, which he developed in the early 1970s, is considered to be the foundation of a more flexible approach to identifying and developing high levels of potential in young people. He has contributed numerous books and articles to the professional literature and has been a series author with the Houghton Mifflin Reading Series. His two most recent books are *Schools for Talent Development: A Practical Plan for Total School Improvement* (Renzulli, 1994) and *The Schoolwide Enrichment Model: A How-To Guide for Educational Excellence* (Renzulli & Reis, 1997). He lists his proudest accomplishment as the Annual Summer Confratute Program at the University of Connecticut, which originated in 1978 and has served more than 8,000 persons from around the world.

Dr. Joyce McPeake Robinson has worked in the areas of English reading and study skills for some thirty years. Her present position is Head of The Dwight School in New York City. A member of Pi Lambda Theta, she received an achievement award from the National Council of Teachers of English and outstanding teacher recognition from The English Speaking Union, National League of American Pen Women and the Propeller Club. Previously membership chair of the Eastern Educational Research Association, she is currently membership chair of The Association for the Advancement of Educational Research and a member of the National Academy for Educational Research. The author of *Wordworks* and editor of *How to Double Your Child's Grades in School,* she has contributed articles to newspapers and periodicals. She also has presented papers at national and local conferences. She received her doctorate in Reading and Language and her Master of Arts Degree in English from Boston University. She holds a Bachelor of Arts Degree in English from Tufts University.

Laura M. Schulkind, M.M., holds a Bachelor of Science from Colorado State University, and a Master of Music in Flute Performance from the University of Northern Colorado. An active performer and teacher, she has performed internationally, at the Aspen Music Festival, and in the Denver metropolitan area. She is currently teaching fourth grade and English as a second language and completing a Master of Education in Literacy at the University of Colorado at Boulder.

Eugenie N. Williams is currently a middle school teacher of Physical Science at the Williams Middle School in Chelsea, Massachusetts, who completed an M.Ed. degree in June 1998 in Educational Research at Northeastern University in Boston. Eugenie has been involved extensively with the Caribbean Examinations Council–Barbados in syllabus preparation/design, educational testing, and evaluation. She has co-authored several science textbooks that are now being used in Caribbean schools. She has more than twenty years' experience in science education and brings to this project a strong interest in how students develop conceptual understandings in science.

Enid Zimmerman is a Professor and Coordinator of Art Education and Gifted and Talented Education at Indiana University School of Education. She has published more than ninety articles, fifteen book chapters, and co-authored twenty-two books and monographs including *Art/Design, Communicating Visually, Artstrands: A program for Individualized Art Instruction, Women Art Educators I, II, III, IV, Educating Artistically Talented Students, Understanding Art Testing, Issues and Practices Related to Identification of Gifted and Talented Students in the Visual Arts, Programming Opportunities for Students Talented in the Visual Arts,* and *Research Methods and Methodologies for Art Education.* Enid Zimmerman was a committee member for the National Art Teacher Exam and Consultant to the National Board of Professional Teaching Standards. She is Chair of the National Art Education Association (NAEA) Commission on Research and an International Society for Art Education World Councilor. She received the NAEA Barkan Research Award, the NAEA Women's Caucus Rouse and McFee Awards, and the National Association for Gifted Children's Paper of the Year Award. She was named Indiana Art Educator, NAEA Western Region and Higher Education Division Art Educator, NAEA Distinguished Fellow, and in 1998 NAEA National Art Educator.

Biographical Sketch of Colum Roznik

Colum Roznik, aged 11, designed the cover art when he was eight years old. Colum has been drawing and painting since the age of four. Colum was born in Canada. He and his parents came to the United States in 1995 and settled in Lexington, Massachusetts. Colum was enrolled in a public school where he was diagnosed as suffering from auditory processing disorder and as an underachiever with average intelligence.

At G.A.T.E.S. Research & Evaluation, he was evaluated and found to be much above average intellectually, with high creativity scores. An interdisciplinary, customized curriculum designed for Colum by Dr. Carole Ruth Harris, with a central focus around his interest in flowers, was implemented by G.A.T.E.S. mentor Dr. Patricia Sollner. Colum would learn through his creative strengths, during curriculum implementation, after he was finished attending class in the Lexington school.

The family moved to North Carolina in mid-semester and Colum's analysis was referred to school authorities there. In his new school, they were enthusiastic about helping Colum to reach his potential and gave him much encouragement. Colum now attends a special magnet school for the arts and has blossomed academically, reading well beyond his grade level and achieving consistently.

Colum's art work, evaluated by experts Gilbert Clark and Enid Zimmerman in 1997, was considered to be "remarkable for such a young child, with special strengths in asymmetrically balanced designs, rich, vivid use of color, the creation of decorative patterning in intricately detailed compositions." Colum continues to pursue his early interest in fashion design, but while he is still able to create elaborate, detailed costumes that are imaginative and unique, his interests have expanded to other art areas and he is encouraged to augment his ability and experiment with a variety of mediums.

Introduction

MERVIN D. LYNCH   CAROLE RUTH HARRIS

The variable of creativity has been widely treated in the literature during the past fifty years. Despite its extensive written treatment, there is little consensus on what it is and/or how it may be developed. The major focus from 1950 to 1975 was on the identification of characteristics of the creative individual; that is, those characteristics that differentiated individuals working in creative occupations like art, poetry, literature, and theater from those working in more mundane occupations (Guilford, 1950, 1956, 1967; MacKinnon, 1956; Maslow, 1959; Rogers, 1961). These studies were made primarily with adults as opposed to children perhaps because adults as opposed to children could be identified with occupations labeled as more or less creative in their products.

From 1975 to date, the focus has been more to identify strategies with which to foster the development of talent for creative productivity in children. Some writers (Feldman, 1980, 1982; Gardner,1983a, 1985a, 1993a, 1998) proposed that all children have creative ability and that we need only to remove the barriers to creative expression in order to foster its development. Other writers proposed that creative thinking is productive thinking and that we need to design strategies with which to develop the talent for productive thinking in children (Feldhusen, 1991, 1993, 1994b, 1995, 1996; Renzulli, 1976, 1977, 1986; Renzulli & Reis, 1994, 1997). These writers have also provided some indications of strategies that may be used to stimulate productive thinking, and these represent a substantial step towards fostering the growth and development of creative talent.

A Brief History of Creativity Research

Descriptions of creativity in children reflect the disparate views of those who have attempted definitions. Creativity has been variously defined as need achievement (McClelland, Atkinson, & Clark, 1953), a tendency to self-actualize (Goldstein,

1939; Maslow; 1954, 1959; Rogers, 1959), cleverness (Stephenson, 1967), divergent thinking (Guilford, 1950, 1956, 1959, 1967, 1986), and bisociative activity (Koestler, 1964).

At least three different theoretical approaches to the study of creativity applicable to children have been described in the literature: cognitive (Sternberg, 1988a, 1997), divergent thinking (Guilford, 1950, 1956, 1967), and associative thinking (Koestler, 1964; Lynch & Edwards, 1974; Maltzman, 1960; Mednick, 1962).

Guilford (1956, 1959, 1967), as part of more general research on the structure of the intellect, characterized creativity in terms of six multidimensional constructs: fluency of thinking, flexibility of thinking, originality, sensitivity to problems, redefinition, and elaboration. He differentiated between two major modes of thinking: convergent thinking representing one solution to a problem or one restricted path to a solution, and divergent thinking representing multiple solutions to a problem or multiple paths to one solution.

Sternberg (1988, 1997) proposed that creativity is the style with which we use our intelligence. Facets of creativity may be found in aspects of intelligence, the application of intelligence in a creative, statistically unusual, and highly appropriate way; in the ways it is utilized in thoughts and actions, especially in legislative forms of mental self-government; and in personality attributes that are more conducive to creative performance than others, such as: (1) tolerance for ambiguity, (2) willingness to surmount obstacles; (3) willingness to grow; (4) intrinsic motivation, (5) moderate risk-taking, (6) desire for recognition, and (7) willingness to work for recognition.

Koestler (1964), in the third theoretical approach—association theory—proposed a process called bisociation that underlies every creative process. In this process, previously unaligned matrices of thought are placed in parallel contiguity and novel associations are drawn. Mednick (1962) defined creative thinking as the formation of associative elements into new combinations that meet specific requirements. For Mednick, a person who is more, as opposed to less, creative would produce more novel associations, and would have a moderately flat, as opposed to steep, associative gradient as shown in free association tasks.

Domains of Creativity

The theories of creativity discussed so far treated creativity as a unidimensional variable with many facets, and held that scores on many creativity tests measure a variable that falls within one general domain (Guilford, 1956, 1959, 1967, 1986; Lynch & Edwards, 1974; Mednick, 1962; Torrance, 1977, 1988, 1990). For Guilford as well as the others cited, children will have higher or lower levels of creative ability on this one dimension. Some of Torrance's research would suggest that this may be the factor of originality.

Other theorists (Feldman, 1980, 1982a; Gardner, 1983, 1993a) proposed that creativity is both multidimensional and domain specific. For Gardner, a creative individual is rarely creative across the board but rather has creativity developed in specific domains such that one could be creative in mathematics but not in painting, in writing but not in carpentry. According to Gardner, a creative individual is one who regularly solves problems, fashions products, and/or poses new questions in a domain in a way that is initially considered novel but that is ultimately accepted in a cultural setting.

Other writers (Amabile, 1982; Amabile & Tighe, 1993) have proposed that creativity is both domain general and specific. For Amabile, creativity is composed of three components: (1) domain-relevant skills composed of factual knowledge, technical skills, and special talents—the individual's complete set of response possibilities that provide the set of cognitive pathways for solving problems or doing tasks; (2) creativity-relevant skills, such as cognitive style, application of heuristics for exploration of new cognitive pathways and working style, breaking perceptual set, breaking cognitive set, understanding complexities, keeping response options open as long as possible, suspending judgment, using wide categories of judgment, remembering accurately, perceiving creatively, and breaking out of performance scripts; and (3) task motivation inclusive of motivational variables that determine an individual's approach to a given task—specifically intrinsic motivation.

An underlying notion of the concept of domains is that the primary effort of a creative individual will be to produce a creative product. It is quite likely that a person who has creative ability but no manual dexterity will not become a creative artist or even pianist. On the other hand, the creative individual may still recognize and appreciate the work of creative persons in all media. Lynch & Kaufman (1974) carried out a study of creativeness judgment using the Remote Associates Test as a measure of creative aptitude, a diverse sampling of written materials, and Q-sort methodology in which respondents sorted materials along a continuum from most to least creative. Findings of their study showed one general typology of creativeness judgment that was defined singularly by individuals of moderate to high as opposed to low creative aptitude. The authors proposed that creative individuals may have a restricted language code such that more creative persons may recognize creative products whereas less creatives may not be able to do so.

Intelligence versus Creativity

The relationship between creativity and intelligence has been widely discussed in the literature. In general, authors have held that creativity and intelligence are moderately correlated but different cognitive variables (Barron, 1969; Getzels & Jackson, 1962; Wallach & Kogan, 1965). Getzels & Jackson (1962) studied the correlational and mean relationships between creativity and IQ test scores for 533 students and found a moderate correlation of $r = .40$ for the IQ/creativity relationship.

When they compared mean IQ scores for high IQ and high creative groups, the mean IQ was 150 for the high IQ and 127 for the high creatives. Terman & Merrill (1937), in the reconstruction and validation of the Binet intelligence test, claimed that those who were at the genius level of IQ—150 plus—did not exhibit the same characteristic of emotional instability as that attributed to high creatives in the literature. Instead, as was later supported by follow-up research by Terman & Oden (1947), high-IQ geniuses were calm, logically ordered, nonemotional, and nonrebellious. Terman & Merrill argued that because of this, the literary definition of genius was likely incorrect. It is more likely that Terman & Merrill were incorrect, not the literary definition, because most high creatives—that is, those who might be called geniuses in the literature—likely had IQ scores in the superior, not genius, range of intelligence.

Typically, correlations between creativity and intelligence measures have ranged between r = .20 and r = .35, which is the range of correlations we found in the development of the Miniscat measure of creativity (1974). In that study, Lynch and Edwards (1974) examined correlations of the Miniscat measure of children's creativity to CATB intelligence test scores and found correlations as follows: r = .20 between creativity and language IQ; r = .35 between creativity and nonlanguage IQ, and r = .27 between creativity and total IQ.

Product versus Process

Some writers have proposed that creativity is a product or content phenomenon, bringing something new into birth. Laswell (1959) defined creativity as the disposition to make and to recognize valuable innovations. Gardner (1993a) proposed a product definition asserting that there is no evidence to support a personality trait of creativity and that all individuals have an ability to be creative as recognized by expert judgments of their products. He proposed a "big C" and "small c" for creative productions, where "small c" stands for the creative productions we do daily and "big C" stands for the creative productivity that occurs very infrequently.

Other writers, for the most part, have treated creativity as a process and not a product (Maslow, 1959; May, 1959; Rogers, 1959; Sternberg, 1988a, 1997). Vivas (1955) proposed that what creative persons do is not to invent something new, but to extricate out of the subject matter at hand its own proper structure or order. Sternberg (1997) described creativity as a process for the application of intelligence in a statistically unusual and highly appropriate way, along with the way intelligence is used in one's thoughts and actions.

Some Characteristics of the Creative Child

Numerous characteristics of the creative person have been identified in the literature that are applicable to children. These include affective characteristics such as anxiety and self-esteem, freedom of choice and openness to encounter, desire for social acceptance, rebelliousness, tolerance for ambiguity, a preference for challenge, intrinsic motivation, and a risk-taking preference.

Anxiety and Self-Esteem

The creative child may operate under higher levels of anxiety and self-esteem than other children. Barron (1969) administered a battery of personality tests to a group of persons identified as creative and found that high as opposed to low creatives were higher on both levels of anxiety and of self-esteem. He found that anxiety levels of high creatives were sufficiently high as to appreciably impair performance. However, high levels of self-esteem acted as a compensatory factor, enabling the highly creative person to perform productively with these high levels of anxiety. That self-esteem or self-concept would play this compensatory role is supported in writings of Coopersmith (1967), who proposed that high levels of self-esteem are essential for creative expression.

Freedom of Choice

Some writers (Maslow, 1959; Rogers, 1959) have written extensively about the greater openness to experience and encounter, the internal as opposed to external locus of evaluation, and an ability to toy with elements and concepts of the creative as opposed to less creative person. The creative child may also demand a greater freedom of choice and openness to encounter.

Freedom of choice or encounter is not a one-sided freedom. Rogers (1959) suggested that it is the permission to be free, to be free to be afraid of a new venture as well as to be free to entertain it, free to bear the consequences of his or her mistakes and as well free to make mistakes. Freedom thus permits encountering bad as well as good and challenge as well as boredom, and presumes a responsible balance between available choices and the child's needs at the moment.

Social Acceptance

The creative child is likely more reliant than other children on his or her own ideas, but also seems more motivated toward and preoccupied with communicating his or her ideas with others and gaining social acceptance and social empathy, especially with peers. Rogers (1959) proposed that the creative person will exhibit a need for greater communication and empathy. Barron (1969) proposed that whereas the creative person challenges others in a rebellious fashion, he or she will still be motivated by social acceptance of his or her products. According to Sternberg (1997), the creative person has a strong desire and willingness to work for recognition. Further support for the need for social acceptance has been shown in studies of high and low creative adolescent and elementary grade level children (Lynch, 1997; Lynch & Lynch, 1996).

Rebelliousness

Many authors have written about the defiance of authority or convention that is typical of the creative person (Hilgard, 1959; MacKinnon, 1961, 1978a; May, 1959; Stoddard, 1959). Carlyle (1959) referred to creative genius as a transcendent capacity for making trouble. Creative children likely exhibit similar forms of rebellion in the educational setting and this behavior brings the creative child into direct conflict with authoritarian and more regimented teachers and school administrators.

Tolerance for Ambiguity

According to Sternberg (1997), the majority of creative people must learn to tolerate ambiguity and incompleteness in the development of creative products. Others (Gruber, 1982, 1993; Gruber & Davis, 1988; Vernon, 1970) have argued that tolerance for ambiguity is a necessity for creative performance. Creative children tend to be somewhat impulsive as opposed to reflective and as a result will often attempt to achieve premature closure in carrying out the creative process. The creative child needs guidance to learn to discipline this behavior so as to keep search processes open during the creative process and thus achieve creatively productive behavior.

Preference for Challenge

The desire for complexity and challenge has often been described as a characteristic of the creative person (Barron, 1969; Heinzen, 1989; Voss & Means, 1989). The desire of the creative child to be challenged is in part shown by the humorous reactions often exhibited by the creative child in response to the presentation of paradoxical thinking. It is also exhibited in the playing of computer games in which the reward for solving one game is the presentation of a more challenging game (Pappert, 1996).

Intrinsic Motivation

The importance of intrinsic motivation for the creative person has been suggested by Amabile (1983a) and support shown in subsequent studies reported by Hennessey (1997) and Hennessey and Amabile (1997). It is a truism that most if not all children tend to be motivated to learn when they enter school and that somehow schools tend to extinguish this motivation during the first three years of school. Creative children, in contrast to most other children, tend to be self-motivated both in terms of pleasing themselves and in terms of self-rewards.

Risk-Taking Behaviors

The tendency for creative persons to take risks has often been noted in the literature (Barron, 1969; McClelland, 1958; Sternberg, 1988a). Farley (1991, 1998) describes a personality trait labeled the "Type T" personality as a tendency toward thrill-seeking behavior. It is likely that highly creative children will also exhibit this tendency toward thrill-seeking or risk-taking behavior. McClelland (1958) found that children who were high as opposed to low in need achievement, which he defined synonymously with creativity, exhibited higher levels of risk-taking behavior.

Taylor, Smith, & Ghiselin (1963) found that such risk-taking behavior was especially prevalent among successful scientists. Sternberg (1997) also proposed that creative persons will have higher levels of risk-taking behavior but that they will have a sense of acceptable levels of risk. The highly creative child will likely exhibit risk-taking and thrill-seeking behavior. For instance, he or she may jump off high structures, swim in dangerous areas, and ski in areas that are off-limits. Perhaps it is by means of these out-of-bounds areas of expression that the creative child finds out the acceptable limits of risk-taking behavior; teachers will need to assist them in these exploration and limit-setting processes.

Creativity Testing

But who is the creative child? Can one test for creativity? Creativity "testing" is actually a gauge of potential that can be developed because of the way in which a person thinks or the uniqueness in the way someone might approach a question or situation.

There are a number of such tests that are useful. Among these are those that concentrate on characteristics, or personality traits, biographical gauges, multidimensional instruments, indices that encompass preference; that is, likes and dislikes in combination with characteristics—and those that are theory-derived, such as Torrance (1966, 1988, 1990), who concentrates on originality, fluency, elaboration, resistance to closure, imagination, synthesis, and divergent thinking. The Torrance tests are verbal or figural, or, in the case of young children, also derive from approach, such as movement.

Torrance Tests of Creativity

Torrance (1966, 1988, 1990) chose four theoretical constructs identified by Guilford—fluency, originality, flexibility, and elaboration—and constructed a creativity test to use with individuals in grades K–12. The Torrance tests, according to a survey of Torrance and Presbury (1984), have been used in more than 75 percent of the published research on creativity for elementary and secondary school students, and in more than 40 percent of published studies for college students and adults.

The Miniscat Measure of Creativity

One of the more easily administered tests is the Miniscat measure produced by Lynch and Edwards (1974). The Miniscat is available in two forms of twenty items each. This test provides one creativity score based on a child's parallel associative processing—that is, the child's ability to identify compound associates using different syntactic and semantic associative paths. Lynch and Edwards have provided evidence on both its validity and its reliability.

Rimm's GIFT, GIFF1, and PRIDE Tests for Creativity

One of the most useful instruments for determining characteristics of creative children is the Rimm GIFT, with GIFFI used for grades 7 and 8, and PRIDE used for preschool and/or kindergarten (Rimm, 1980, 1981; Rimm & Culbertson; Rimm &

Davis, 1976, 1980, 1985; Rimm, Davis, & Bien, 1982). Easy to administer and non-threatening, requiring only yes or no answers, these instruments concentrate on preference and personality characteristics, and assess interests, independence, and imagination, and, in older children, values associated with creativity, such as challenge, independence, confidence, and inventiveness. PRIDE is for preschool and is directed to parents, who answer the inventory.

Behavioral Observations

Clark (1979) proposed identification of attributes of the creative child that become apparent during the course of classroom interaction. Among these may be noted the child who is self-disciplined, has a zany sense of humor, is able to resist group pressure, and exhibits adaptability. The child who is adventurous, with a tolerance for ambiguity and discomfort, a low tolerance for boredom, and a preference for complexity, asymmetry, open-endedness, divergent thinking, and attention to detail, is likely to be creative.

Creativity Rating Scales

There are two basic types of rating scales for creativity. One type identifies characteristics of creativity. Scales for creativity need not use numerical values or letter "grades" but can make use of constructive criticism, which actually *encourages* creativity and excellence in stimulating refinement in linguistic expression. In teaching, and in trying to stimulate creativity in language arts, for instance, the use of rating scales is important; however, this should be developmental, qualitative, student-centered, and individualized as well as product-oriented. Wigginton (1986), for instance, both writes letters and journals and uses scales of creativity by demanding standards of his students.

Conclusions

Most conceptions of creativity are certainly not neat, and do not fall into logical, straightforward patterns; however, they describe a quintessentially human characteristic. Although Eliot's poetry on cats is creative, one may not say that the animals that inspired it have even a modicum of creativity. Creativity has attributes, stages, and a genetic basis. It is influenced by environment; however, to such a degree that the environment does not foster creativity, then the attribute will probably not be optimized. At worst, it will be lost. It therefore devolves on those who have the opportunity to encourage its growth to do so, and parents, teachers, mentors, and schools have both the obligation and the rewarding task to nurture it for the sake of a fuller, more enriched world with fulfilled children as they make their way through the early years of learning. This book is dedicated to the development of talent for creative thinking in children in the hope that teachers, parents, and mentors may find it especially useful in their work with talented children.

Section *I*

Teaching for Creative Growth

The development of a child's talent to be creatively productive or to recognize creative products is the focus of the chapters in Section I. Four chapters presented in this section present procedures for stimulating the development and growth of creative talent. These include chapters in which Feldhusen emphasizes multiple options approaches; Reis and Renzulli present schoolwide enrichment programs; Lynch, Harris, and Williams discuss uses of refutational processes; and Piirto presents both parent and school practices.

Feldhusen in Chapter 1, entitled "Multiple Options as a Model for Teaching the Creatively Talented Child," proposes that creative thinking is productive thinking with a continuum of creativity ranging from the new and useful—such as solutions to problems or works of art—to ideas and solutions that enhance daily living. Feldhusen states that the school's primary mission is to teach declarative and procedural knowledge and productive motivations. For Feldhusen, creative thinking manifests itself through talents that emerge from general physical and intellectual abilities.

Reis and Renzulli in Chapter 2, entitled "The Schoolwide Enrichment Model: Developing Students' Creativity and Talents," propose that creative productivity is the interaction among three clusters—above-average ability, task commitment, and creativity. They suggest that teachers modify instruction based on student interests and that this will foster the development of creatively productive talents in three ways: (1) student interests can help teachers identify highly motivating, representative topics that address core curriculum objectives; (2) student interests can help teachers offer alternative resources, a choice of assignments, and homework activities that will enrich the students' development; and (3) student interests can help teachers plan individual enrichment activities that a child may not be able to identify. The principles that underlie the recommendations of Reis and

Renzulli are: each learner is unique; learning is more effective when students enjoy what they are doing; learning is more meaningful and enjoyable when the content learned is that of a real and present problem. A major goal of this approach is to enhance knowledge and thinking skill acquisition that result from students' own constructions of meaning.

Lynch, Harris, and Williams in Chapter 3, entitled "Stimulating the Development of Talent for Creative Productivity in Children through the Use of Refutational Processes," propose that exposing children through systematic instruction to grammatical or conceptual errors that they are expected to refute will stimulate the development of talent for creative productivity and its recognition. The use of refutational processes for this purpose, the authors suggest, will involve the use of higher-order mental activities such as those involved in creative production, including: error-detection procedures, error-resolution procedures, heightened ego-strength or self-concept, increased levels of intrinsic motivation, and increased reliance on humor associated with incongruities or errors. They provide examples of refutational uses that may be used in instruction in language arts, history and social studies, and mathematics at grade levels from kindergarten through grade 8.

Piirto in Chapter 4, entitled "How Parents and Teachers Can Enhance Creativity in Children," presents twelve procedures for enhancing creativity based on her Pyramid of Talent Development Model: provide a private place for work to be done; provide materials with which to work; encourage and display the child's work; do your own creative work and let your child see it; set a creative tone; value the creative work of others; discuss your family mythology; avoid emphasizing sex-role stereotypes; use life's hardships positively; emphasize that talent is only a small part of creative production and that discipline and practice are important; allow the child to be odd; and develop a creative style using kind humor.

Multiple Options as a Model for Teaching the Creatively Talented Child

JOHN F. FELDHUSEN

Developing children's creative abilities and motivations is a complex task that is still poorly understood and guided mostly by guesses and assumptions. Although it is clear that some children are born with greater potential for creative and/or productive thinking than others and acquire cognitive skills and motivational sets more rapidly than others, it is also clear that there are essential learning processes in which potentials are evoked, new skills are learned, and motivations are developed on the way to a career involving creative, productive thinking.

Creative thinking is productive thinking (Treffinger, Feldhusen, & Isaksen, 1990); at the high end, it leads to the new and useful, solutions to problems, works of art, inventions, theories, designs, legislation, social organizations, and business or economic plans; at the low end, it yields ideas and solutions that enhance daily living. In between are diverse products of creative thinking that are more or less original, inventive, artistic, or innovative. In short, creative thinking is not simply the business of Picassos and Edisons—it is operative in all lives as we adapt, cope, and live proactively in a complex world of challenges, problems, opportunities, and resources.

The School's Tasks

Developing creative, cognitive abilities goes on at home, at school, and in the broader context in which the child lives—the world of peers, television, relatives, and the broad culture. All influence emerging creative abilities and motivations, and all influences commingle with one another in interactive, productive, and sometimes nullifying ways. Thus, in looking at the role of school in developing children's creative abilities, it is essential to recognize that other forces are also at work, sometimes enhancing and sometimes diminishing what school is trying to do.

School's primary mission is to teach declarative and procedural knowledge (Schunk, 1996) and productive motivations (Dweck, 1986). Just as the computer does not function without data or information, so also the human mind cannot function creatively without a knowledge base of stored information and skill routines. In all creative, productive thinking, information is acted on, used, combined, manipulated, or processed on the way to new ideas, plans, designs, solutions, and so on.

Brainstorming, for example, is a clear illustration of the role of the knowledge base, information, or data in the process of creative thinking. Given a problem or an idea to develop, brainstormers use recall fluency to come up with information that connects or relates to the problem and then—using creative, adaptive, or inventive thinking processes—they combine, alter, extend, modify, or elaborate that information to general, potential solutions, new ideas, inventions, designs, and so on. Such creative brainstorming goes on not only in formally organized group-thinking sessions in school, but also in individuals and small, informal work groups as problems are encountered and/or new ideas are sought.

The Creativity Component of Talent

Creativity is the innovative aspect of talent that is often characterized as fluency, flexibility, originality, and elaboration (Torrance, 1987) or divergent thinking (Guilford, 1967). It resides in the person as productive thinking and behavior. It also resides in or grows out of the locale or setting. New York City, Chicago, and San Francisco are great centers of creative productivity in the arts. Creativity is also time- or age-dependent. The Renaissance and the Age of Enlightenment were periods of immense creativity in art and philosophy. Some periods or eras seem to be encouraging for creative production whereas others are negative or discouraging (Feldman, Csikszentmihalyi, & Gardner, 1994). Creativity also yields a product, but the product might be entirely conceptual or in the spoken or written words of the creator. A stage design may be translated to a model or to words on paper. Solutions to a problem in chemistry or physics may reside in an article in a professional journal or a patent right that foresees the practical payoffs of the solution. For the creative composer, the essence as a product is the notes on paper. All of these acts of creative behavior grow out of the creative talent of individuals and the surrounding physical and intellectual environment.

Talent and Creativity

Creative thinking manifests itself through our talents. Talents emerge from general physical and intellectual abilities as learned skills and behaviors. Talents are general, pervasive abilities that guide and facilitate human behavior in practical and career-related domains of human activity. Gagne (1997) defines talent as follows:

> *Talents are the outcome of a developmental process: they progressively emerge from the transformation of high aptitudes into the well-trained and systematically developed skills characteristic of a particular field of human activity (p. 83).*

They are the product of genetic predisposition and learned skills. To have creative talent in photography means that an individual has aesthetic perceptual abilities, potential for originality or inventiveness, and a set of learned skills regarding cameras, films, development, printing, and so on. Creative talent in writing reflects high general verbal ability and creative productivity as well as specific, acquired skills in grammar, punctuation, spelling, plot structuring, and characterization and literary tools such as alliteration and metaphor. Thus, natural talent or potential in a talent domain combines with specific learnings to determine the course of talent development.

Creative Talent versus Interest

Creative talent in a domain usually parallels high interest in the domain. The initial interest that led to acquisition of skills in a domain grows as a result of successes in learning and behavioral operations in a domain. That interest then motivates individuals to continue growth and performance in the talent domain (White, 1959).

Creative talent and interest are often confused or thought to be synonymous. Whereas talent embraces the relatively natural abilities such as verbal facility or aesthetic sensitivity and learned skills such as structuring short story plots or dyeing fabrics, interest is essentially a motivational condition of positive affect or inclination toward the practices and activities of the talent domain. That positive affect may result from specific positive or reinforcing experiences in the talent domain, preoccupying experiences like "flow" (Csikszentmihalyi, 1990b) in the domain, as well as the emerging sense of competence or mastery in it (White, 1959).

Levels of Talent

It is important to recognize that levels of creative talent differ between and among individuals and at different times and stages in their development. A high school student may exhibit outstanding talent in writing short stories as compared with the efforts of his peers, but his stories are far inferior to those of mature, publishing writers of short stories. A fourth grader may exhibit talent strength in dramatics but far less dramatic talent than a high school student who has taken several courses in acting. Thus, at any point in time, a creative talent may be emerging, growing in the individual, and conversely might be as far developed as it will ever be. The levels of talented behavior, performance, or production vary widely.

Talent versus Talent Strength

The term *talent* is often used to denote a quite clearly defined area of ability whereas *talent strength* is used to refer to a still ill-defined and relatively weak area of ability that nevertheless shows promise. A middle school student may show some skill in writing stories and poems but does not demonstrate high-level interest nor commitment to writing activities. Thus, we refer to his/her ability as a *talent strength*. On the other hand, a fifth grader who has become highly proficient in chess, seeks opportunities to play every day, and enters all the competitions she can find may be said to be developing talent for chess.

The Role of Talents in Developing Creativity

Youth have the greatest potential for the development of their creative abilities in the areas of their talent strengths. Although creative thinking operates in all aspects of our daily lives as we face and cope with exigencies, it is especially in the areas of our special talent (Feldhusen, Wood, & Dai, 1997) that creativity is manifested. Thus, we see high school students adapting old clothing to serve as costumes in a play, elementary school students devising a plan to gather information from recent German immigrants for a report on post–World War II life in Germany, or college students planning a psychological study of the motivations of pro-choice abortionists. In all such activities, talents provide the base or springboard for creative productivity.

Creative Talent and the Knowledge Base

Talents grow as an interaction among genetic predisposition, emerging general abilities, potential for originality, and the emerging knowledge base. The roles of procedural and declarative knowledge become more salient in talent development as children reach school age. Major influences on early creative talent development and development of the knowledge base are peers, siblings, and the physical environment surrounding the child. Wachs (1992) suggests that children's development results from several types of interaction between child and environment. In many instances, the child is proactive in evoking responses from the world around him, and he learns or experiences growth thereby. Other instances are passive influences on the child. That is, he or she does not evoke, but rather is the recipient of, an environmental influence.

The growth of the knowledge base involves development in long-term memory of cognitive structures—for example, ideas, facts, conceptions, and understandings—otherwise called declarative knowledge and skills or procedural routines for using that knowledge in thinking about, interpreting, and solving problems, also known as procedural knowledge. The knowledge base provides both the data and the procedural guides for using data or information in creative thinking and productivity.

Creative Talents and Expertise

The ultimate career goal of creative talent may be expertise as the latter is defined by Bereiter and Scardamalia (1993). Whereas the usual conception of expertise is skill at the level of excellence, Bereiter and Scardamalia go on to define the ultimate level of expertise as creative, inventive, and/or innovative within the domain of skilled performance or expertise. Thus, the highest-level expert devises new problem solutions not heretofore known that turn out to be creative and accepted within the particular domain of expertise as a breakthrough. This is the skilled photographer who captures nuances of personality in pictures, unlike any photographers before her; or the skilled writer of plays who pioneers a new plot design to enhance the emotionality of the drama. Creative talent undergirds this highest level of expertise.

Multiple Options as a School Model

There is no single, theoretically based, and research-validated model for teaching creative thinking in school (Feldhusen & Clinkenbeard, 1996). Parnes (1987), Isaksen, Dorval, and Treffinger (1991), Feldhusen (1994), Renzulli (1994), Torrance (1987), and others can give us valuable insights. We can also borrow eclectically from these models to suggest multiple options for creativity development. Our multiple options will also include a number of national programs and competitions that provide specific structures and organization for youth to experience and learn both the skills and motivations of creative thinking.

The basic methods of teaching are all relevant to teaching the procedural skills of creative ideation and behavior. These are: (1) Didactic exposition in which a teacher tells a student how to perform a skill or transmits conceptual information; (2) Modeling in which a teacher, mentor, or parent demonstrates skilled performance; (3) Constructive engagement in the skill activity and opportunities to develop self-understanding and self-regulation of the skilled behaviors; (4) Reinforcement, either intrinsic or extrinsic, of behaviors appropriate to the creative behaviors to be learned; and (5) Corrective feedback to eliminate inappropriate aspects of the creative behavior to be learned. For the creatively talented student, there will also be a need for learning experiences to develop the metacognitive skills of self-regulation and self-direction (Schunk, 1991b), and the motivations and skills of the "autonomous" learner (Betts, 1986).

A wide variety of experiences in classes, extracurricular programs, and out-of-school activities can provide the opportunities for developing creative talents. Figure 1–1 presents suggested options at the elementary, middle, and high school levels for the in-school experiences. Although there is no definitive route to high-level creative achievement, productivity, expertise, or a career that is marked by creative successes, we can use individual profiles and growth plans as shown in Figures 1–2 and 1–3 to chart the course rationally. The profile in Figure 1–2 is completed by entering test scores, ratings, and audition evaluations and/or product assessments. The Growth Plan shown in Figure 1–3 is used by students, with guidance by a counselor or teacher, to inventory current class enrollments, test scores, awards and honors, interests, and learning styles to help students understand their own talents and motivations. The bottom section of the Growth Plan is used to help students learn how to set goals and plan appropriate classes and activities to facilitate the development of their creative talents (Feldhusen & Wood, 1997).

Special classes and schools for students of high academic aptitude or artistic talent offer ideal settings for the development of creative talents. In such academic settings, students are taught the knowledge base at a high level commensurate

Elementary Services	Junior High or Middle School Services	High School Services
1. Full-Time Classes	1. Counseling	1. Counseling
2. Pullout	A. Group	A. Group
A. Cluster Groups	B. Individual	B. Individual
B. IEPs	2. Honors Classes	2. Honors Classes
3. Jr. Great Books	3. Future Problem Solving	3. Advanced Placement Classes
4. Future Problem Solving	4. Jr. Great Books	4. Foreign Languages
5. Odyssey of the Mind	5. Odyssey of the Mind	5. Seminars
6. Career Explorations	6. Career Education	6. Mentorships
7. Mentors	7. Seminars	7. Internships
8. Saturday Classes	8. Mentors	8. Concurrent College
A. Arts	9. AP or College Classes	Enrollment
B. Academics	10. Acceleration	9. College Classes in High School
9. Summer Programs	A. Math	10. Special Opportunities
10. Foreign Language	B. Science	A. Art
11. Early Admission	C. English	B. Music
12. Grade Advancement	11. Special Opportunities	C. Drama
13. Talents Unlimited	A. Art	D. Dance
14. Spelling Bee	B. Music	11. Special Projects for
15. Knowledge Master	C. Drama	Vocationally Talented
16. Drama Club	D. Dance	12. Debate
17. Curriculum Compacting	12. Special Projects	13. Correspondence Study
18. Chess Club	13. Foreign Language	14. Independent Study
	14. Correspondence Study	15. Math Olympiad
	15. Independent Study	16. U.S. Academic Triathlon
	16. Chess Club	17. Academy for Creative
		Exploration

FIGURE 1–1 Talent Development Services

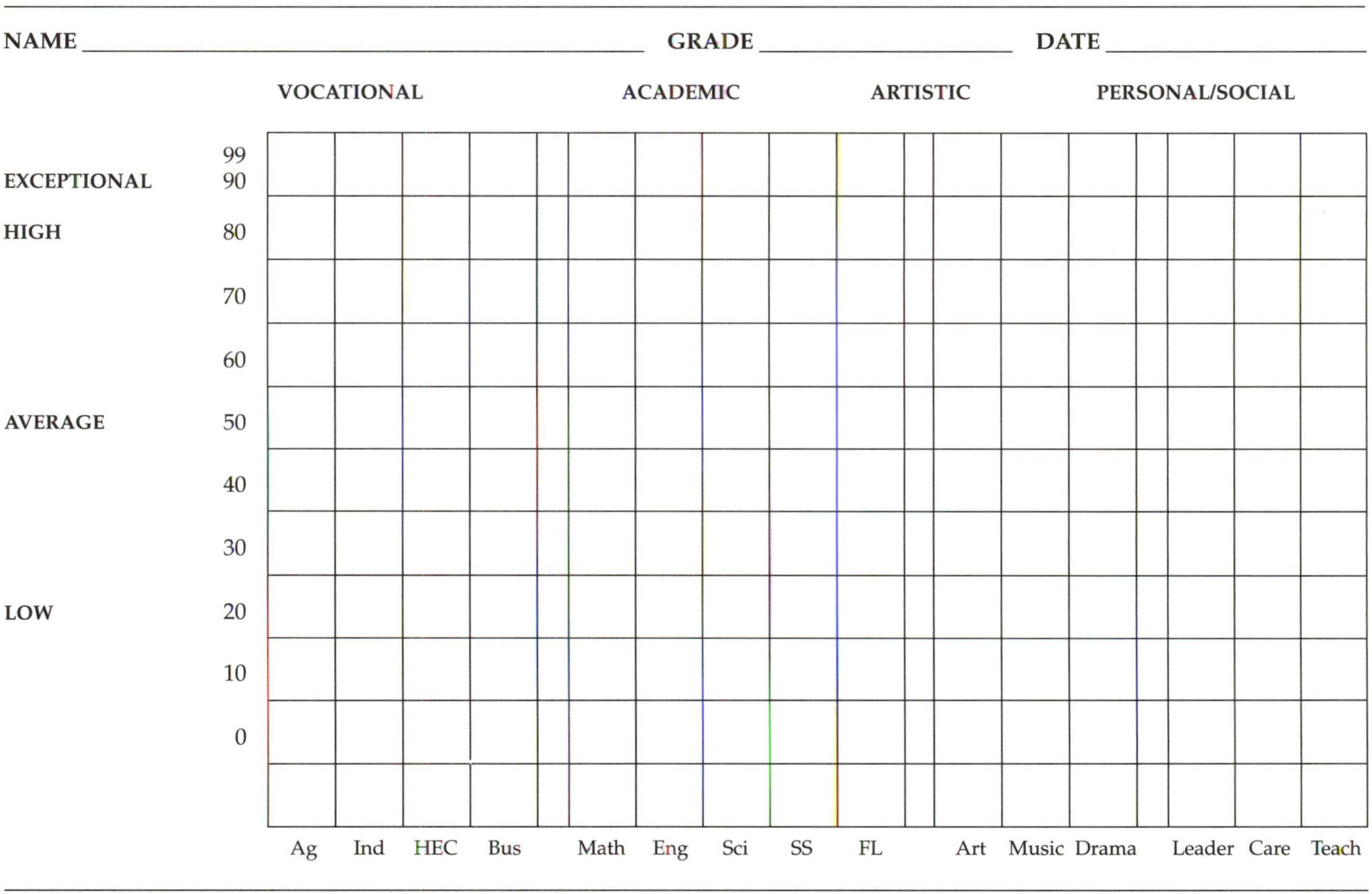

FIGURE 1–2 Talents Profile

Name _____   Home Phone _____

Grade Level _____   Date _____

<u>Current Courses</u>   <u>Current Extracurricular Activities</u>
_____   _____
_____   _____
_____   _____
_____   _____

<u>Test Scores</u>   <u>Awards, Honors</u>
_____   _____
_____   _____
_____   _____
_____   _____

<u>Interest Analysis</u>   <u>Learning Styles</u>
_____   _____
_____   _____
_____   _____
_____   _____

<u>Student's Goals</u>
Academic   Personal   Social   Career
_____   _____   _____   _____
_____   _____   _____   _____
_____   _____   _____   _____

<u>Recommended Classes for Next Year</u>
_____   _____
_____   _____
_____   _____

<u>Recommended Activities</u>
<u>in School</u>   <u>Outside School</u>
_____   _____
_____   _____
_____   _____
_____   _____

FIGURE 1–3   Growth Plan

with their levels of ability, and they profit especially from the opportunity to learn the metacognitive skills of self-regulation and self-direction and the motivations that characterize high-level creative careers. There is also substantial value in the peer relationships that serve as supportive models and commitment to high-level creative careers. In such classes and/or schools, the teachers and resources (for example, libraries, computers, and technical equipment) are also likely to be commensurate with the emerging capabilities of the students.

The Crucial Role of Mentors in Creativity Development

Mentors serve as role models and motivational stimulators of youth (Bandura, 1997). They can be formally related to youth by programmatic arrangement (Haeger & Feldhusen, 1989), informally as natural cultural influences (Pleiss & Feldhusen, 1995), or some combination of the two. In the formal approach, an agency—often of the school—arranges for youth to spend time observing, working with, and/or experiencing persons who are already mature exhibitors of creative, productive behaviors. At the most advanced level, the mentorship may be an internship with a highly creative person or group in an organization. The intent, in such mentorships, or internships, is clearly to provide opportunities for a young person to observe and learn creative skills and motivations from the mentor and to emulate the mentor's behavior, hopefully in new and creative ways for the protégé.

Lesser or lower levels of the formal mentor experience include role-model speakers in the classroom, short-term visits to observe mentors in action at their work sites, movie and video representations of mentors/models, and reading biographies and other written descriptions of models of creative functioning. Always the focus will be on the model/mentor in his or her work site, but Ellingson, Haeger, and Feldhusen (1986) emphasized that ideally the mentoring exposure should include opportunities to observe the mentor in a broader social, community, and family context and opportunities to understand and emulate the motivations of the mentor.

Informal mentoring includes all opportunities youth enjoy to see family members; school personnel; and community, national, and international leaders exhibiting creative behaviors. Although there may be no formal direction to observe and learn from such models, family and school can urge youth to seek and profit from such experiences, and it is probably the case that some youth will spontaneously reach out to mentors and models for guidance, counsel, and direction as they face challenges calling for creative thinking and production.

The Wide Range of Types and Levels of Creative Talent Development as Career Goals

Talent potentials vary widely, and the potential levels of ultimate career and creative achievements growing out of talent potentials also vary widely. On one end may be the skilled waiter in a fine restaurant whose technical efficiency in taking orders, social aplomb, and capacity to get food out on time and at the proper temperature are all unsurpassed. At the other end is the research biologist with a Ph.D. whose laboratory is developing new enzymes as potential medications.

The creative talents of one individual may be verbal and used in writing well-worded want ads for a newspaper, whereas another may use verbal creative talents in writing award-winning poetry. There are creative talents in all the areas related to traditional academic disciplines, such as science, mathematics, English, foreign languages, social analysis, and history; in the arts, such as oil painting, photography, dance, and drama; in the personal/social domains, such as leadership, caregiving, teaching, and counseling; and in the technical realms, such as computer programming, equipment design, or mechanical engineering.

Classroom Applications

Teaching creative thinking and problem solving can be both didactic and constructive. In didactic teaching, teachers offer guidelines for creative thinking processes and then engage students in using those guidelines in situations as realistic as possible. The guidelines for brainstorming, for example, include: (1) making sure that students understand the task dimensions; (2) indicating that many ideas or responses are the goal; (3) stating that there will be no evaluation or judgment of responses while ideas are being produced; (4) assuring students that they should feel free to proffer unusual and original ideas; (5) urging students to strive to connect, relate, or alter their own and others' ideas; and (6) suggesting that students should be brief in responding; lengthy statements should be avoided. These guidelines should be presented to students with clarifying discussion to be sure that they are well understood.

The teacher can then model good brainstorming by showing a video of a group brainstorming. The modeling of children brainstorming displayed on the tape should be discussed and related to the guidelines to see how well they were or were not illustrated.

The time is then at hand to engage students in brainstorming on a simple problem followed later by more complex and realistic problems. Ideas are generated and recorded by a leader on the chalkboard. They should be encouraged to look back, after the session, at their own experience (self-understanding) and how they personally utilized the guidelines (self-regulation) as they went about the task of brainstorming. The goal is to become personally skillful in working with a group using brainstorming to generate creative solutions to problems.

Reinforcement of the learning experience can be both intrinsic and extrinsic. Students who see themselves as functioning well and using the guidelines effectively in videotaped brainstorming sessions can derive strong intrinsic motivation from the learning experience. The teacher can also point to specific student behaviors that were good illustrations of effective brainstorming behavior and thereby provide extrinsic motivation to students.

The latter reinforcement process is linked closely to the final teacher function of providing corrective feedback. The teacher may note that some students talked far too long when they offered an idea. Several others may have shown negative signs by groaning when other students offered ideas. There also may have been very little evidence of linking with or extending ideas that were already on the board.

In closing a brainstorming session, the teacher should encourage students to remember the guidelines, be sure they understand them, and see them as self-regulating guides that they can use when next they participate in brainstorming sessions. The teacher might also try to stimulate further motivation by pointing out that brainstorming is widely used in business, industry, government, and education settings to generate creative solutions to real problems.

Conclusions

Creative thinking and productivity are cognitive and affective processes that operate in the lives of all people. Levels and types of creative thinking and production vary widely. Although there may be some natural or genetic potentials that make it possible for some students to learn and exhibit very high levels of creative talent, it is also clear that creative talent is learned. Parents, schools, and teachers can help children learn the declarative and procedural knowledge that is essential to creative thinking at all levels.

Chapter 2

The Schoolwide Enrichment Model
Developing Students' Creativity and Talents

SALLY M. REIS   JOSEPH S. RENZULLI

When Caroline was in fourth grade, she participated in an enrichment opportunity in which she was exposed to a wide variety of possible design projects. Caroline decided to pursue the development of a design project that interested her, the idea of designing a playground that would be accessible to children with physical disabilities. She spent a great deal of time learning more about this topic and worked with a local design firm to finalize her plan. She applied to the City Council for funds for a feasibility study of the costs associated with building such a playground. Two years later, Caroline's dreams were realized when her playground design became a reality. Caroline's work was a Type III study, one of the components of the Schoolwide Enrichment Model described in this chapter.

Was Caroline gifted? The term *gifted* evokes a variety of responses from parents, teachers, and community members. A chapter about the Schoolwide Enrichment Model (SEM) (Renzulli, 1977; Renzulli & Reis, 1985, 1997) must include an explanation of the conception of giftedness on which the model is based, and this chapter begins with a discussion of the following questions: (1) What do we mean by the term *gifted*? (2) How do we develop creativity and gifted behaviors in young people? (3) What is the purpose of the SEM? and (4) Which students should receive which gifted education services? This chapter provides an overview of the philosophy of the SEM and summarizes the major components of the model.

The SEM is based on a philosophy of gifted education that emphasizes the importance of developing, and not just identifying, creativity and gifted behaviors. Educators and parents achieve this goal through prolonged attention to children's individual interests and strengths; by nurturing a taste for challenge, rigor, and inquiry; and by providing a modified, differentiated, and enriched learning environment that fosters academic achievement, creativity, and real-world problem solving and productivity.

The Three-Ring Conception of Giftedness: The Basis for the Schoolwide Enrichment Model

The Schoolwide Enrichment Model (SEM) (Renzulli & Reis, 1985, 1997) was based on Renzulli's research (1978) regarding prevailing and emerging conceptions of giftedness. At that time, most researchers and practitioners defined giftedness as superior intellectual ability, usually measured by administering academic aptitude tests, and often restricted participation in gifted education programs to only those students who scored in the superior ranges. Renzulli (1978) suggested that a review of the research on creatively productive adults did not support such an exclusionary approach to identification. Instead, he indicated that academic aptitude and achievement tests could be used to identify students with superior academic ability, but that this ability did not necessarily predict adult creative productivity. Renzulli believed that adult creative productivity is more closely associated with an interaction of three clusters: above-average general and specific abilities, high degrees of task commitment to specific projects and problem-solving initiatives, and the ability to develop creative solutions and products to address these problems (see Figure 2–1).

Research on creatively productive people has consistently shown that although no single criterion can be used to determine giftedness, persons who have achieved recognition because of their unique accomplishments and creative

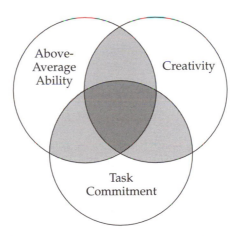

FIGURE 2–1   The Three-Ring Conception of Giftedness

contributions possess this relatively well-defined set of three interlocking clusters of traits. It is important to point out that no single cluster "makes giftedness." Rather, it is the interaction among the three clusters that research has shown to be the necessary ingredient for creative productive accomplishment (Renzulli, 1978, 1986). This interaction is represented by the shaded portion of Figure 2–1.

Individuals capable of demonstrating creative productive behavior are those possessing or capable of developing this composite set of traits and applying them to any potentially valuable area of human performance. Persons who are capable of developing an interaction among the three clusters require a wide variety of educational opportunities and services that are not ordinarily provided through regular instructional programs.

This point of view suggests that gifted behaviors can be developed in a far broader spectrum of the school population than the small percentage of students who are usually identified by high scores on aptitude or achievement tests. It clearly and unquestionably recognizes such obvious abilities as those displayed on achievement and aptitude tests, but it also recognizes several other factors that contribute to the development of superior cognitive or creative productive behaviors. These factors include many types of abilities and potentials that cannot be measured as precisely as IQ and scholastic achievement. The fact that these abilities can be developed, to varying degrees, in larger segments of the population than is usually included in special programs makes it imperative that we reconsider the entire concept of "giftedness" and the ways in which we go about developing a service delivery system for the best possible education for students with various and multiple potentials.

The SEM does not "forget about" those students who earn high scores on traditional measures. However, it does not assume that high scores automatically "make" a person creatively productive, nor does it assume that creative productive behaviors can be displayed only by persons with extremely high scores. Instead, students with high academic aptitude or achievement scores receive services specifically designed to address their needs for a faster-paced and more challenging curriculum. When appropriate, these students are offered opportunities for interest-based enrichment and talent-development activities, experiences that are also relevant for larger segments of the student population.

An increasing percentage of SEM schools also offer interest-based enrichment activities to more, if not all, of their students in an attempt to provide talent-development opportunities for as many students as possible. In addition, many also believe that the "high-end" curriculum offered to many academically able students in gifted education programs may prove beneficial in increasing the academic achievement of all students. Although a more challenging, authentic, and active academic curriculum may need to be accompanied by increased teacher support and professional development, it seems likely that a rich and complex curriculum may actually be more beneficial than the singular, remedial approach currently used to enhance the achievement of students who are functioning at or below grade-level expectations. Several research studies have supported the use of the SEM with a more diverse population, including high-ability students with learning disabilities (Baum, 1988), underachieving gifted students (Baum, Renzulli, and Gilbert, 1995), and several other special population groups (Renzulli and Reis, 1994).

Research by Gardner (1983) and Sternberg (1987) supported this broadened conception of intelligence and giftedness. Gardner's work focuses on the identification of multiple, rather than singular, conceptions of intelligence. His work with conventional aptitude and academic achievement tests lends credence to the premise that these tests largely measure abilities related to linguistic or logical mathematical skills. His work in a variety of cultures also supports his theory that these two intelligences are part of a constellation of at least seven intelligences that are necessary for advanced performance in a variety of settings and fields. Sternberg's research enlarged conceptions of general intellectual ability to include creative and practical intelligence, in addition to the analytic abilities commonly measured by traditional achievement and aptitude tests.

In addition, Bloom's (1985) studies of adult creative producers suggested that talented young people are more likely to display interests and preferences that, if properly nurtured, can lead to the development of strengths and talents in the adolescent and adult years. Bloom's research indicated that fewer than 10 percent of the talented adults in his studies could have been reliably identified as 10-year-olds. These findings about a broader conception of giftedness have significance for the development of an appropriate philosophy and a set of student goals to guide the identification of giftedness and the services within an early childhood gifted education program. The SEM program philosophy incorporates the following beliefs: (1) The term *gifted* can refer to either extraordinary academic or creative talent. (2) These talents can be latent, emergent, and manifest in young children. (3) Appropriate school, community, and home enrichment activities can enhance creative productivity and academic achievement. (4) Enrichment and acceleration services typically offered to students with demonstrated strengths and abilities may prove useful in developing talents and increasing academic achievement in all students.

The goal of the SEM is to develop gifts and talents in as many children as possible by teaching and encouraging creative productive behaviors. Rather than identifying only those students who score well on standardized tests, we encourage some level of participation in enrichment activities for all students. In this way, we can encourage our youngsters to identify their individual interest areas, to become "resident experts" in these topics, and to find and creatively solve real-world problems in these interest areas. We believe the development of these types of enrichment opportunities will increase adult creative productivity by providing opportunities for all students to become independent, lifelong learners who will have an impact on their world through innovative thinking, creative problem solving, product development, and involvement in real-world problem solving.

Teachers of SEM programs focus attention on challenging curriculum, talent development, interest enhancement, and differentiated instruction. They help youngsters articulate their academic or fine arts interests and then respond to these interests through exploratory, group training, and investigative activities.

Their role becomes that of a facilitator who responds to individual students' interests, a teacher who helps students acquire appropriate skills and knowledge, and a guide who instructs students in the process of creative productivity; but above all, a teacher's role is one of a talent developer.

Identification in the SEM

In addition to decisions about a guiding conception of giftedness and philosophy, gifted education program developers also struggle with issues related to identification and assessment. The practice of identifying students as gifted—and by default, as nongifted—is difficult. Although many state departments of education require the identification of gifted students as a prerequisite for receiving state funds to support gifted programs, the procedures for identifying these students vary widely. Although most states recommend the use of multiple assessment procedures, the use of norm-referenced achievement and aptitude tests often prevails. Most current research supports the use of alternative assessment procedures, but this practice is more frequently recommended than implemented. To address these issues the Schoolwide Enrichment Model emphasizes assessment over identification, and stresses the importance of identifying students for enrichment opportunities and services, rather than identification for the purpose of labeling students as gifted or nongifted.

Identifying Students to Receive Various Services

Identification should always be linked to the specific services that students should receive. In other words, we believe that students should be selected for participation in specific program services and activities, based on the perceived benefits, not on a global acknowledgment of "giftedness." All students might benefit from one or more of the services offered in an SEM program, although the particular services might vary from student to student. For example, if a school offers interest-based exploratory activities, workshops, visitations, and presentations for the purpose of increasing students' knowledge base about specific fields or disciplines, it seems likely that the vast majority of students might benefit from attending one or more of these activities if the topic is of wide interest. Assessing or identifying students' interests seems more valid for such purposes than restricting participation to students by using a predetermined achievement test score. Other services, such as the availability of an accelerated math curriculum, or a workshop for highly able writers should be offered to students who have demonstrated not just interest but also expertise in these areas. In this case, math or writing assessments, teacher nominations, and grades are relevant criteria for participation.

The schedule of services can also guide identification procedures. A balance can be achieved through the development of a wide range of services, a variety of scheduling options, and a broad base of staff, faculty, and community involvement in program services, if interest-based projects, talent-development training, or exploratory activities are offered after school or during school hours when time is made available for all children to participate in interest-based offerings. Most

SEM programs identify 10 to 15 percent of their student population, called the Talent Pool, for participation in services. Once the Talent Pool has been established, certain programming modifications should also be considered or implemented. Students who have been placed in the Talent Pool should participate in an orientation meeting about the program with the resource room teacher and their classroom teacher. We have found that explaining the SEM to these youngsters helps them understand the various services that are available to them.

It is important to remember that students with above-average academic ability comprise only one set of students who will receive SEM services—specifically, those students who could benefit from curriculum modification and differentiation, and those who can spare time from the regular curriculum in order to participate in interest-based talent-development activities in the resource room. Students with average or below-average academic achievement should also receive enrichment opportunities. Depending on the school's philosophy, this might include enrichment activities during noninstructional time, and participation in curriculum differentiation services that address their preferences, styles, and prior knowledge. In addition, some SEM schools report increases in the achievement of all students, regardless of prior academic ability, when exposed to the modified and highly challenging, authentic, and active curriculum that is standard fare in gifted education pullout or magnet school programs (Gentry, 1996). Rather than discouraging students from less advantageous homes from participating in various enrichment activities, we must make special efforts to increase the number of students who participate in these modification, differentiation, and enrichment experiences through increased exposure, self-nomination, parental involvement, teacher conferences, and expanded attention to student interests. We are clearly aware that if we are to truly achieve our goal of talent development (as well as talent identification), we must continually remind ourselves that not all youngsters with the potential for creative productivity will be star pupils. We should encourage as many students as possible to pursue various enrichment activities. We do not, however, abandon identification procedures. These efforts help us find the most advanced readers, the able young mathematicians, the talented artists, and the above-average underachievers who are least likely to need the review, repetition, and drill that frequently accompany some grade curriculum units.

An Overview of the Schoolwide Enrichment Model

The SEM provides three services. These services involve procedures for: (a) assessing students' strengths, interests, preferences, and styles; (b) modifying and differentiating the core curriculum to address individual variations in prior knowledge, learning rate, learning styles, motivation, or interests; and (c) enrichment teaching and learning through offering talent-development activities based on students' strengths, interests, and related core curriculum or community opportunities.

These services are offered within three different school structures: (1) within the regular classroom; (2) through a variety of specially organized programs (competitions, expositions, seminars, visitations, minicourses, mentorships, and so on) that are facilitated by gifted education specialists, a volunteer team of teachers, parents, community members, administrators, and a K–12 plan for a continuum of services; and (3) talent-development opportunities provided to all students during a regularly scheduled time of the school week, in a newly designed component called Enrichment Clusters.

These services and school structures are illustrated on the front fact and the top face of the cube diagram (see Figure 2–2). This diagram also lists the organiza-

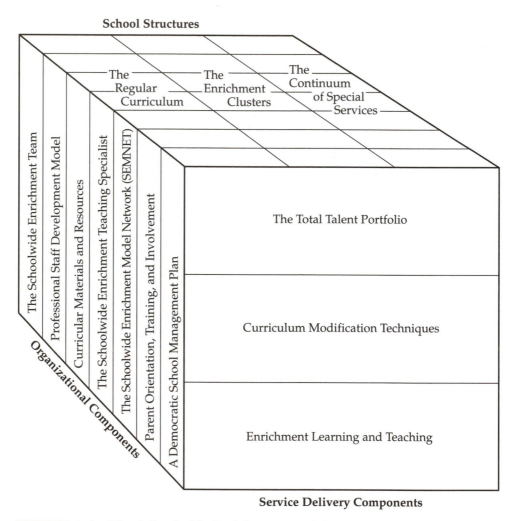

FIGURE 2–2   The Schoolwide Enrichment Model

tional components that must be available to ensure the delivery of program services. These organizational components include such things as a professional staff development model; an educational school management plan; vehicles for promoting parent orientation and community involvement; and the availability of vital curricula resources, materials, and instructional references. The three dimensions within the SEM—the school structures, the service delivery components, and the organizational components—interact to achieve student goals related to academic achievement, talent development, intrinsic motivation for learning, and the acquisition of independent learning skills.

Dimension One: Service Delivery Components

The three service delivery components represent the centerpiece of this model, and provide goals for implementation.

The Total Talent Portfolio

Educators in gifted education programs that adopt SEM as their programming model share similar perspectives about the role of assessment in determining appropriate program services for individual students. The purpose of these assessment procedures is to recognize and analyze early childhood interests, experiences, and preferences for the express purposes of using this information not to identify students as gifted or not gifted, but instead to provide services and activities that are related to a child's creativity and potential. To offer these services, teachers must first collect, analyze, and make decisions based on relevant student information. The Total Talent Portfolio (see Figure 2–3) provides the vehicle for these systematic gathering, assessing, and planning activities.

The first stage of this process involves the collection of items, examples, and information to place within the portfolio. The contents of the portfolio focus specifically on a child's strengths—information that synthesizes "best case" evidence about a child's interests, strengths, product preferences, learning and thinking styles. Because most SEM programs create services on the basis of a teaching philosophy that suggests we derive higher achievement and more enjoyment and motivation for learning, when we concentrate on children's strengths, and teach core knowledge through related interest areas, the very nature of the portfolio must revolve around data related to these strengths and interests.

Informal information about co-curricular experiences, hobbies, collections, personal goals, special lessons, and trips is as important to a portfolio's quality as the more formal information provided from test scores, teacher ratings, grades, surveys, questionnaires, and work and product samples. Although basic data from tests, grades, surveys, and checklists can be gathered during the beginning of the school year and updated annually, the various work samples, products, and anecdotes that form the bulk of the portfolio must be carefully chosen and included across a child's years in school. Students should play an integral role in helping to select work samples and products that represent their best work or the work that typifies their greatest interests, strengths, and talents. Photographs,

Abilities	Interests	Style Preferences			
Maximum Performance Indicators	*Interest Areas*	*Instructional Style Preferences*	*Learning Environment Preferences*	*Thinking Style Preferences*	*Expression Style Preferences*
Tests • Standardized • Teacher-Made Course Grades Teacher Ratings Product Evaluation • Written • Oral • Visual • Musical • Constructed *(Note differences between assigned and self-selected products)* Level of Participation in Learning Activities Degree of Interaction with Others	Fine Arts Crafts Literary Historical Mathematical/ Logical Physical Sciences Life Sciences Political/ Judicial Athletic/ Recreation Marketing/ Business Drama/Dance Musical Performance Musical Com- position Managerial/ Business Photography Film/Video Computers Other *(Specify)*	Recitation and Drill Peer Tutoring Lecture Lecture/ Discussion Discussion Guided Indepen- dent Study* Learning/ Interest Center Simulation, Role Playing, Dramatization, Guided Fantasy Learning Games Replicative Re- ports or Projects* Investigative Re- ports or Projects* Unguided Inde- pendent Study* Internship* Apprenticeship*	Inter/Intra Personal • Self-Oriented • Peer-Oriented • Adult-Oriented • Combined Physical • Sound • Heat • Light • Design • Mobility • Time of Day • Food Intake • Seating	Analytic *(School Smart)* Synthetic/ Creative *(Creative, Inventive)* Practical/ Contextual *(Street Smart)* Legislative Executive Judicial	Written Oral Manipulative Discussion Display Dramatization Artistic Graphic Commercial Service
Ref: General Tests and Measurements Literature	Ref: Renzulli, 1997	Ref: Renzulli & Smith, 1978	Ref: Amabile, 1983b; Dunn, Dunn, & Price, 1981; Gardner, 1983	Ref: Sternberg, 1988a, 1990	Ref: Renzulli & Reis. 1985

FIGURE 2–3   Dimensions of the Total Talent Portfolio

audiotapes, and videotapes provide information about three-dimensional products or performances that cannot be described with paper or pencil.

The second stage of the Total Talent Portfolio process involves data analysis. Once collected, the information within the portfolio provides vital data that teachers, parents, and gifted education specialists use to assess the ways in which students prefer to learn and prefer to share their learning. Each child's academic strengths, talent areas, and individual stage of talent development can also be determined through an analysis of the contents of the Total Talent Portfolio. This analysis process can be conducted jointly by a team of teachers, or by an individual classroom teacher working in conjunction with the gifted education specialist.

When the adults who work with a given child identify the child's academic strengths, styles, preferences, interests, talents, and stage of talent development, they are ready to move to the third step of the Total Talent Portfolio process.

This last stage of the Total Talent Portfolio process provides the basis for any curriculum modification, differentiation, or enrichment services that an individual child receives in an SEM school. Teachers use the descriptors collected in the second step to make decisions and plans for individual students or small groups of students with similar interests, strengths, or talent development needs. For example, if portfolio information suggests that a child enjoys math and performs two or more years above grade level, teachers might decide to provide this student with a continuous progress math curriculum, access to sophisticated math software, and/or supplementary opportunities to learn more about math applications, problem solving, or career opportunities.

Another child's portfolio might suggest strengths in art, high levels of creativity, preferences for visual, hands-on, and small group learning, product preferences that include conferences, drawing, and open-ended activities, but only average or below-average academic performance. In this case, art talent can be nurtured during the enrichment component of the SEM program. This service addresses the child's need for talent development, recognition, and self-esteem. In a similar vein, information about learning style strengths and product preferences can be used to improve academic performance through differentiated and modified large-group and small-group instruction that encompasses the student's preferences and does not overly rely on tests, lecture, or worksheets to assess, teach, or practice learning objectives.

Together, modification and differentiation of curriculum and enrichment experiences can improve the quality and the breadth of daily learning activities if changes are made on the basis of individual student strengths and preferences. Attention to learning style preferences, especially when students are working on a difficult learning objective, leads to changes in instructional strategies and involves the increased use of small-group teaching activities or, at the very least, small-group learning activities.

Teachers can modify instruction based on student interests in at least three ways. First, student interests can help teachers identify highly motivating, representative topics that address core curriculum objectives. A teacher might use students' fascination with sharks by using the shark as a representative topic in a beginning unit on ichthyology. This creates more attention to learning, and the increased attention usually results in increased learning. Second, a teacher can use students' individual interests to offer alternative resources, choice within assignments, and optional center or homework activities that revolve around central objectives or a key topic, while still permitting sidetrips connected to individual preferences and strengths.

Third, student interest information, specifically related to the child's previous talent development opportunities, helps teachers plan individual enrichment activities. For example, if a child cannot yet identify his or her interest or strength areas, teachers will use this information to plan regular participation in a broad range of exploratory, hands-on experiences in order to help students identify areas of strength or interest.

Traits and behaviors associated with strengths and talents include an avid curiosity and intense involvement in specific kinds of activities or subject areas and a large storehouse of information in areas of personal strength or talent. Children who have reached this stage of talent development do not generally need varied enrichment activities as much as they need opportunities to learn more advanced technical information, skills, and processes. Interest information from children at this stage also helps teachers suggest specific real-world problems, projects, investigations, research, or mentoring opportunities that can be used to encourage a child's talent development.

Teachers, parents, and students should collaborate on much of the information in the Total Talent Portfolio. Although test scores may be unavailable, data about performance on informal reading inventories, information from kindergarten screenings, and pre- and post-unit tests or assessments can substitute for standardized test information. Teachers' observation notes, parent surveys about home and community activities, and parental perceptions of strengths, interests, and learning styles also provide vital data for the collection process. The students, regardless of their age, should be involved in decisions about which work samples and projects will be stored in the portfolio to demonstrate their strengths and interests. We have had success using simplified checklists to self-rate styles, product, and interest preferences.

Used together, data about interests, styles, preferences, and academic strengths can help teachers and parents appreciate the unique strengths, experiences, and talents of each child as a special and valued member of the school community. Using this information, not merely collecting it, helps educators make the curricular changes and create the enrichment opportunities and alternatives for small groups or individual students that are vital to the SEM approach. The Total Talent Portfolio enables us to treat children as individuals, enabling us to respect and appreciate the variation and diversity within our school community.

Curriculum Modification

Students also receive curriculum modification services in a school that adopts the SEM. The second service delivery component of the SEM is a series of curriculum modification techniques that are designed to: (1) adjust levels of required learning so that all students are challenged, (2) increase the number of in-depth learning experiences, and (3) introduce various types of enrichment into regular curricular experiences. The procedures that are used to carry out curriculum modification are curriculum compacting, textbook analysis and surgical removal of repetitious material from textbooks, and a planned approach for introducing greater depth into regular curricular material.

Curriculum modification involves changes and enhancements in the core curriculum. To elevate the core curriculum relates to the lackluster track record of remedial education in helping disadvantaged students "catch up," academically, with their age mates. Years of drill and repetition, worksheets, and isolated practice activities have not resulted in better scores for these children. Instead, it seems more likely that they require both an interesting and a challenging curriculum, based on high expectations and the belief that all children can achieve more with proper support and motivation. Instead of expecting students who perform below the average academically to merely memorize facts and recall details, SEM encourages the use of concept-based and problem-oriented curriculum units for all students. Although some students may need more support (in the form of varied questioning strategies, more small-group teaching or individual assistance, smaller steps, and greater use of advance organizers) than other students, the use of these enhanced features is more advisable than restricting some students' interaction with sophisticated content and in-depth learning.

Team planning and brainstorming make it easier for more teachers to modify their core curriculum. The involvement of the school librarian, the gifted education specialist, the art or music teacher often helps teachers identify additional alternatives that were not readily identified during the early stages of the process.

Curriculum Compacting for Above-Average Ability Students

When schools embrace the role of talent developers, differentiation can be used to find the time students need to pursue self-selected, interest-based enrichment activities that help them develop their individual talents. To create the time for these activities, teachers must eliminate or modify instruction, learning activities, and/or assignments. We refer to this process as curriculum compacting (Reis, Burns, & Renzulli, 1992; Renzulli & Smith, 1978) (see Figure 2–4).

How to Use the Compacting Process.

Defining goals and outcomes. The first of three phases of the compacting process consists of defining the goals and outcomes of a given unit or segment of instruction. This information is readily available in most subjects because specific goals and outcomes usually can be found in teachers' manuals, curriculum guides, scope and sequence charts, and some of the new curricular frameworks that are emerging in connection with outcome-based education models. Teachers should examine these objectives to determine which represent the acquisition of new content or thinking skills as opposed to reviews or practice of material that has previously been taught. The scope and sequence charts prepared by publishers, or a simple comparison of the table of contents of a basal series, will provide a quick overview of new versus repeated material. A major goal of this phase of the compacting process is to help teachers make individual programming decisions; a larger professional development goal is to help teachers be better analysts of the material they are teaching and better consumers of textbooks and prescribed curricular material.

Identifying students for the compacting process. The second phase of curriculum compacting is identifying students who have already mastered the objectives or outcomes of a unit or segment of instruction that is about to be taught. The first step of this phase consists of estimating which students have the potential to master

INDIVIDUAL EDUCATIONAL PROGRAMMING GUIDE
The Compactor

Prepared by Joseph S. Renzulli
Linda M. Smith

NAME _____ AGE _____ TEACHER(S) _____

SCHOOL _____ GRADE _____ PARENT(S) _____

Individual Conference Dates and Persons Participating in Planning of IEP

_____ _____ _____ _____

CURRICULUM AREAS TO BE CONSIDERED FOR COMPACTING Provide a brief description of basic material to be covered during this marking period and the assessment information or evidence that suggests the need for compacting.	PROCEDURES FOR COMPACTING BASIC MATERIAL Describe activities that will be used to guarantee proficiency in basic curricular areas.	ACCELERATION AND/OR ENRICHMENT ACTIVITIES Describe activities that will be used to provide advanced-level learning experiences in each area of the regular curriculum.

☐ Check here if additional information is recorded on the reverse side

FIGURE 2–4   The Compactor

new material at a faster than normal pace. Knowing one's students is, of course, the best way to begin the assessment process. Scores on previous tests, completed assignments, and classroom participation are the best ways of identifying highly likely candidates for compacting. Standardized achievement tests can serve as a good general screen for this step because they allow us to list the names of all students who are scoring one or more years above grade level in particular subject areas.

Being a candidate for compacting does not necessarily mean that a student knows the material under consideration. Therefore, the second step of identifying candidates consists of finding or developing appropriate tests or other assessment techniques that can be used to evaluate specific learning outcomes. Unit pretests or end-of-unit tests that can be administered as pretests are ready-made for this task, especially when it comes to the assessment of basic skills. An analysis of pretest results enables the teacher to document proficiency in specific skills, and to select instructional activities or practice material necessary to bring the student up to a high level in any skill that may need some additional reinforcement.

The process is slightly modified for compacting content areas that are not as easily assessed as basic skills, and for students who have not mastered the material, but are judged to be candidates for more rapid coverage. First, students should have a thorough understanding of the goals and procedures of compacting, including the nature of the enrichment and acceleration activities. A given segment of material should be discussed with the student (for example, a unit that includes a series of chapters in a social studies text), and the procedures for verifying mastery at a high level should be specified. These procedures might consist of answering questions based on the chapters, writing an essay, or taking the standard end-of-unit test. The amount of time for completion of the unit should be specified, and procedures such as periodic progress reports or log entries for teacher review should be agreed on. And, of course, an examination of potential acceleration and/or enrichment replacement activities should be a part of this discussion.

Another alternative is to assess or pretest all students in a class when a new unit or topic is introduced. Although this may seem like more work for the teacher, it provides the opportunity for all students to demonstrate their strengths or previous mastery in a given area. Using a matrix of learning objectives, teachers can fill in test results and establish small, flexible, and temporary groups for skill instruction and replacement activities.

Providing acceleration and enrichment options. The final phase of the compacting process can be one of the most exciting aspects of teaching because it is based on cooperative decision making and creativity on the parts of both teachers and students. Efforts can be made to gather enrichment materials from classroom teachers, librarians, media specialists, and content area or gifted education specialists. These materials may include self-directed learning activities, instructional materials that focus on particular thinking skills, and a variety of individual and group project-oriented activities that are designed to promote hands-on research and investigative skills. The time made available through compacting provides opportunities for exciting learning experiences such as small-group, special-topic seminars that might be directed by students or community resource persons, community-based apprenticeships or opportunities to work with a mentor, peer tutoring situations, involvement in community service activities, and opportunities to rotate through a series of self-selected minicourses. The time saved through curriculum compacting can be used by the teacher to provide a variety of enrichment or acceleration opportunities for the student.

Enrichment strategies might include a variety of Type I, II, or III or a number of options included on the continuum of services. Acceleration might include the use of material from the next unit or chapter, the use of the next chronological grade-level textbook, or the completion of even more advanced work. Alternative activities should reflect an appropriate level of challenge and rigor that is commensurate with the student's abilities and interests.

Decisions about which replacement activities to use are always guided by factors such as time, space, and the availability of resource persons and materials. Although practical concerns must be considered, the ultimate criteria for replacement activities should be the degree to which they increase academic challenge and the extent to which they meet individual needs. Great care should be taken to select activities and experiences that represent individual strengths and interests rather than the assignment of more-of-the-same worksheets or randomly selected kits, games, and puzzles! This aspect of the compacting process should also be viewed as a creative opportunity for an entire faculty to work cooperatively to organize and institute a broad array of enrichment experiences. A favorite minicourse that a faculty member has always wanted to teach, or serving as a mentor to one or two students who are extremely invested in a teacher's beloved topic, are just two of the ways that replacement activities can add excitement to the teachers' part in this process as well as the obvious benefits for students. We have also observed another interesting occurrence that has resulted from the availability of curriculum compacting. When some bright but previously underachieving students realized that they could both economize on regularly assigned material and "earn time" to pursue self-selected interests, their motivation to complete regular assignments increased. As one student put it, "Everyone understands a good deal!"

The best way to get an overview of the curriculum compacting process is to examine an actual example of how the management form that guides this process is used. This form, "The Compactor," presented in Figure 2–4, serves as both an organizational and a record-keeping tool. Teachers should fill out one form per student, or one form for a group of students with similar curricular strengths. Completed Compactors should be kept in students' academic files and updated on a regular basis. The form can also be used for small groups of students who are working at approximately the same level (for instance, a reading or math group). The Compactor is divided into three sections:

- The first column should include information on learning objectives and student strengths in those areas. Teachers should list the objectives for a particular unit of study, followed by data on students' proficiency in those objectives, including test scores, behavioral profiles, and past academic records.
- In the second column, teachers should detail the pretest vehicles they select, along with test results. The pretest instruments can be formal measures, such as pencil and paper tests, or informal measures, such as performance assessments based on observations of class participation and written assignments.

  Specificity is extremely important. Recording an overall score of 85 percent on ten objectives, for example, sheds little light on what portion of the material can be compacted, because students might show limited mastery of some objectives and high levels of mastery of others.

- Column three is used to record information about acceleration or enrichment options. In determining these options, teachers must be fully aware of students' individual interests and learning styles. We should never replace compacted regular curriculum work with harder, more advanced material that is determined solely by the teacher. Instead, students' interests should be taken into account. If, for example, a student loves working on science fair projects, that option may be used to replace material that has been compacted from the regular curriculum. We should also be careful to help monitor the challenge level of the material that is being substituted. We want students to understand the nature of effort and challenge and we should ensure that students are not simply replacing the compacted material with basic reading or work that is not advanced.

When teachers differentiate the core curriculum and provide varied teaching or learning activities that are still related to the regular grade-level curriculum, they alter the breadth or the depth of their teaching or learning activities, the student resources, or their assignments. If pretesting suggests that the most influential difference among students relates to learning rate, prior knowledge, or cognitive ability, teachers usually make changes in depth. In other words, they retain the gist of the original learning objective, and instead teach the objective to students with varying degrees of sophistication.

When teachers differentiate instruction by varying the depth of instruction or assignments, they usually "tier" the work for two to three small groups of students, rather than creating individual assignments or contracts for each student in the class. Each group of students gains knowledge, despite their entry level. It is unrealistic, however, to expect that all students will start or complete most units at the same level of competency; what they should all do is make reasonable gains in their knowledge or skill base. Differentiation does not eliminate differences among students—it addresses them.

Enrichment Learning and Teaching

The third service delivery component of the SEM is enrichment learning and teaching, which is based on the ideas of a small but influential number of philosophers, theorists, and researchers such as Piaget, Bruner, and Dewey. The work of these theorists, coupled with our own research and program development activities, has given rise to the concept we call enrichment learning and teaching. The best way to define this concept is in terms of the following four principles:

1. Each learner is unique; therefore, all learning experiences must be examined in ways that take into account the abilities, interests, and learning styles of the individual.
2. Learning is more effective when students enjoy what they are doing; therefore, learning experiences should be constructed and assessed with as much concern for enjoyment as for other goals.
3. Learning is more meaningful and enjoyable when content (that is, knowledge)

and process (that is, thinking skills, methods of inquiry) are learned within the context of a real and present problem; therefore, attention should be given to opportunities to personalize student choice in problem selection, the relevance of the problem for individual students at the time the problem is being addressed, and authentic strategies for addressing the problem.

4. Some formal instruction may be used in enrichment learning and teaching, but a major goal of this approach to learning is to enhance knowledge and thinking skill acquisition that is gained through formal instruction with applications of knowledge and skills that result from students' own construction of meaning.

The ultimate goal of learning that is guided by these principles is to replace dependent and passive learning with independent and engaged learning. Although all but the most conservative educators will agree with these principles, much controversy exists about how these (or similar) principles might be applied in everyday school situations. A danger also exists that these principles might be viewed as yet another idealized list of glittering generalities that cannot be manifested easily in schools that are entrenched in the deductive model of learning. Developing a school program based on these principles is not an easy task. Over the years, however, we have achieved a fair amount of success by gaining faculty, administrative, and parental consensus on a small number of easy-to-understand concepts and related services, and by providing resources and training related to each concept and service delivery procedure. Numerous research studies and field tests in schools with widely varying demographics have been carried out (Renzulli & Reis, 1994). These studies and field tests provided opportunities for the development of large amounts of practical know-how that are readily available for schools that would like to implement the SEM.

In 1977, Renzulli developed the enrichment Triad Model (see Figure 2–5), which included three different types of enrichment opportunities. Type I enrichment activities expose children to new and exciting topics and ideas not ordinarily addressed in the core curriculum. These exploratory activities help many children begin to identify their interest areas, and possibly their future strength and talent areas. For students who can already identify their interest areas, Type I experiences help students acquire more sophisticated and technical knowledge and expertise in these areas.

The enrichment experiences can stem from classroom learning activities, from the environment in general, or they can be specifically organized around the most frequently mentioned interest areas on students' Total Talent Portfolio. Schoolwide or large-group Type I activities usually involve presentations, visitations, workshops, performances, or video offerings. Type I individuals use books, Web sites, shadowing experiences, interviews, or other print resources to deliver interest-based content knowledge. Classroom-based Type I activities usually emanate from core curriculum units and provide opportunities for students to investigate highly interesting subtopics related to these units.

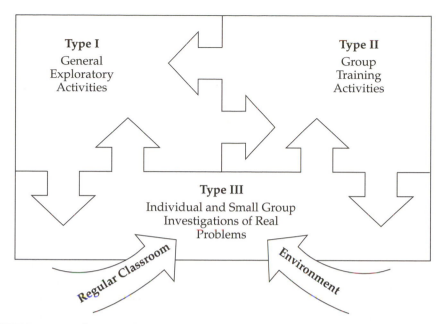

FIGURE 2–5   The Enrichment Triad Model

Type I enrichment is designed to expose students to a wide variety of disciplines, topics, occupations, hobbies, persons, places, and events that would not ordinarily be covered in the regular curriculum. In schools that use this model, an enrichment team consisting of parents, teachers, and students often organizes and plans Type I experiences by contacting speakers; arranging minicourses, demonstrations, or performances; or ordering and distributing films, slides, videotapes, or other print or nonprint media.

Type I enrichment, and the debriefing that accompanies this type of enrichment, also provides an invitation for some students to reach beyond these exploratory or knowledge-acquisition activities to pursue methodology or process skill training experiences. Type II training activities provide young talent with opportunities to learn the cognitive skills, the research processes, and the discipline-based methodologies of practicing professionals in their interest area. These training activities help students develop more expertise, become more skillful, and become capable of firsthand research.

Type II enrichment consists of materials and methods designed to promote the development of thinking and feeling processes. Some Type II enrichment is general, consisting of training in areas such as creative thinking and problem solving, learning how to learn skills such as classifying and analyzing data, and advanced reference and communication skills. Type II training, usually carried out both in classrooms and in enrichment programs, includes the development of (1) creative thinking and problem solving, critical thinking, and affective processes; (2) a wide variety of specific learning how-to-learn skills; (3) skills in the appropriate use of advanced-level reference materials; and (4) written, oral, and visual communication skills. Other Type II enrichment is specific, as it cannot be planned in advance and usually involves advanced instruction in an interest area selected by the student. For example, students who become interested in botany would pursue advanced training in this area by doing advanced reading in botany; compiling, planning, and carrying out plant experiments and more advanced methods of training would be necessary for those who want to go further.

Type II training activities can be offered as schoolwide minicourses, as supplemental units in the regular classroom, in tandem with appropriate core curriculum units, to individual students on an "as-needed" basis, or during the course of student involvement in their own research projects or investigations. Enrichment specialists often serve as peer teachers or coaches to classroom teachers who express interest in incorporating these training opportunities within their curriculum or during enrichment cluster opportunities. An increased knowledge or skill base is of little use in talent development if this information and these skills are not transferred and applied by students.

Type III opportunities provide students with an apprenticeship in real-world problem solving. Type III enrichment occurs when students become interested in pursuing a self-selected area and are willing to commit the time necessary for advanced content acquisition and process training in which they assume the role of a firsthand inquirer. The goals of Type III enrichment include:

- providing opportunities for applying interests, knowledge, creative ideas, and task commitment to a self-selected problem or area of study.
- acquiring advanced-level understanding of the knowledge (content) and methodology (process) that are used within particular disciplines, artistic areas of expression, and interdisciplinary studies.
- developing authentic products that are directed primarily toward bringing about a desired impact on a specified audience.
- developing self-directed learning skills in the areas of planning, organization, resource utilization, time management, decision making, and self-evaluation.
- developing task commitment, self-confidence, and feelings of creative accomplishment.

Type III participants identify and focus on real-world problems related to their interest or talent areas. Under the mentorship of a community member, a classroom teacher, a cluster facilitator, or the gifted specialists, students involved in Type III projects gather raw data and related information about their problem area. They propose solutions to unmet needs or unanswered questions. Then they use their methodological, cognitive, and research skills to produce a product that will ameliorate the problem. Later, they present their solution and product to a real-world audience. Type III enrichment is the highest level of enrichment in which a student can engage because they exchange their role from traditional lesson learner to firsthand inquirer. Type III enrichment is distinguished from other types of enrichment by five essential elements: (1) a personal frame of reference, (2) a focus on advanced-level knowledge, (3) a focus on methodology, (4) a sense of audience, and (5) authentic evaluation. One Type III investigation (a group of students developed a local history book) is included in Figure 2–6.

Although some teachers can offer whole-class modified Type III experiences, most Type III products are completed during enrichment cluster opportunities or in the gifted education resource room during compacted time. The amount of time students can spend pursuing these investigations is highly correlated with increases in problem-focusing ability, enhanced self-efficacy for creative problem solving, and greater tolerance for risk-taking, task commitment, and self-discipline. For these reasons, the extent to which students have Type III time available to them is a crucial predictor of SEM success in a given school. Research has been conducted on the SEM for twenty years with a variety of populations and in a

---

An Illustrated History of
Albertville, Alabama

by Beth Gurrard, Ashley Williams, Jana Rucks, and many others
Alabama Avenue Middle School, Albertville, Alabama

Description of Type III

This book originally began as an independent study project for a third grader. Because of the interest it generated, this study soon became a class project. After receiving a grant from the National Endowment for the Humanities, it later involved 120 students from the town. The project required three years to complete and the resource teacher, Jane Newman, found that each year, more students became interested in becoming involved. Each student or group of students selected a topic of interest for small group investigation and research. The senior high students served as editors and completed the photography and art work. Several area residents served as mentors including an amateur historian who had pursued individual research for fifteen years and a local resident who was a history professor and an associate director of a center for the study of southern history and culture.

Jane Newman, the project teacher, also had a teacher at each of the five schools in **Albertville who** coordinated the research completed by students. Jane found that because the project was so large, students had to be reminded often of the benefits of their contribution. She and the other project teachers also learned to divide the project into smaller segments so that students could experience some closure periodically.

The printed copies of the book were distributed to the Albertville Historical Society, newcomers to the community by the Chamber of Commerce, interested citizens of the Albertville area, and all third and fourth grade classes in Albertville for use in conjunction with their Social Studies book.

FIGURE 2–6 (*continued*)

CONTENTS

LOCATION

Albertville is located in the northeastern part of Alabama. It is the largest city in Marshall County and is called "the heart of Sand Mountain." Sand Mountain is a foothill of the Appalachians. The Sand Mountain plateau covers an area about 25 miles wide by 75 miles long.

GENERAL HISTORY

Imagine you were walking through Albertville about 200 years ago. Instead of paved sidewalks, you would use Indian trails. Instead of brick buildings, you would see tall hickory, oak, and popular trees.

You might stop to drink water from a cool stream where ferns and moss grow along the creek banks. You might also see more wild strawberries growing than you could count!

Black bears, cougars, deer, and many other kinds of wild animals would be roaming about. The Albertville area was also home to the Cherokees at this time. You may have been invited to spend a night at an Indian Village.
As a matter of fact, that's just what happened to Davy Crockett when he crossed Sand Mountain in 1812.

FIGURE 2–6   Type III Enrichment Sample—Illustrated History of Albertville, Alabama

variety of settings, and this research has been summarized in various research articles (Renzulli & Reis, 1994).

Dimension Two: School Structures

Schools need to use existing configurations, or to create new ones, in order to provide the services previously described. Within an SEM school, these components range from services within the regular classroom, to services in specially designed interest and talent development groups (called enrichment clusters), as well as incorporate a continuum of special services, programs, and competitions typically associated with gifted education programs.

Enrichment Clusters

Enrichment clusters bring together nongraded groups of students who share common interests. Like extracurricular activities and programs such as 4H and Junior Achievement, the clusters meet at designated times of the school day (during a mutually agreed-upon time) and operate on the assumption that students and teachers (or community resource people) want to be there. Enrichment clusters place a premium on the development of higher-order thinking skills and the creative and productive application of these skills to real-world situations. As a result, the learning environment supports the development of talent and student strengths. To put it another way: Every child is special if we create conditions in which that child can be a specialist within a specialty group.

Enrichment clusters revolve around major disciplines, interdisciplinary themes, or cross-disciplinary topics. A puppetry production group, for example, might include puppeteers, writers, stage designers, and costume designers. Clearly, the clusters deal with how-to knowledge, thinking skills, and interpersonal relations that apply in the real world. Student work is directed toward producing a product or service. Instead of lesson plans or unit plans, three key questions guide learning: (1) What do people with an interest in this area—for example, pet care—do? (2) What knowledge, materials, and other resources do we need to authentically do activities in this area? (3) In what ways can we use the product or service to affect the intended audience?

SEM schools use enrichment clusters to varying degrees. The Webster Elementary School in St. Paul, Minnesota, for example, has a broad array of interdisciplinary clusters every day. The Southeast School in Mansfield, Connecticut, offers enrichment clusters once a week. Teachers and parent volunteers jointly teach the clusters. The superintendent of schools, who is also a licensed pilot, organized one of the most popular clusters, Flight School. Students enter a cluster based on interests and other information learned from the Total Talent Portfolio. Students who develop a high degree of expertise in a particular area are sometimes asked to serve as assistants within a cluster that relates to their talent area.

One golden rule exists for enrichment clusters: Everything students do in the cluster is directed toward producing a product or delivering a service for a real-world audience. This forces the issue of learning only relevant content and using only authentic processes within the context of student-selected product or service development activities. Common goals make cooperation a necessity and divisions of labor within the clusters allow for differentiated levels of expertise and involvement, varying levels of challenge, and opportunities for different types of leadership to emerge among students.

Continuum of Special Services

Although enrichment clusters and the modification, differentiation, and enrichment services provided within the regular classroom help meet individual needs, a program for talent development still requires supplementary services. These services, which challenge the students capable of working at the highest levels of their special interest areas, typically include individual or small-group counseling; direct assistance in facilitating advanced-level work; mentor relationships; and other programs that connect students, families, and out-of-school resources or agencies (see Figure 2–7).

The SEM teaching specialist, or a team of teachers and parents, has responsibility for providing options for advanced learning. One school enrichment teaching specialist in Barrington, Rhode Island, estimates she spends two days a week serving as a resource to the faculties of two schools; on the other three days, she provides direct services to students. The school corporation developed a parent-teacher enrichment guide that describes opportunities in the city and surrounding area. Direct assistance often takes the form of encouraging students, faculty, and parents to participate in programs such as Future Problem Solving, Odyssey of the Mind, and Model United Nations, in addition to essay, mathematics, and history contests sponsored at the state and national levels. Typically, SEM specialists also make arrangements for students interested in summer programs, on-campus courses, special schools, theatrical groups, special expeditions, and apprenticeships.

Dimension Three: Organizational Components

The Schoolwide Enrichment Model uses several different resources, within an underlying organization of human resources and materials, to provide the prescribed student services within the previously described school structures. These seven resources include: the availability of a Schoolwide Enrichment Team; the creation of a comprehensive and effective professional staff development model; the acquisition and distribution of supplemental curriculum materials and enrichment resources; the employment of a trained SEM specialist; participation in a network of SEM schools; opportunities for parent orientation, training, and involvement; and the existence of a democratic school management plan.

The Schoolwide Enrichment Team is composed of volunteer parents, teachers, administrators, and sometimes students. They help to organize schoolwide talent-development activities such as speakers' series, workshops, demonstrations, summer programs, after-school offerings, and special programs and competitions. They can also assist with identification and assessment procedures, and offer advice on program evaluation, planning, and improvements.

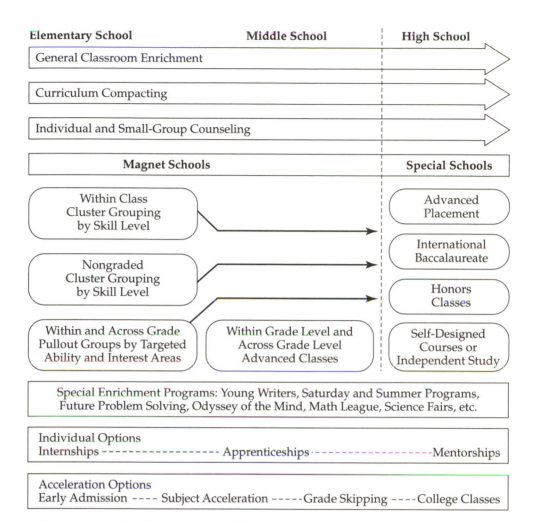

FIGURE 2–7   The Continuum of Services for Total Talent Development

A sound professional development plan is crucial to the successful implementation of an SEM program, but these offerings must include more than workshops and presentations. Effective staff development also requires the services of a support team that addresses individual teacher needs, goals, and implementation problems. Professional development can involve coaching, brainstorming, planning, and action research activities. Most importantly, sound professional development means that each teacher is treated as an individual, and his/her own learning styles and professional goals for SEM implementation should govern any subsequent services and help.

Teachers who provide talent-development activities usually need not only a regular curriculum but also additional materials and enrichment resources. The same is true for classroom teachers who modify or differentiate the core curriculum. Supplementary teaching materials, kits, and raw supplies do not have to cost an exorbitant amount, but they are necessary to permit the kinds of activities that are above and beyond traditional school offerings.

The employment of a well-trained enrichment teaching specialist is vital to the successful implementation and the longevity of an SEM program. This person serves as the "chief worrier" for program activities, and coordinates and facilitates student services. The SEM specialist also works with classroom teachers to plan or implement classroom-based modification, differentiation, and enrichment services.

An informal network of schools and districts across the nation helps participating SEM schools share information, ideas, and problem-solving strategies. The University of Connecticut coordinates this network and readily refers interested schools to other educators who provide similar services, or who work with similar-age students. Using the old adage that "two heads are better than one," the SEM Network links interested schools for visitations, phone conferences, and the sharing of program documents and student products.

Parents must be integrally involved in these activities in school, in the community, and at home, and feel as if they are partners in talent-development activities for their children. Orienting parents to the SEM philosophy and services helps them understand their role in providing their children with more challenging learning experiences. Parents also assist SEM implementation by providing valuable information about children's interests, their home-based enrichment experiences, and specific strengths or prior knowledge with regard to the core curriculum.

The last organizational component within an SEM program may be the most important. If we want to increase ownership and staff participation in modification, differentiation, and enrichment services, the school faculty must work within a management system that welcomes their ideas, their assessments, and their problem-finding and creative problem-solving abilities. Administrators must share responsibility for program development and implementation, and they must regularly check progress and collect data to assess growth and document accomplishments. Their leadership is crucial, but only within the confines of a governance structure that listens to and respects alternative propositions and varied approaches. Each teacher, like each student and each administrator, will initiate their SEM involvement with different levels of prior knowledge and expertise. Within a democratic management plan, these developmental differences are expected and welcomed.

Conclusion

SEM doesn't replace existing structure, but, rather, seeks to improve them by concentrating on the factors that have a direct bearing on learning. Evaluations indicate that the model is inexpensive to implement and has a common-sense practicality that appeals to professionals as well as laypeople (Olenchak & Renzulli, 1989). SEM takes a gentle and evolutionary approach to change. In the early stages of implementation, minimal but specific changes are suggested for existing schedules, textbooks, and curricular activities. These strategies have already demonstrated favorable results in different types of schools and with groups from varying ethnic and economic backgrounds.

Think of an automobile as a metaphor for SEM. The school is the car's body—preferably a Porsche—and the principal is the driver—preferably as bold and daring as Mario Andretti. The faculty represents the engine, loaded with power and constantly being tuned to become as efficient and effective as possible. Members of the Enrichment Team serve as the spark plugs, bringing energy to all activities. And the SEM specialist is the ignition and the distributor, initiating new developments and directing the flow of resources and energy to appropriate places. That automobile performs well on the track known as "special programs," but the model operates equally well in all schools that wish to be laboratories for talent development.

Chapter **3**

Stimulating the Development of Talent for Creative Productivity in Children through the Use of Refutational Processes

MERVIN D. LYNCH   CAROLE RUTH HARRIS   EUGENIE N. WILLIAMS

Various writers have linked the development of talent for creative productivity to that of independence; that is, the ability of a child to stand behind his or her convictions with courage (Coopersmith, 1967; Daniels, 1997; Davis, 1992; Sternberg, 1989). For some writers, an individual, to produce creative products or ideas, must trust his or her own perception of truth and reality and believe in the validity of his or her opinions to order and deal with uncertainty (Barron, 1969; Coopersmith, 1967). Coopersmith (1967) proposed that an individual who is learning to produce new ideas or products must believe that what he or she is doing is valuable and that he or she can tolerate adverse reactions that may result from public scrutiny of the innovations or ideas.

One way that this may be accomplished is through the use of refutational processes. The concept of refutation has been generally associated with Socratic reasoning; that is, a false argument is presented and an individual through systematic questioning proceeds to refute these arguments. Refutational processes have been successfully used in research to stimulate critical thinking (Fritz &

Weaver, 1986; Maria & MacGinitie, 1987); to immunize against persuasion attempts (Hennessey, 1997; McGuire, 1961; McGuire & Papageorgis, 1961); and in the teaching of science concepts (Govindarajan & Wright, 1994; Iran-Nejad, 1990; Maria & Johnson, 1990; and Wright & Govindarajan, 1994a, 1994b, and 1995). They have also been used in teaching as an occasional diversion from routine teaching methods but not as a consistently used curriculum tool.

The logic of the use of refutational processes in teaching of science concepts seems pertinent here. According to Wright and Govindarajan (1995), the successful use of refutation in teaching of science concepts assumes that "such an experience should ensure that students acquire meaningful knowledge and useful conceptual understanding; develop cognitive skills in directing thought patterns toward independent, creative, and critical ventures; and secure confidence in their potential toward applying their acquired knowledge in solving problems and making well-balanced judgmental decisions in ever-changing environments" (p. 26).

The uses of refutation, as in these science studies, apply to the teaching of critical insights that would seem to have merit for individuals who are at the secondary or college level or beyond, and who have learned to develop and trust their refutational processes at earlier grade levels. That children will learn to trust their own refutational facilities may not occur. Iran-Nejad (1990) reviewed research on students' approaches to learning and concluded that more than two-thirds view learning as knowing more, memorizing for later reproduction, or acquiring and using facts. According to Iran-Nejad, these students tend to take a surface approach to learning, which contrasts to the one-third who believe that learning involves new ways of thinking, insights into the subject matter, and personal growth.

Theoretical Rationale for the Efficacy of Refutational Techniques

The use of refutational processes requires many of the same mental processes as those involved in creative productivity. Such skills include (1) the use of critical thinking and error-detection skills, such as the ability to recognize errors; (2) the development of skills for suggesting solutions for and resolutions of erroneous information; (3) the development of a level of ego strength to be able to stand on his or her own convictions in correcting erroneous information; (4) the utilization of intrinsic motivation to stimulate creative productivity in the face of dissent or disagreement; and (5) the use of a highly developed sense of humor.

Refutational processes involve the development of error-detection skills; that is, the ability to recognize errors when they occur. Similar notions of error-detection skills provided the basis for tests developed by Gray (1915) in his oral reading test, Durrell (1937) in his measure of dyslexia, and Goodman and Burke (1970) in their Reading Miscue Inventory. However, the use of error-detection skills in those instances was for testing decoding skills and not for instructional purposes as proposed here.

Error-detection skills are required as part of the decoding process. According to Levin (1957), a child in decoding communications forms a hypothesis about an incoming communication and attempts to confirm this hypothesis on the basis of prior and present experience. Early discrimination learning may take place in instances in which a match-mismatch occurs when a child is expected to identify a color as incorrectly named or the number of objects on a table as incorrectly counted. In these instances, the child forms a hypothesis about the name of the color or the number of objects on the table, and attempts to confirm or refute that hypothesis. If he or she is unable to confirm the hypothesis, then the child may need to modify his or her representation of prior experience of the color name or number of objects so as to resolve these discrepancies. The child should be able to do so on the basis of available cognitive match-mismatch rules. The discriminations made with these rules may be fine-tuned or sharpened through the consistent use of refutation and elaborated on as the child grows and develops using more complex hypotheses-testing systems.

The development of error-detection systems as in refutational uses will likely involve neural network models that rely on error detection to develop a distributed representation of knowledge (Masson, 1990). Heuristics involved in some research applications of these detection strategies have been shown to be more likely applied to reduce costly errors than to detect simple inaccuracies (Friedrich, 1993), more effective when used by reflective than by impulsive children (Walczyk & Hall, 1989), and enhanced when subjects strived for accurate performance but diminished when response speed was emphasized at the expense of accuracy (Gehring et al., 1993).

When a child recognizes that an error has occurred, the child may require the development of new or specialized rules or codes for handling this discrepancy or the child may modify existing rules to handle the discrepancy. That children will likely use the latter approach is attributable to the contingency that individuals tend to be cognitive misers; that is, children will use a few cognitive rules to handle a wide range of situations. The child may also perform a search for common features with existing rules and adopt a new or different rule with which to resolve errors. For instance, if the child is given a mathematics problem such as $4 + 3 = 9$, the child, having detected the error, may resolve it by changing the 4 to 6, the 3 to 5, or the 9 to 7 and each of these three strategies will have worked.

It is likely in many instances that the child will not detect errors, and this is where training is needed. Results of a study by Plumb, Butterfield, Hacker, and Dunlosky (1994) illustrate the paucity of error-detection strategies that may be available to an individual to resolve errors. Plumb et al. found that the major decoding problem experienced by a sampling of high school and college students given exposure to texts with errors was not knowledge of how to correct the errors but the likelihood of detecting them. Plumb et al. attributed this to the possible dearth of error-finding strategies, a possible lack of motivation, and/or a failure to perceive the nature of the task.

The efficacy of refutational processes may be due to their ego- or self-enhancing effects. In general, individuals learn to master their environments by overcoming frustrations with which they are faced. As children learn to refute erroneous information, they not only will learn rules with which to master uncertainty in their environment, but will be motivated to make sense out of this mastery. Ego-enhancing effects of refutation such as these have been shown in studies of attitude immunization (Maria & MacGinitie, 1987; McGuire, 1961; McGuire & Papageorgis, 1961; Swan & Hill, 1982).

Coopersmith (1967) proposed that the development of self-esteem or self-concept would be essential for creative expression. According to Coopersmith, an individual will need a high self-concept in order to explore ideas and strike out in new directions, and this will require the belief that one can discriminate between sense and nonsense, that one can impose order where disorder exists. It is likely through the testing and validation of cognitive rules such as those for error-detection that a child through refutation will develop a confidence in his or her own ability to detect and resolve errors and also will learn to rely on the adequacy of these rules for handling new and more complex discrepancies.

The efficacy of refutational processes may also be due to intrinsic motivational effects. Hennessey (1997) and Hennessey and Amabile (1988a, 1988b) proposed that creative productivity is related to the nature of the child's rewards. According to Hennessey, children or adults will be most creative when they feel motivated primarily by interest, enjoyment, satisfaction, and the challenge of the work itself and not by external pressures. Refutational processes if successful should arouse interest, enjoyment, satisfaction, and challenge and as a result stimulate the arousal of intrinsic motivation.

According to Hennessey, one cannot teach intrinsic motivation to children; rather, one needs to eliminate possible deterrents to the expression of their intrinsic motivation. In contrast, one can teach the use of refutational techniques and processes, and through the development of refutational skills stimulate the arousal of intrinsic motivation with or without the removal of deterrents. Hennessey argued that one cannot teach intrinsic motivation to individuals; rather, one needs to eliminate possible deterrents to the expression of the intrinsic motivation. In contrast to Hennessey (1997), the refutational approach assumes that one can teach refutational techniques to children, which should, if successful, stimulate the arousal and use of intrinsic motivation.

Humor may play an important role in the child's use of refutational processes. A number of writers have listed humor as an important characteristic of the creative child (Daniels, 1997; Davis, 1992). Getzels and Jackson (1959) in their research showed that high as opposed to low creative high school students were more likely to inject humor into stories they are asked to make up in response to pictures, and this may also be true of younger children. The humor associated with incongruities may be in part a determinant of the increased motivation with which children react to refutational opportunities and should for this reason result in a higher extent of error detections and resolutions, but this remains to be shown.

Developing Refutational Skills

The development of skills in refutation may proceed in an increasingly complex manner. In early grade levels, this may take the form of presenting children with erroneous material that they should be easily able to refute. As a child develops, his or her refutational activities may move from refutation of simple errors to the refutation of discrepant information, or in social situations the refutation of communications that acceptable behaviors are inappropriate. This is essential for the child, who may be often seen as disputational and antisocial. Noncreative individuals may make disparaging comments about the creatively gifted child, and refutational techniques provide the creatively gifted child with a means of coping with this input in a well-adjusted manner.

As children become successful in the use of refutational processes, they may learn to trust their own refutational systems; this will likely enhance the development of their self-concept and their self-identity. It should be possible for the child to apply refutational processes to increasingly ambiguous discrepant events, thus enhancing the motivational utility for purposes of learning and application to complex concepts.

The basic premise in this chapter is that children need to be trained to learn refutational skills and rewarded for appropriate refutational use through instructional practice. Too often creative students, either because they are late bloomers or argumentative, are required by teachers to learn in a rote manner, and as a result, their refutational processes are underdeveloped or not developed at all. This is accentuated by the possibility that if these skills are not developed at the elementary grade level, it may be difficult if not impossible to develop them at a later date.

A second notion is that to start children at early grades in refutational activity, one needs to focus on tasks that are more easily refutable. Typically, this will not take the form of conceptual refutation. Rather, children can be encouraged to utilize their refutational processes by presenting them with erroneous materials that are designed to stimulate their use of refutation. For instance, if first graders are told that today is Monday, October 42, most children will question this outright. If they were told that America was discovered by Superman, they should also have considerable doubt.

Some Applications of Refutation

To date, we have applied refutational processes on a limited albeit meaningful basis to instruction in history, science, and math. One such use of refutation was by a graduate student who was an instructor in a remedial history course at the seventh grade level in one of the suburban Boston schools. The seventh graders were turned off by history and would not listen to any of the material presented by the instructor no matter how imaginative the presentation.

Refutation was applied in practice to test the theory, and positive results followed. The teacher walked into her classroom and announced that today she was going to discuss the Declaration of Independence. According to her, it was signed on July 4, 1996; the signers were Thomas Edison, Thomas Jefferson, and Sarah Caldwell.

The change in atmosphere that took place in the class was dramatic. Students immediately questioned 1996 as the date of signing, and there was considerable discussion. When the students asked about the signers, Thomas Jefferson was a possibility. Thomas Edison did things with electricity, but he did not seem right. But who was Sarah Caldwell?

The instructor said that Sarah Caldwell works in the "Combat Zone" area light district in Boston. A discussion of the "Combat Zone" ensued, as well as a discussion of Sarah Caldwell who was the director of the Boston Opera Company located in the Combat Zone in Boston. By utilizing refutation, students who were apparently turned off to history were suddenly motivated toward learning historical material as well as incidental content that accompanied it.

We carried out similar exercises in elementary mathematics courses. In general, mathematics tasks at the elementary level present the student with problems, and the student is required to solve each problem and fill in the answer in a blank space provided for that purpose. The use of blank spaces for some children may be accompanied by performance anxiety. When we inserted incorrect answers and had children correct them, we found that apparently children not only were less anxious about the tasks that required the same skill, but were more motivated to perform this work.

Finally, the efficacy of motivational stimulation of refutation was demonstrated in a middle school science course. The teacher had her students read the unit on chemicals from a class textbook which introduced students to basic concepts in chemistry. She discussed these concepts with the students and then presented contradictory statements such as "examples of acid include limewater, vinegar, and detergent." The students disagreed with vinegar because vinegar had a pH level of two and made many indicators red. Limewater and detergent are bases because their pH levels were seven or above.

She then asked a student if a farmer should add crushed limestone to his soil because he was told it was too basic. The student's response was, "I think that is wrong because limestone is a base and his soil was a base too. If you combine them, it's still a base. Also too much alkali will burn the crops so it is wrong." The student suggested the farmer add vinegar because acids neutralize bases and make the soil neutral and good for crops. The refutational approach stimulated both reasoning and reported satisfaction with the learning process.

When asked about the use of refutational methods, students reported that this approach "feels great. . . . Not only do we make mistakes but the teachers do too." Also, "I had to concentrate because the questions had some tricky parts and I really had to concentrate." Some students reported that they believed that this would help them to "improve their thinking ability and logic for later in life." Others stated, "We like correcting the teacher's wrong mistakes." [sic]

Some Examples of Refutational Strategies by Grade Level by Content Area

It should be possible to apply refutation in a large number of different ways and instances in the instructional process. Some practical examples will illustrate how refutation may work in areas of mathematics, English and language arts, history and social studies instruction by grade levels kindergarten through two, three through five, and six through eight.

In classroom uses of refutation, we have been careful to query all students to make sure that they are not carrying errors away with them. It is interesting to note that it may be more likely that students will carry such errors with them if we did not use refutation with subsequent queries.

I. Grades Kindergarten through Two

A. Mathematics

Children may be asked to correct the following examples, which will require that they not only recognize what is wrong but be able to solve the problems.

$$
\begin{array}{cccc}
1 & 2 & 4 & 3 \\
\underline{+4} & \underline{\times 8} & \underline{+12} & \underline{-2} \\
7 & 8 & 5 & 4
\end{array}
$$

B. English and Language Arts

Children may be asked to edit writing samples for incorrect facts and misspelled words.

The wulf huffed and puffed and blue the hous up.

The cat sat undr the dore and cryed moo, moo.

The bog darked and darked.

The dall was hit with a dat.

C. History and Social Studies

Children may be asked to correct historical facts.

Magellan discovered America.

Columbus was elected President of Israel.

II. Grades Three through Five

A. Mathematics

Children may be asked to correct answers to word problems as well as to equations.

Suppose Mary was four years older than Jane was three years ago and Mary is presently ten years old. How old is Jane now? Answer: Eight years old.

Correct the following equation:

$$8 + 4/2 = (8 + 4)/2$$

Henry runs five miles and ends up ten miles ahead of Sally. If they run at the same speed, how far ahead of Sally was Henry at the start? Answer: Seven miles.

B. English and Language Arts

Children may be asked to edit paragraphs so as to correct for misuse of punctuation and misspelled words.

Tom; the janitors' son swept the flour befour going to skol. The principle mr adams could not beleave that Tom had spilled flower over the flour from his choose. After talking with Tom principle adams now new that Tom needed to wash down befour coming to skol.

C. History and Social Studies

Children are asked to correct facts such as in the following paragraph:

After traveling for months through the steamy jungles of Canada, Dr. Livingston and Miss Stanley spotted each other in the moonlight and Dr. Livingston was heard to say, "Aha, Miss Stanley, at last I found you. They each then displayed the collection of Angolan monkeys they had obtained in Mongolia, and discovered that they were approximately identical.

III. Grades Six through Eight

A. Mathematics

Students at this level may be asked to correct solutions of equations or probability problems.

$$\text{If } x + y = 2 \text{ and } y = 3 \text{ then } x = 5$$
$$\text{If } X \times Y/3 = 7 \text{ and } Y = 9, \text{ then } X = 4$$

If you were to flip a coin 250 times and you were to get 240 heads on the 250 flips than the probability of getting a head on the 251st flip would be 240/250.

B. English and Language Arts

A student might be asked to correct inappropriate facts from literature.

One might propose that Hamlet wounded Ophelia with a razor blade obtained from a Stop and Shop in Picadilly Square.

One might also propose that it was a woodpecker (not a raven) that was knocking, knocking, knocking at Poe's condominium door.

C. History and Social Studies

Students at this age are required to learn about American history and to establish causes for historical events. One might ask for corrections on conceptual materials as follows.

The Civil War was fought to protect the South's interest in the stock market, especially the markets in Europe and Asia. The fact is that with each point rise in the Dow Jones, 200 soldiers died in the Civil War. A second cause was that there was need for the development of medical treatments for yellow fever. It was possible for doctors to learn extensively about its cause from the large number of soldiers who were bitten by rattlesnakes during the Civil War.

Summary

It should be possible to design individual procedures for all academic areas utilizing refutation as an instructional process in the implementation stages. It should also be possible to evaluate the effectiveness of such curriculum for stimulating the development of talent for productivity and its recognition for children. The proof of the utility of the refutational process will be in such applications and evaluations.

In the meantime, teachers themselves will need to learn risk-taking behaviors, and this may necessitate the development of increased ego strength. It is important that teachers need to learn that they do not always have to be factually correct in the classrooms. It may be the case that children find teachers more human when they make errors, and in fact the children likely will learn better from teachers who present erroneous materials with sufficient opportunity for refutation.

One concern that may occur to some is that children will become cynical rather than critical in their behaviors as refutation is more frequently and consistently utilized as an instructional tool. To date, we haven't seen the emergence of cynical behavior as a result of the use of this technique. But with increased use, this is always possible. As teachers become more sophisticated with the use of refutation, it should be possible to moderate the level of criticism so as to produce a child with a talent for producing and recognizing creative products who is a sensitive, informed, and courageous critic.

How Parents and Teachers Can Enhance Creativity in Children

JANE PIIRTO

These thirteen suggestions for enhancing creativity in children are based on my Pyramid of Talent Development Model, encompass the "suns" of home and school, and focus on creativity within domains (Piirto, 1995a, 1999). Feldhusen's TIDE (Talent Identification and Development) model also focuses on creativity within domains, rather than creativity as a general factor or creativity as merely divergent production (Feldhusen, 1996). The assumption is that creativity is the underpinning, the basement, the foundation that permits talent to be realized. Creativity is here viewed more as an aspect of personality than as the cognitive propensity to be fluent, flexible, or the like.

To be creative is necessary in the realization of a fulfilling life, but with all due respect to Mensa, having scored high on an intelligence test is not necessary. We are all creative. Those who are more creative than others have learned to take risks, to value complexity, to see the world, or their own surroundings, with naïveté. They have learned to be creative even if their creativity has been pushed down, stifled, and diminished by sarcasm and abuse. Creativity is often a matter of tone, of attitude. The following thirteen precepts illustrate this. They are appropriate, with your own modifications, for all ages of children at all developmental levels. They are precepts and not prescriptions.

Provide a Private Place for Creative Work to Be Done

For Teachers

If you are a teacher, take a look around your room. Mentally reconfigure the room so that you have a loft or a place where children can go. Create a hideout beneath a table or a desk in the back or front of the room. Pitch a tent in the room. Get an upholstered chair that faces the wall. Replace the desks with soft chairs and couches. Use your own creativity to imagine a place where good schoolwork can get done and yet there is a place to read, to think, to draw. Use access to this place as a reward, distributed fairly to all students, of course.

For Parents

I have done a little informal research on the need children have for a private place. "Where do you go when you want to think?" I ask. "Have you ever built yourself a place that is just yours?" Almost all the students have. As a parent, I remember the places my own children built—beneath the staircases, in the garage, in the living room with blankets and pillows. In my work as a National Endowment for the Arts Poet in the Schools, I often used my own poem about children's love of secret hideaways.

Forts

there's one beneath the basement steps
carpeted with a crib mattress
closed off with a worn out bedspread

there's one in the attic
secret in the junk and jumble
small hollow under caving boxes

there's one in the garage
where this week's neighborhood club
exchanges officers
"No Grils Allowed"

there's one this rainy Sunday
hung from the television
over chair and stool, one quilt's

drooping width to the beanbags
holes shut with towels
corners pegged with books

the cat slips in to visit
reclining brother and sister
covered inside a warm soft roof

whispering and bickering
in the world of the marxes
three stooges

they told me
when I peeked
I'm too big to fit

© 1979 Jane Piirto, from *mamamama* (Sisu Press)

One of my students told a story after reading this precept: She said she would scold her youngest child, who wouldn't keep her room to the immaculate standard of the household. She said the child kept running away to hide on the rock beneath the porch, and she had made a vow to close off that space next summer. After reading this, she felt tears rising in her throat. She loosened her immaculate standards, and the house became a home for the child as well as for the mother. "I let her begin being a person who lives there, and not just a hotel resident," my student said.

Provide Materials

For Teachers

If the child has talent in a certain area, and if the parents do not have the means to develop that talent, the school has a responsibility to try to do so. Does your schoolroom have supplies, and are the children encouraged to be free with the supplies? Teachers are known for their propensity to gather odd pieces and bits of materials and to recycle them for use in the classroom—oatmeal cartons, scraps of cloth, milk bottles, discarded containers—all become part of the teacher's supply closet. Put clothes into costume boxes for dramatic play. The school should not only have materials, but should provide musical instruments and make sure sketchbooks are available as well.

For Parents

Yes, it costs a lot and takes a year or two to pay it off—those time payments for the piano, the trumpet, the saxophone—but do it. No one started to be creative in adulthood without having some thread for that creativity leading back to childhood.

Let your house be the house where the kids hang out. Besides knowing where your children are, the richness your life acquires with a houseful of teenagers cannot be duplicated. Junior high school boys who are creative often get involved in role-playing games such as Dungeons and Dragons or Magic. However, if as a parent you don't like to have hordes of kids around, don't fake it. Kids can tell. Just remember to provide supplies, private places, and encouragement.

Encourage and Display the Child's Creative Work, But Avoid Overly Evaluating It

For Teachers

Do you as a teacher know what talents your students have, and do you praise them for themselves; or are you in the dark? Many a child has stopped singing or drawing because of a teacher's or other students' sarcastic comments. Look back at your childhood in school for a moment. What did a teacher or a peer say to you that made you stop singing, stop drawing, stop writing? Are you that same teacher, making remarks to children? Your remarks will live forever in those children's minds. A colleague told me this story the other day. He wrote on a student's paper that she was very talented in mathematics, and he forgot about the comment. A few years later, she sent him a card, telling him that she was finishing studies for her Ph.D., and that his comment had given her inner permission to go to graduate school. Your words have legs, wings, and immense power. Use them for good.

For Parents

So what if it doesn't look like a dog? I have a theory that many people stop attempting to draw when they view their work and see it lacks verisimilitude, doesn't look like the object being drawn. The child knows; you don't have to rub it in. Is the refrigerator door an art gallery, covered with your child's work? How about the walls of the child's room? Would someone entering your house know that your child lives there? My children and I used to draw portraits of each other. Here is a poem about it:

A Profile

practicing profiles
with charcoal
on drawing pads

my children and I
buffoons at the hippodrome
before the chattering TV

doing ballet-to-commercials
and somersaults
we are giggle boxes

now it's her turn.
she hushes me
sits right-angled

squinting at me
slowly setting lines
to my portrait

"Mama you will love this!"

later she shows me coded
a squat pumpkin
with clenched teeth

full face front
carol burnett's smile
pigtails with triton ends

"I can't draw curly hair"
philodendron-leaf eyes
a pig's snout

and stars on my crown!

© 1979 Jane Piirto, from *mamamama* (Sisu Press)

Along the same lines, does your child's practicing of his musical instrument drive you nuts? My sister's violin practice used to do that to me. But she had to practice.

Some people say you shouldn't force lessons on your children, but I'm the living grateful example that it didn't hurt me. Although I never had the raw talent or practice obsession to become a professional musician, my piano goes with me whenever I move houses, and it provides hours of solitary pleasure as I improvise and sing and feed my soul. I play well enough for my own pleasure and those of the people who like to sing old songs and show tunes behind me.

Do Your Own Creative Work, and Let the Child See You Doing It

For Teachers

So what if you're a math teacher? Do your students know you are also a cabinet-maker? A painter? A writer? That you sew, or knit, or design boats? The wee bit of humanizing that such information about you does for you with your students can make a big difference in their feelings of freedom of expression with you. Try it. The cooking, the crafts, the building, the refinishing of furniture, the designing of exercise routines and gardens all emerge in these teachers' descriptions as times when they feel creative. Teaching itself is a creative activity.

The postmodern idea that teaching is meandering pleasurably with students in a river of knowledge where the ideas to be pursued arise from the context of the discussion supports the idea of teaching as a creative activity, but the curriculum planners who make teachers hand in detailed behavioral lesson plans and check off detailed task boxes have taken the creativity out of what is essentially an art form, a form of skilled craft raised to the sublime when the teacher is really in there with the kids (Slattery, 1995). Teaching itself feeds on your creativity, and if it were only an activity where you "deliver" curriculum, you would atrophy and die, become disillusioned. Teaching is an art, the teacher's art.

For Parents

Does your house have a special place where the parents (as well as the children) can do their creative work? The writer Lucia Nevai is author of the 1997 book of short stories, *Normal*. She also won the prestigious Iowa Short Fiction Award in the late 1980s. She lives in a small apartment in New York City and supports herself with a job in media. When she writes, she goes to her room and puts this sign on the door: "Lucia's writing." The message machine on her telephone has this message. "Lucia's writing. She'll get back to you later. Leave a message." She values her own creativity, and her family values creativity also.

This is especially difficult for women to do. Loeb (1975) called it the "If I haven't dusted the furniture do I have the right to begin carving?" syndrome. We think that we have to sneak our creative work, and not tell anyone that we're doing it. Here is a poem I wrote in the early 1970s.

Poetmother

the afternoon is calm
silence time to write
the paper is green
like the summer

the mind floats into itself
like distanced birdsong
with images bright
as the kitchen sink

the polished coffee table
slowly right there
the words twist
from the images

and the fingers
take dictation
fast and willing
then the back door slaps

and his feet
in dirty sneakers tramp
and the voice begins

"Mom where are you?
I can't find anyone to play with
Where's the juice?"
(Mom I want)
(Mom I own you)

"You can't catch me!"
and the front door crashes
and a little girl runs
shrieks laughing

through the twisting words
and out again
the back door slams
on my resentment

a child's voice yells
"Bye Mom!"
I sit up and try again
for stillness

Now I write in the morning. For me, such morning writing time is a joyous luxury. The point is that people must make space and time for their creative work and to let children see this.

Set a Creative Tone

For Teachers

When I was a school principal, I tried administratively to set the tone of the school as one of valuing creativity. I encouraged the kids to write a lot of poems and stories. Besides hiring professional writers to work with the students, through Teachers and Writers Collaborative, I myself wrote for them.

Many of the teachers in that school likewise set examples of creativity, and it showed in their rooms. The halls were filled with artwork; the bulletin boards were replete with children's efforts. The rooms were filled with learning centers, and every week there was a performance or a class project. The *atmosphere* was creative. The teacher's lounge talk was often of movies, plays, books, and musical performances, with opinions freely given about the latest pan by the local theater critic. The teachers were interesting people, interested in creative things, and it showed in their interactive teaching. When you enter a school, you can just tell what the atmosphere is. What do the administrators and teachers value? Are there stern signs ordering you to go immediately to the principal's office, but no directions as to how to get there? Are there institutional lockers and gray walls? Is the school more nearly like an army barracks than a joyful place where children learn to value their own creativity and humanity?

One school I remember well. There was an actual waiting room near the entrance, with couches, lamps, magazines, and bulletin boards of children's work. When parents came, they chatted with each other, shared the gossip of the day, and felt as if they, too, had a place in the school their children attended.

Value the Creative Work of Others

For Teachers

Yes, I know you live in some small rural town miles from any *real* cultural life. I know. I grew up there. So why, in my hometown of Ishpeming, Michigan, is there a project that has preserved the local history, the accomplishments and experiences of the whole community? And why has that research been done by seventh graders? And why has it won national awards? Called The Red Dust Project, a small junior high school has since 1975 been collecting the stories of the local residents and publishing them in an illustrated book.

This project was initiated by a teacher. Teachers are usually the most stable part of a community. The administrators leave, the parents are involved in the school only while their children are in school, but the teachers often stay for twenty, twenty-five, thirty years. What one teacher and her supportive administrator have done has been to teach the children to interview and write up the interviews. The children have had their work displayed at the Smithsonian. They have been interviewed themselves, for national television. All because a teacher had an idea that rural junior high school students from the wilderness could do a creative project with the people in this small mining community.

For Parents

Is your house filled with books? Do you subscribe to any magazines? Do your children subscribe to any magazines? Do you visit the public library? Does your child have a library card? When was the last time you went to a museum? A live performance of theater or music? You say you live in South Dakota and have two radio stations on the dial, both of them country-western? Do you have Internet access from your home? Provincialism is a state of mind, not geography.

Examine Your Family Mythology

For Parents

Your family mythology is important. Finish this sentence. "In our family, we—." "In our family we—*value the arts, and talk about art.*" "In our family we—*go to col-*

lege." "In our family we—*read books.*" "In our family we—*go to museums.*" "In our family we—*play on sports teams.*" When parents ask me how to get their kids to do certain things, I ask them what their family mythology is. In my family, I knew I was going to college from kindergarten, even though my parents were children of Finnish immigrants and neither had been to college. In fact, my parents couldn't speak English when they went to kindergarten.

What family mythology made all my cousins, my sisters, and me believe we could go to college? The motivation of immigrant families is not new, and my family's story is probably similar to your family's story. The story is still happening. Asian American families in particular have succeeded, by and large, within our U.S. school structure.

For Teachers

If your students don't have a family mythology that encourages cultural activities such as museums, concerts, or books, then your role is crucial. Field trips are a bother, yes, and busy school administrators often discourage efforts to take students to cultural events; but this should be a priority and a necessity, not a burden. Even if there is no encouraging atmosphere for field trips, videos of cultural events can be used.

At the very minimum, each student should have a public library card, and each classroom should have a set of encyclopedias. As teachers, you can make sure that this happens. And model for your students that research and learning are part of your life, as well. Here is what one writer I studied said about her favorite teachers:

> *My "creative writing" teacher in high school was certifiably senile; I switched out of the class, an honors one, to a regular English class with a teacher who loved grammar. I hated grammar, but I learned there to love learning, precision with words. Other memorable teachers were so only because they loved what they taught; thus I, who cannot draw a straight line with a ruler, recall the electricity and excitement of geometry class; I have a lot of buried knowledge and continuing fanaticism about Alexander the Great, because of an ex-jockey-turned-history-teacher whose love of that period of history sent me to the most obscure and advanced of resources, gave me a knowledge of library sources that has served me since, and gave me an absolute adoration of the whole process of knowledge: from the atmosphere in libraries to love of books for their new bindings and type as well as for their contents. It was not, I emphasize, WHAT these people taught, but HOW that worked the miracles—and I try to remember that every day I go into a classroom. (Navarre, 1978)*

Remember what the writer quoted above said about it not being what her teachers taught, but how they taught.

Avoid Emphasizing Sex-Role Stereotypes

For Teachers

The presence of red ribbons on the lapels of entertainment stars at award ceremonies on national and international television is not just a political statement that there should be research on AIDS; it is a personal statement that good friends and colleagues have died, and the wearer is wearing a token in memoriam. This should not be forgotten by jaded television viewers who think that the entertainers are self-promoting. One characteristic of creative people is emotionality and empathy, and every red ribbon probably means a friend has died. The creative fields of the arts, fashion design, and theater have been visited by a great plague in the past two decades.

Many people who are homosexuals, regardless of gender, seem to have always known this about themselves, though some repress the knowledge. Surveys show that the middle class is less accepting of homosexuality than of heterosexual infidelity, lack of church attendance, and single parenthood. They believe that homosexuality is a choice and not a biological preference. Nevertheless, some literature disagrees. A book about how a talented boy discovered his homosexuality is the cult classic, *Best Little Boy in the World,* by Reed (1977). The works of the prizewinning fiction writer Leavitt (e.g., 1997; 1990) are also instructive in the description of coming to awareness of one's homosexuality. Whether homosexuals are more creative than other people is not known; however, it would seem that creative fields are more open to sexual divergence.

The point is that following rigid sex-role stereotyping limits creativity. The personality attribute of *androgyny* should be emphasized here. In order to succeed in the world of visual arts, for example, a female artist needs to be willing to exhibit what are typically called masculine characteristics (Getzels & Csikszentmihalyi, 1976). The profession of artist demands an extraordinary commitment in terms of willingness to take rejection, to live in poverty, and to be field-independent. Those are often typical traits of committed males, but not of committed females, who often choose careers as art educators and not as artists.

Girls' problems come when they try to reconcile the stereotypical paradox of the nurturing, recessive, motherly female with that of the unconventional artist (Piirto, 1991b) or other aggressive, creative, and productive professional. According to Bem (1974), success in most areas seems to require traditionally masculine traits. Boys' problems come when they try to reconcile the stereotypical paradox of the six-shootin' muscle-flexing "real" man with that of the sensitive, perceptive, and insightful artist. There is no evidence that creative people in the arts are more often homosexual than people in other fields, such as teaching, politics, the military, or athletics. There is evidence that creative girls are more tough-minded and that creative boys are more tender-minded than their peers (Piirto and Fraas, 1995).

For Parents

I'll bet the Marlboro Man and the Sweet Young Thing aren't very creative, for they represent the extremes of masculinity and femininity. More highly creative men and women are more androgynous than noncreative men and women, according to Bem (1974). On a continuum of masculinity-femininity with the most masculine and most feminine at either end, creative children and adults are more toward the middle. The humorist, screenwriter, and movie director Nora Ephron in her essay "Breasts," described her childhood thus: "I did not feel at all like a girl. I was boyish. I was athletic, ambitious, outspoken, competitive, noisy, rambunctious, I had scabs on my knees, and my socks slid down into my loafers and I could throw a football" (p. 468).

Androgyny may be one of the keys. Or to put it another way, creative people seem to have both yin and yang. We did a study of creative adolescents using the HSPQ (Junior-Senior High School Personality Questionnaire) and OPQ (Occupational Personality Questionnaire) that indicated that yes, indeed, high school boys in the arts were more tender-minded and more nonconforming than a comparison group of other boys (Piirto, Cassone, Ackerman, & Fraas, 1998d; Piirto and Fraas, 1995). Myers-Briggs Type Indicator (MBTI) data indicated a similar personality preference as the creative boys preferred Feeling to a greater extent than academically talented boys and a comparison group of other boys (Piirto, 1998a). Our studies support the research of Barron (1968, 1972, 1995) and others at the Institute for Personality Assessment and Research (IPAR) that showed that creative men had traits of sensitivity and creative women had traits of assertiveness and intellectuality (compare Helson, 1983; MacKinnon, 1961, 1978b).

Provide Private Lessons and Special Classes

For Parents

Most schools, unless they are special schools for the arts or sciences, are not going to provide all of what your child needs to truly develop his/her talents, and so you must be the one to do so. This means lessons as well as materials. Even if your child plays in the band, the orchestra, jazz band, or string ensemble, if your school is fortunate enough to have such groups, your child also needs private lessons in order to develop musically. This is usually understood in the field of music and dance, but is less understood in writing, visual arts, and theater. Few children who have talents and the desire to learn get private lessons or tutoring in these fields, and this is a terrible shame.

The Development of Talent Project described by Bloom (1985) documented well the sacrifices and provisions that parents went through for their talented children. Parents are the first and most important influences on their children's talent development. Talented children who become successful adult professionals study and practice the skills of their field to the point of automaticity. The notion that creativity is separate from what is produced by the adolescent, that it springs from exposure to general exercises in fluency, flexibility, brainstorming, and elaboration, without specific nurturing in the field in which the creativity is exhibited, seems not to have influenced, at this time, the curricula of special schools for talented adolescents such as Juilliard or the LaGuardia High School for the Arts.

Actually, the role of parents and specialized teachers in these adolescents' talent development seems more important than whatever structured creativity training they have had. Parents often nurture and direct their children in the fields in which the parents themselves have interest and talent. The talented child is then taught by a teacher, who passes on what knowledge he or she can, and then the teacher passes the child to another, more masterful, teacher. That is the path of creative adult production. In the very depth of their special training, these children are developing automaticity. In their adolescent years, spontaneity in young creatively talented students often gives way to conformity.

For Teachers

The value of mentors is often spoken of in the literature for the talented. Researchers such as Simonton (1995) and Zuckerman (1977) have gone so far as to say that a person will not reach eminence in science without apprenticing himself to a mentor scientist, without studying with the right teacher. Kogan (1987) also discussed the importance of having the right teacher, who will have access to the right connections.

The classroom teacher and the specialist in talent-development education also have a role, that is, to provide the child and the parents with information about suitable mentors. Although the relationship between mentor and mentee is deeply personal and cannot be legislated or mandated, efforts can be made. Schools must also play a part in the development of talent, helping find private teachers and mentors for talented children from families without financial resources.

If Hardship Comes into Your Life, Use It Positively to Teach the Child Expression Through Metaphor

For Teachers

Try to notice and be sensitive to the situations of the children you teach. Don't be under the impression that a child will not be creative because he is poor or disheveled. A student of mine, a bilingual Spanish-English teacher, discovered the creativity of one boy who lived in extreme poverty, but who was almost always reading, even at seemingly inopportune moments. She took photographs of him reading in the bus line, in the lunchroom, in the hallways, in math class, on the playground. She then identified him as having potential writing talent by asking him to write stories, which were extraordinary blends of Mexican and Central American mythological characters. She recommended him to the specialists in talent-development education in his district, even though his IQ scores did not meet the threshold cutoff (see Piirto, 1999, for further details).

Release of emotion through the arts is often indirect, and may be more therapeutic than therapy itself. The depth psychologists, the archetypal psychologists, the neo-Platonists speak of the fire within that is turned into an *image,* a thing *out there* (Hillman, 1996; Jung, 1965, 1976); compare Plato's *Ion* (Hamilton & Cairns, 1996). The expression is itself enough. Remember the life of Christy Brown as shown in the movie, *My Left Foot* (Sheridan, 1989)? Brown's family refused to let him be institutionalized for his profound handicaps and provided him with materials, company, support, and a neighborhood full of loving friends.

Singer/songwriter and high school teacher F. Christopher Reynolds has created an extracurricular program called Creativity, Inc. (Reynolds, 1990, 1997). He works with selected students in ten areas that combine their personal experience with the creation of images in poetry, music, clay, paint, and the like. Many of the suggestions and books on how to enhance creativity focused on the "springtime" of creativity, but the creative person must visit winter as well. Many speakers about creativity celebrate the joy of creativity, using such words as *enhancing, unlocking,* and *tapping,* with images of leaps, flights, openings, growings, and increases. These metaphors are good and useful and necessary. Creativity is also a reflection as to what has occurred, and this is felt in a receptive mode—returning what has been received.

In this way, creativity can be permitted to be somber and to sing the blues, drawn inward toward gravity. Creativity and productivity across a lifetime should not only mean optimism and excitement, the idea of constant improvement with no regrets and wrong turns, for creativity also involves the dark side, the introversive, contemplative, intuitive, insightful side, in order to round out the whole picture.

When the *image* is created, a metaphor, a personal poem, story, song, painting, theater piece, clay sculpture—anything that objectifies the emotion that is churning—the young creator can begin to have some peace. One of the teams that visited Kuwait after the Gulf War was a team of art therapists, who asked Kuwaiti children to draw the horror they had seen, of invading soldiers breaking down the doors of their homes and raping their mothers. The therapeutic value of creative work should not be overlooked. Self-therapy is one powerful reason for creativity. After all, the word *create* means *to make.*

However, the biographer Joan Dash (1988) differentiated between ordinary autotherapeutic creativity and the creativity of very talented people. She said of Edna St. Vincent Millay, American poet/playwright:

> *If Edna Millay had been only a neurotic woman, death-haunted, claustrophobic and sexually ambiguous, she might have found considerable satisfaction as well as worthwhile therapy in whatever art form she took up in her spare time. . . . But she had also been born with the peculiar genetic equipment that can become high talent, perhaps even genius, and in her earliest years had acquired the habit of hard and precise observation of the world around her, as well as the discipline that leads to transmuting experience into something more than therapeutic art. Her fears of death became everyman's fear of death, her longing for love and her denial of it became the universal cry of the spirit to be part of something greater than the single self. Just as the poetry transcended her own individual nightmares, so did the poet herself, in the very act of writing, push back the cage of self to join humanity at large. (p. 156)*

For Parents

The challenge of personal hardship often leads to creativity. "Aren't there normal creators?" people have asked. Can't a person be creative and live in a happy family, have a happy life? This question of whether trauma is necessary to creative expression is certainly debatable. One new study has shed some light on this. Aren't there normal people who are creative? Yes, of course. But in some domains—for example, creative writing, music, and visual arts—the preponderance of turmoil in the creatives' lives comes through loud and clear (compare Andreason, 1987; Jamison, 1993, 1995; Piirto, 1990, 1995b, in press).

Normal creatives come from homes rich in books, with lively discussions and lessons in art and music. The parents are themselves creative, and their style of discipline is either authoritative or permissive. The students had a voice in the home and were raised to be independent decision-makers. It may not be out of line to say that teachers make good parents of creative children. A look into biographical literature shows that many normal creative people had one or both parents who were teachers (Piirto, 1991a, 1991b).

If trouble comes into your family, try to help your child or yourself create an image of it. Writer and storyteller Marie Vogl Gery told of her yearlong residency at a junior high school where the mother of one of the boys she worked with committed suicide. This boy demonstrated talent and expressed his feelings through poetry that didn't specifically refer to the suicide, but that permitted him indirectly to defuse his feelings of sorrow, confusion, and sadness. The creation of an image, a metaphor, is helpful and even necessary in bringing the hurt outside without having to talk about it. Indeed, "talking therapy" often does not work with young people, who, when asked what is wrong, may not be able to say. However, by the creation of an image, the hurt can be diffused into the metaphorical, and thus healing can begin.

Emphasize That Talent Is Only a Small Part of Creative Production, and That Discipline and Practice Are Important

For Teachers

Teachers of the talented especially must realize that such children are often overly praised and rewarded just for possessing the talent. Teachers of the artistic disciplines—the visual arts, writing, music, dance, theater—know what it takes to realize that talent, but often such talented students are not given special help by the school. They are instead thrown in with far less talented students in art, music, math, and science. This would never happen in athletics, where talented students are permitted to advance according to their abilities, competing with people at their own levels of expertise. Accurate and qualified feedback is important in the development of talent, and the child should have access to people who have some expertise. Thus, mentoring is important.

Talented people often are talented in many dimensions, and it is hard to choose which field to pursue. The clue is often found in passion. If a person likes to practice, likes to work at the domain, loses track of time while doing it, thinks of it when not doing it, the answer may be found. If the doing is more play than work, the "gift" is poking toward consciousness. Although absolutely necessary, the presence of talent is not sufficient. Although many people have more than one talent, and wonder what to do with them, what is the impetus, what is the reason, for one talent taking over and capturing the passion and commitment of the person who has the talent? A useful explanation comes from Socrates, who described the inspiration of the Muse (Plato, *Ion*) (see Piirto 1998b, 1999, in preparation). Carl Jung (1965) described the passion that engrosses; Csikszentmihalyi (1990a) described the process of flow; depth psychologist James Hillman (1996) described the presence of the *daimon* in creative lives; and E. Paul Torrance (1987) described "the blazing drive." All these give clue to what talent a person will choose to develop.

Hillman (1996) described the talents in a way similar to Plato's and Jung's: "The talent is only a piece of the image; many are born with musical, mathematical, and mechanical talent, but only when the talent serves the fuller image and is carried by its character do we recognize exceptionality" (p. 251). Hillman's idea is similar to the notion of "vocation" or "call." I would call it *inspiration* or passion for the domain. Philosophers would call it *soul*. Thus I have put an asterisk, or "thorn," on the pyramid to exemplify that talent is not enough for the realization of a life of commitment. Without going into the classical topics of Desire, Emotion, Art, Poetry, Beauty, Wisdom, or Soul (Adler, 1952), suffice it to say that the entire picture of creativity in talent development ensues when a person is pierced or bothered by a thorn, the *daimon,* that leads to commitment. Feldman was close when he described the *crystallizing experience* (Feldman, 1982b), but the thorn is more than crystallizing; it is fortifying.

Another challenge for teachers is not to counteridentify. Often the teachers of talented students are almost as jealous and anxious as parents are. When teachers counteridentify, they feel horrible when the student doesn't perform or when the child makes a mistake. They are as narcissistic as the parents described by Alice Miller in *The Drama of the Gifted Child* (1997). This is particularly difficult when the teaching relationship becomes a coaching relationship. Teachers can be temperamental and cruel, pushing hard until the students hate the field. True realization of creativity comes through hard work, tolerance for ambiguity, preference for complexity, passion, motivation, and discipline. That has been emphasized repeatedly through studies of creative people and their interactions with their domains of creativity. A child gradually realizes that talent comes through habits of hard work. Remember that there are two stages in the development of talent. The first stage is the natural stage, when everything seems to come easily; during the second stage, the adolescent learns the formal aspects of the discipline—the talent becomes consciously developed (compare Bamberger, 1986; Feldman & Goldsmith, 1986; Feldman & Piirto, 1995; Piirto, 1989a, 1989b, 1990, 1991b). The world is full of talented people, but fully creative people do a lot of hard work.

Avoid Emphasizing Socialization at the Expense of Creative Expression; Allow the Child to Be "Odd"

For Teachers

The schools often see their major roles as socializing children so they fit into a mold and become acceptable to the society that the schools serve. This is considered to be as important as teaching the children to read and write and figure, for this is what the real world demands, say some educators. But creative people are often at odds with the world and are prickly, rebellious, and nonconforming. Often their nonconforming is actually conforming, but conforming to a stereotype similar to how they perceive creative people to behave. Often, creative students act out in class, are argumentative, and consciously underachieve—that is, they do well in classes they like but don't care about classes they don't like or don't see as relevant to their futures.

Some may recommend that such creative students need therapy. But they view themselves as *too* different, *too* creative, *too* cool for any intervention from the schools. Often their rebelliousness carries over to the therapist's office as well. One teenage creative writer I know said she sat silently and stubbornly when she was sent to a therapist. Another creative child videotaped for a case study by one of my students said that even though her mother made her go to therapy because of her nonconforming behavior, she didn't feel she had benefited because she felt smarter than the therapist. Thus the selection of the therapist is also quite important. Creative people generally understand creative people, recognize kindred spirits. Sending a creative child to a rigid therapist may not work.

For Parents

So your daughter didn't get to be Clara and had to settle for being a mouse in *The Nutcracker*. So your son didn't get his brilliant short story accepted for publication by that magazine of children's writing. Is this the end of the world? Is it your child's or your own ego that is hurt? Parental narcissism, counteridentification— that is, parents investing so much of themselves in their children's successes and failures that they lose sight of the purpose of the practice—can be very harmful.

At the other end of the continuum, some parents either deny that their children have talent, seemingly fearful of what might be the implications for their future development, or they don't see their children's talent as important. Or, like the mother of a talented young actor, who told the teacher never to put him into another play because all actors are weird homosexuals, they fear the child's talent will lead him/her down paths the parents do not want. The need to get along with others is not paramount in creative people. Most creative people weren't president of the club or queen of the prom or the one voted most likely to succeed. Often, they were odd. For many, high school was the most painful time, as the pressures for conformity beckoned. Often, too, high school creative youth will band together in what they call nonconformity but will still dress the same as their other non-conformist friends, listening to the same music, reading the same books, and rebelling together. College youth do so also; my interdisciplinary studies creativity class always has an inordinate number of students with pierced tongues and punk hair.

Develop a Creative Style: Use Kind Humor and Get Creativity Training

For Parents and Teachers

Besides enjoying and being frustrated by that child's sense of humor, we as parents and teachers should monitor our own ways of dealing with creative children. Do we enjoy children? Do we laugh with children (or at them, if appropriate)? Do we have fun with children? In other words, is being with creative children the pleasure it can be?

If school districts are serious about effectively teaching creative thinking, they must provide the necessary backup training. There are many commercial programs available and many trained people who can provide creativity training for school districts. School districts also should provide the rigorous instruction in the fields and domains in which the creativity training can be applied. Many opportunities for teaching students to be more creative exist. Some of these are extracurricular, and some of these are curricular. The techniques and lessons must be integrated with and incorporated into the courses as they are taught. Every school has experts who can help the student who is creative in some domain to be nurtured in that domain.

Many people do not believe that the school is the place to work to enhance student creativity, and in fact, they doubt whether any such exercises do really train people to be more creative. I am of mixed opinion on this; on the one hand, doing such exercises can make people aware of what goes into creativity, if the exercises are based on the research about creative people. These would be likened to the drills that athletes practice or the scales that musicians practice or the skills that one seeks to acquire to get automaticity in an area in which one wants to be expert. On the other hand, perhaps such exercises are too abstract to promote transfer.

After all, does practice in risk-taking encourage the risk-taking that creative people must have in doing their creative work, as well as in pursuing their careers? Is risk-taking teachable through a creativity-enhancement exercise? If one begins to think about this, though, one realizes that the "ropes courses" through which many businesses send their employees to build a sense of trust in each other also encourage physical risk-taking as a "safe" rehearsal for "dangerous" life. With these caveats in mind, I have compiled a list of possible activities teachers could use to construct educational experiences for their students in hopes they will learn to be more creative (see Table 4–1). They are organic to the creative process and not imposed from outside, they are nonlinear rather than linear, and the results lead to a deepening of an understanding of the power of inner creativity.

Thus it can be seen that enhancing creativity is possible with careful attention to opportunity, attitude, and environment.

TABLE 4–1   Exercises to Enhance Creativity

Divergent Production
  Brainstorming
  Fluency and Flexibility
  Novelty/Originality
  Elaboration
Core Attitudes
  Cultivating Risk-Taking
  Cultivating Naïveté or Openness
  Building Group Trust
  Making It Habitual: Thoughtlogs
The Five I's
  Imagery
    Guided Imagery
    Ten-Minute Movie
  Imagination
  Intuition
    Intuition Probe
    Psychic Intuition
    Dreams and Intuition
  Insight
    Grasping the Gestalt
    Aha!
    Zen Sketching
  Inspiration
    Visitation of the Muse
Creativity Rituals
  Solitude
  Creating Ideal Conditions
  Background Music
Nature
  I Am a Naturalist
  This Is the Day Which the Lord Hath
    Made
Meditation
  Meditate on Beauty
  Meditate on the Dark Side
  Meditate on God

Improvisation
  Jazz
  Theater
  Word Rivers
  Writing Practice
  Creative Movement to Rock 'n' Roll
  Rhythm and Drumming
  Scat Singing
  Doodling
Use of Humor
  Telling Jokes
  See the Sunny Funny Side
  I Am a Worm
Synaesthesia
  Seeing
  Hearing
  Smelling
  Tasting
  Touching
Exercise
  A Walk
  A Run
  Aerobics
  A Team Game
  Trance Dancing
Passion
  Stepping into the River
  Flow
Conversation
  A Salon
A Visit to a
  Bookstore/Library
  Museum
  Concert
  Play
  Movie
  Reading or Lecture
  Place (Travel)
Individual Creativity Project
  Other

Personality Considerations

This section includes two chapters that focus on some personality correlates of the creative child. Farley proposes that creativity is an ability that is a combination of genetic and environmental factors. Levin and Greenwald propose that creativity often expresses itself as late blooming.

Farley in Chapter 5, entitled "A Genetic Model of Creativity and the Type T Personality Complex with Educational Implications," proposes that the Type T trait plays a major role in creative functioning. For Farley, extremely high levels of creativity involve risk-taking behaviors, leaving the rules behind, and letting go of the status quo. He suggests that there is a model of genetic influence operating from genes through the Type T Personality Complex to creativity. In this context, he warns that Type T youngsters should not be lost to education through rebellion, dropout, or burnout behaviors. He proposes that Type T youngsters may require instruction by Type T teachers or at least Type T teaching to enhance the growth of their creatively productive talents.

Levin and Greenwald in Chapter 6, entitled "Swimming against the Tide: The Creative Child as a Late Bloomer," propose that children who have talent for creative productivity may not exhibit this talent early in school but may do so at a later age. According to Levin and Greenwald, these children may fail in the classroom because they are not ready to perform at a consistently high level early in school and teachers' expectations of their performance may be set at that stage. The authors state that cultural standards may suppress creative development in that children are taught that there is only one right way of doing things. Children with this talent may not make deadlines and are often involved in activities that are considered to be out of the mainstream, and this may provoke anxiety with teachers. Levin and Greenwald suggest that the extrinsic rewards often offered for performance for many children may not work with creative youngsters who find satisfaction in pursuing their own creative inclination. The authors suggest that we need to develop techniques for early discovery so as to facilitate the development of creative talent on an early as opposed to late bloomer basis.

A Genetic Model of Creativity and the Type T Personality Complex with Educational Implications[1]

FRANK FARLEY

In educational research and educational psychology, two of the more neglected topics are creativity and personality. For example, there has been negligible coverage of either topic in the American Educational Research Association convention program over the past many years. There is only one listing under creativity in both the 1996 and 1998 convention Subject Indexes; personality is not listed at all.

We need new thinking in solving the problems of education and society at large because many of the old ideas are not working. Major creativity is required. We need it to solve the seemingly intractable problems of horror and violence, personal and public failure, social disconnectedness, and declining civility. The schools could be a major influence on our creativity capital, but they are not. It would be easy to give up on schools as we know them ever becoming major stimuli for creative growth; creativity is not edugenic in the United States.

---

[1]Revised version of a paper presented at a symposium at the American Educational Research Association Annual Meeting, New York City, April 8, 1996. Author's Address: 213 Ritter Addition, Temple University, Philadelphia, PA 19122.

What about personality? The current state of personality science is one of the crowning glories of twentieth century scientific psychology. In my view, personality is becoming our central individual differences concept. Dramatic but unheralded advances in personality theory and research have produced validity and reliability as high as or higher than any area of differential psychology and with underlying theories that are powerful in extending the role of personality into major facets of human functioning, including creativity. We now know the main outlines of personality structure—no small feat given the complexity and importance of personality—and we have evolving theories as to what these structures mean for a range of psychological functioning. The near-universal convergence of data and interpretation on a structure of personality ranging from three to seven fundamental dimensions, with the presently favored conception being the so-called Big Five, is an intellectual and scientific accomplishment potentially as important as the so-called "Grand Synthesis" in physics, the near universally agreed-upon idea that there are four fundamental forces in nature. But these powerful conceptions of personality are essentially unknown in education, and in the learning sciences generally. They need to be incorporated into our conceptions of creativity and thinking, and into the educational psychology of school achievement.

Which brings this chapter to my small corner of psychology.

Some years ago (Farley, 1986), I proposed the terms Type T Personality and Type T Theory to reflect a risk-taking, thrill-seeking, stimulation-seeking, novelty-seeking, arousal-seeking, openness-to-experience personality dimension. This is seen as a trait of temperament and as being in part genetic. Think of a continuum of human behavior characterized at one extreme by high risk-taking, stimulation-seeking, thrill-seeking, excitement-seeking, openness-to-experience—what I call the Big T or Type T end. The other extreme is characterized by risk aversion and little or no openness-to-experience, what I call the small t end. The use of T is shorthand for thrill-seeking, chosen on the belief that the motivation at the base of most risk-taking and openness-to-experience is simply the thrill of it, the excitement of it. The assessment device we have used the most, historically, was that of, or a variant of, Zuckerman, Kolin, Price, and Zoob (1964), or on occasion similar measures (see Farley, 1971), and more recently we have used our own measure or have been engaged in participant-observation research without traditional assessment. The factors that I believe motivate the Type T versus Type t person are summarized in Table 5–1. Not all Type Ts or Type ts are motivated by all the factors listed in Table 5–1, but I believe most of the factors are involved. It should be noted that most of the factors listed in each column in Table 5–1 tend to be conceptually related. I also believe that Type T persons tend to be high in energy, show strong independence of judgment, are self-confident, and believe they are in control of their destiny. There is T-positive (T+) behavior and T-negative (T–) behavior. I believe the T+ represents healthy, constructive, and positive forms of risk-taking and thrill-seeking, and significantly underlies human creativity. Examples of T+

TABLE 5–1 Factors Presumed to Motivate the Type T Personality

Motivates Big T	Motivates Small t
Uncertainty	Certainty
Unpredictability	Predictability
High risk	Low risk
Novelty	Familiarity
Much variety	Little variety
Complexity	Simplicity
Ambiguity	Clarity
Low structure	High structure
High intensity	Low intensity
High conflict	Low conflict

behavior include most entrepreneurship and capitalism, most creativity, and healthy, developing relationships, to name a few. T– behavior represents the destructive and negative side of this persona. Examples of T– behavior might include aspects of delinquency and crime, unrestrained experimentation with dangerous drugs, drinking and driving, and unsafe sex in the era of AIDS, to name a few. I believe a major determinant of the Type T temperament is heredity, but that the positive or negative direction this trait displays (T+ versus T–) is primarily due to the environment. This conception is represented in Figure 5–1.

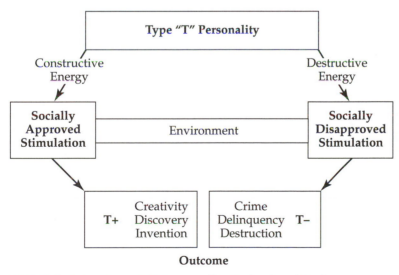

FIGURE 5–1 Type "T" Personality Behavioral Pathways

In addition to the T+ versus T– distinction, it is proposed that a distinction can be made between T mental (Tm) and T physical (Tp) aspects of risk-taking, thrill-seeking, and openness-to-experience. Addressing the ancient mind/body distinction, the Tm and Tp distinction suggests that some Type T individuals tend to emphasize psychological aspects of Type T behavior (for example, cognitive creativity, entrepreneurship), and others tend to emphasize physical aspects of Type T behavior (for example, thrill sports, adventure). It is realized, of course, that at the level of personality, mind and body cannot be perfectly discriminated. For more details on T+, T–, Tm, and Tp, see Farley (1991).

The evidence for a genetic factor in openness-to-experience and thrill-seeking is strong. Two studies—one at the National Institutes of Health (NIH) (Benjamin, Li, Patterson, Greenberg, Murphy, & Hamer, 1996) and the other in Israel (Ebstein, Novick, Umansky, Priel, Osher, Blaine, Bennett, Nemanov, Katz, & Belmaker, 1996)—have independently confirmed a significant connection between alleles of the D4DR dopamine-receptor gene and novelty-seeking in at least one fairly large sample (Benjamin et al., 1996) using blood assays. This goes way beyond earlier twin studies also implicating genetics in risk-taking and novelty-seeking or Type T behavior. It also is the *first ever* identification of a specific gene being related to "normal personality."

Despite genetic involvement, the role of the environment remains very strong, as it does in all traits for which some genetic role has been established. Indeed, Hamer (1997) reported that D4DR accounted for 4 percent of the novelty-seeking trait. He estimates that ultimately there might be shown to be as many as ten genes involved. Knowing the genetic contribution helps us to know better the environmental contribution and to know better what we *can do about* the trait or the behavior.

I believe the Type T Personality is a factor in many forms of creative functioning (Farley, 1974, 1985, 1986, 1991), especially perhaps the exceptionally high levels of creativity—as in Picasso, Einstein, Elvis, Churchill, Crick, Chomsky, Ted Turner, Margaret Mead, Bird, and Bach. I don't believe you will ever show the highest levels of creativity unless you are willing to enter the realm of the unknown, the uncertain, leaving the rules behind, letting go of the handrails and the status quo, in a word—*taking a risk*. Thus I put risk-taking and the Type T Personality at the center of creative functioning. Of course, many writers have given personality a significant role in creativity. I would give it an even more major role, connecting creativity to the incredibly rich network of concepts and research in contemporary personality science.

Feldhusen (1994b) in a major paper identified personality variables as one of the three main factors in creativity. Many of the personality variables he identified as critical are also part of the Type T Complex, including intense independence, high energy, and an internal locus of control. Martindale (1989) also identified crucial personality elements—many of which are found in the Type T Complex—including self-confidence, high energy level, wide range of interests, curiosity, preference for complexity or ambiguity, problem finding, disinhibition, unconventionality, and *openness to experience*. Martindale especially identified the last three as crucial. Note that it is openness to experience for which a gene has now been identified! Amabile (1987) has emphasized the "passionate interest in their work" (p. 224) and the intrinsically and internally motivated characteristics of creative individuals. Barron (1995) (see Farley, 1998) is one of the pioneers in the study of the creative personality, identifying such factors as independence of judgment, preference for complexity, tolerance of ambiguity, and risk-taking—again, characteristics also of the Type T Personality. If what I call the Type T Personality Complex is a major factor in creativity, what are some implications of this?

First, I would open a debate on the genetics of creativity, and propose a model of genetic influence operating from genes through the Type T Personality Complex to creativity. The proposed model of genetic influence might look like Figure 5–2.

The D4 + T = Cr figure suggests that several genes, especially D4, influence the Type T Complex, which is also influenced by the environment, and Type T itself is a factor in major aspects of creativity. I believe the role of the Type T Complex has been established for creativity, and the role of at least the D4 gene in the Type T Complex has been implicated; therefore, I believe we need to give some attention to what might be called the *New Genetics of Creativity*. There will be a lot of further research needed in pursuing the New Genetics of Creativity and in sorting out the implications of the model proposed here.

For example, research is needed that incorporates measures of creativity, measures of the Type T Complex, and the same kind of genetic analyses Hamer (1997)

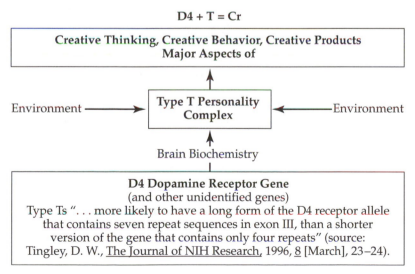

FIGURE 5–2   Influences on the Type "T" Complex

has employed, all on the same sample. It would need to conform to Hamer's requirements of a within-family design "... comparing children born to and raised by the same parents ... eliminate the effects of ethnicity, and ... minimize the effects of differences in rearing environment" (Hamer, 1997, p. 113). Such a study would directly test our proposed model. One problem will lie in measuring creativity, ensuring that a variety of approaches to assessing this often-ineffable quality are used. Where the Type T Complex is concerned, the relevant measures from Benjamin et al. (1996) and Ebstein et al. (1996) as well as other measures employed by Farley (1974, 1986, 1991) in his research would need to be included.

Second, the Type T and creativity connection suggests that *adaptive education* must be considered for Type T youngsters so that they are not lost to education through rebellion, dropout, burnout, or *misdiagnosis by well-meaning professionals* as having a behavior disorder, conduct disorder, antisocial personality, ADHD, or some other questionable DSM-IV diagnosis. The genetic involvement makes it even more mandatory for the educational interventions to be adaptive and precise. To engage the Type T's in schooling and keep their interest and commitment high will require a *passionate pedagogy* not usually seen. These T Types are easily bored by routine or overdetermined teaching. This can be a deadly boredom in that there are many stimulating, thrilling, and exciting alternatives in this high-option society, and some of the options are deadly, including drugs and delinquency. Boredom is eating away at American education in general. It may be the No. 1 problem of contemporary schooling, and education reform as proposed won't arrest this cancer in the classroom. Teachers increasingly cannot compete with TV, the Internet, and related media, and for Type T students the situation is acute. Therefore, *Type T Teaching* is imperative for Type T kids. That is, *passionate pedagogy* involving Type T personalities as teachers—flexible, inventive, enthusiastic, risk-taking, experimental, open-minded and nonauthoritarian. Techniques for Type T Teaching would include discovery learning, inductive instruction, fast pace, variable pace, dramatic and challenging presentation, high regard for autonomy and independence, and acceptance of ambiguity.

School teachers reading this would say: "Dream on, professor. It ain't going to happen." They're right. And because they are, we will increasingly lose much of the creative potential in school performance as we lose the attention or engagement of our T Types.

In one hundred years, we have gone from the intimate instruction of the little red schoolhouse to the impersonal pedagogy of the big brown school factory. Few attempts to reinvent have arisen from educational research, and shame on us for that. We have been too much the compliant technocrats serving the system and staying close to narrow empirical efforts. We have shown too little of the questioning spirit and the risk-taking of true creativity.

But there is hope. As one glaring possibility, American schooling is going to be changed from the outside, beyond the factory gates, by Bill Gates and all those creative T Types, often poor students descended from smokestack schooling, who are creating the computer and communications revolution that will issue in cyber-schooling. With cyberschooling, the potential for individual initiative, autonomy, independence, intrinsic motivation, risk-taking, challenging the rules, and so on that motivate T Types may usher in a golden age of global creativity, where personality will be a major and sustaining factor in creativity in cyberspace. The present creativity/personality/genetics model may be helpful in facilitating this transformation.

Chapter **6**

Swimming Against the Tide

The Creative Child as a Late Bloomer

JACK LEVIN   *NINA L. GREENWALD*

Norms of proper timing create socially accepted deadlines for the completion of life's transitions, achievements, and occasions. Because of the presence of such norms, the members of society are in general agreement as to when they are supposed to arrive at business appointments, by what age they may date and marry, and even precisely when they are expected to feel hungry. Indeed, the presence of time constraints provides a degree of stability and predictability without which organizing collectively would be extremely difficult, if not impossible (Levin and Levin, 1991).

According to Shekerjian (1990), "staying loose" is, over the long term, very uncomfortable. Ambiguity makes many people confused to an intolerable extent. As a result, they tend to frame their analyses and queries in clearly delineated terms having yes or no answers. In this way, individuals can exclude the fuzzy middle area of gray—everything can be reduced to a more reassuring "either/or," "black and white" dichotomy. At the same time, this reduction in ambiguity serves to satisfy a need for closure that characterizes most people.

Like other achievements in life, success in school has been given a socially constructed deadline. Students who achieve by the expected time are considered to be acting in a socially acceptable manner, and those who do not succeed "on time" may be labeled as "off schedule" and regarded as failures. If they eventually do attain success, albeit exceeding the deadline, such students may still be regarded as "time deviants" and labeled as "late bloomers."

Research on late bloomers has focused mainly on violations of the agreed-upon timing of the transition from high school to college. Levin and Levin (1991) have identified two criteria on which success in making this transition is usually measured. The first is the chronological age at which individuals matriculate and complete their educational requirements. In the United States, for example, most college students have conformed to time standards—some 80 percent of all American college students begin their freshman year by the age of 19. The second criterion concerns the timing of the demonstration of academic excellence. By their high school years, students are expected to have achieved the grades and standardized test scores necessary to be admitted to college; all postsecondary institutions with admissions standards require applicants to submit their high school academic records. In the United States, approximately 79 percent of all students enrolled in four-year colleges and universities were A or B students in high school (U.S. Bureau of the Census, 1995).

The Expectation for Consistency

From a very early age and long before they begin to think about attending any college, academically talented children are expected to demonstrate a consistent level of competence in the classroom. The expectation for consistency can be so strong that parents of early readers might make plans for their kindergartners to attend an Ivy League university, and elementary school teachers may respond to their "gifted" students from previous years in a manner that is quite different from the way in which they treat their "average" students. Tracking into homogeneous ability groups may, as a result, institutionalize this widespread tendency, so that students who begin in a low track continue, from year to year, to be viewed as intellectually deficient. Conversely, students who begin with the "gifted" label may be able to maintain their lofty academic status throughout their years in school (Howe and Lauter, 1972; Rosenthal and Jacobsen, 1968).

Children who fail at an early age are expected to fail again and again throughout their academic careers. It should come as no surprise, therefore, that the prophecy of consistency is generally fulfilled—most students who do well in the first grade also do well in the twelfth grade and beyond. Late bloomers are not expected nor accommodated in the academic system.

The presence of a socially constructed schedule for academic success permits detailed planning, on an annual basis, for the quantities of textbooks to be used in a class and for the training required by teachers, as well as the size and number of classrooms. In addition, strict norms of educational timing make possible methods of evaluation of student progress measured against norms for their chronological age (Levin and Levin, 1991).

This perhaps explains what amounts to an almost universal preference for scheduled age-graded educational achievements. The expectation for blooming on time is extremely rigid in most societies. Thus, in England, India, and Japan, students who have not achieved high grades by their early teens are effectively eliminated from the pool of college eligibles. In France, Germany, England, Japan, China, and throughout Latin America and Africa, students are generally separated into secondary schools that lead to a college education and secondary schools that do not. In Germany, France, England, and Sweden, students may be tracked by the high school subjects they study. In France, for example, only in mathematics does academic excellence assure a path to every area of higher education (Clark, 1985; Levin and Levin, 1991; Neave, 1985).

Americans have at least some tolerance for late blooming, though they too strongly prefer succeeding by a deadline. As a result, some students in the United States can still attend college, even if they do not fulfill their academic potential early in life. For many late bloomers, the community college becomes the only bridge between their mediocre high school record and admission into the four-year college of their choice (Levin, 1993; Levin and Levin, 1991).

According to Lynch, Scotti, and Rindler (1973), many late bloomers are actually creative learners who, for one reason or another, realize their potential only later in life. Early on, they simply do not fit the expectations for "normal" behavior. As soon as they are perceived as unconventional, they are likely to get into trouble with teachers, parents, and friends (Gardner, 1993a).

Winner (1996) similarly emphasizes that late bloomers are not seen as "gifted" when they are children, but go on to make a creative contribution as young adults, if and when they discover a field of particular interest. Indeed, they often wait until college before expressing their creativity and intelligence in a discernible way. As young children, potential late bloomers may show great curiosity, unusual interests, a willingness to take risks, and a tendency toward nonconformity—but they hardly appear to be the talented individuals they eventually become. In high school, late bloomers may become almost fanatically preoccupied with a project, job, or activity outside of the requirements of the classroom (Levin, 1996). As young adults, however, they discover their "calling" as a result of some "life-changing" event in which their confidence is reinforced and their talents are encouraged (Winner, 1996).

The Influence of Sociocultural Forces

Cultural standards often work against developing creativity. The creative impulse is reduced whenever the members of a society place too much emphasis on teaching their children *the* "right" way of doing things (Barron, Montouri, and Brown, 1997). Youngsters fear ridicule from their peers for being different; they also fear having "crazy hunches" that might indicate they are somehow psychologically unbalanced. By establishing a single standard of correctness for everyone, society discourages efforts to be adventurous, to experiment in uncharted intellectual waters, to be original, to look at things in an unconventional way. Valued instead are children who can be conventional and who are afraid to take intellectual risks—in other words, children who lack a creative impulse.

Another cultural bias against creativity involves the preference for immediate results. Americans tend to be impatient with long-term objectives in general. They prefer a quick-fix—"Give me an answer now"—mentality and short-term payoffs (as in the joke, "Question: When is this report due? Answer: Yesterday"). In the classroom, the preference for immediate results translates into rewarding students who are able to arrive at a specified conclusion during a finite period of time (the average "wait time" for student responses to a teacher's question is not more than one second)—hence, the widespread use by teachers of timed tests to measure various abilities (Purkey, 1978).

Many creative children do not operate well under time-bound circumstances. Others discover that their creative abilities go unrecognized. Indeed, many of the world's greatest creative breakthroughs were generated over long periods of time. Creativity is about good thinking, rather than quick thinking. Creative ideas typically require time to come to fruition. This is the reason that many important creative contributions are made later in life. For example, Mozart struggled a decade or more before producing his major innovative accomplishments in music composition; he struggled another decade before developing a second stylistic breakthrough (Gardner, 1993a).

Environmental Factors

There are at least two kinds of environmental factors involved in explaining why many creative children bloom late. First, there are occurrences leading to the failure to develop an ability by a socially constructed deadline. Armstrong (1994) argues that many such occurrences in the life of a young child consist of what he calls paralyzing experiences—experiences that "shut down" various forms of intelligence by means of emotions such as shame, guilt, fear, or anger—for example, a student who is humiliated by her teacher in front of her classmates, or a child who is rejected by his friends for acting like a "geek."

Clearly, children from an early age are told that it is unnecessary, or even a drawback, to be creative. In many classrooms, creative thinking is discouraged, punished, and impeded. Those children who have the courage to express their creativity risk being labeled as failures at school as well as in their personal lives. They may be stereotypically perceived by teachers or age-peers as bizarre, noncompliant, unproductive, inefficient, impractical, lazy, or misfits.

By definition, creativity requires a deviation from the mainstream—something different, something unusual, something new. By choosing to pursue a creative approach, a child is no longer squarely "in step," in a given field of study or in life generally. He or she may resist the rules, appearing strange to those who choose to conform.

The presence of creativity therefore provokes considerable anxiety around the need for stability and predictability in life's events. Those individuals who dare express their creativity may be perceived as threatening the smooth functioning of an institution (for example, a classroom). Because they are frequently discouraged by teachers who prefer conformity, creative youngsters are not typically at the top of their class, nor do they score well on standardized tests. Indeed, they may be asked to repeat a grade, punished with detention, and ignored by their teachers (Gardner, 1993a).

Even the sorts of rewards so effective in motivating other students may instead discourage truly creative youngsters. Forms of extrinsic motivation designed to get students to comply with learning standards may, for creative students, only decrease the pleasure associated with learning. A creative student who finds satisfaction in pursuing a creative inclination may feel punished by the external constraints that his or her classmates find rewarding (Amabile, 1983a).

Throughout history, most societies have been less than kind to some of their creative citizens who might be perceived as a threat to the status quo rather than as innovators in any positive sense of the word. In some cases, creative individuals were only shunned or ridiculed; in other cases, they were killed (Cszikszentmihalyi, as quoted in Shekerjian, 1990, p. 53).

All of this is hardly lost on creative children. According to Gardner (1993a), there are what he calls "creatophobic" factors that inhibit the expression of creative potential. Some individuals become so self-absorbed and worried about themselves that they have little psychic energy left over for channeling into creative pursuits. In some cases, they may even become hopeless about possibilities for changing anything. Gardner suggests that such potentially creative but "neurotic" individuals engage in psychotherapy in order to free their energy for creative purposes. He also suggests that models for creativity may be especially helpful to someone who has the potential for creative ideas but lacks the courage to go against conventional thinking about a topic or issue.

Although not immune to paralyzing experiences with people and institutions, certain sustaining characteristics of creative children, such as their cognitive skills, habits of mind, and flexibility, frequently help protect them from total devastation. A key characteristic of creative individuals, from the early years, is that they set their own goals and standards for achievement and successes, goals that are typically at odds with sociocultural expectations.

Creative students tend to be intensely inner-directed and unconventional. They are much more likely to comply to the idiosyncratic standards they have internalized than to any social construction. Creative children generally refuse to be pushed around by what other people think. Instead, they create their own measures for achievement and success, becoming only more self-assertive and less conventional in response to their rejection by others.

In addition to paralyzing experiences, Armstrong (1994) also suggests a number of environmental factors that may prevent on-schedule intellectual development. In the case of delayed musical talent, a child's family may be so impoverished that he or she cannot afford to own a musical instrument. In the event of retarded logical-mathematical talent, a child may grow up during a period of time when math and science programs are being underfunded. In the case of bodily-kinesthetic ability, a child may grow up in a big-city high-rise where his or her exposure to the natural environment is restricted. In the event of delayed artistic talent, a child's parents may encourage certain more "practical" pursuits (for example, linguistic intelligence) at the expense of his or her spatial abilities.

On the other side of the ledger, Feldman (1980) has referred to circumstances leading to success as crystallizing (as opposed to paralyzing) experiences. Such "turning points" can, of course, occur in early childhood, but they can also occur after the deadline for success has long passed. Whenever they take place, crystallizing experiences "are the sparks that light an intelligence and start its development toward maturity" (Armstrong, 1994, p. 22).

There is a wide range of crystallizing experiences—a relationship with an encouraging adult who recognizes a child's particular form of intelligence, a therapist who encourages a youngster to succeed in a neglected area, or a course that inspires a child in a previously unexplored area. In addition, some crystallizing experiences may take subtle forms. Certain children experience developmental lag in areas that are regarded as essential for success. They may have learning disabilities that improve over time, especially through active remediation. Still others may receive effective counseling for emotional problems that reduced their academic effectiveness earlier.

Creative students who wait until they are in their college years to express a talent or ability may be stimulated by a negative experience. In previous research, misery was seen as a turning point for academic success—that is, as an important precipitant in the process of encouraging profound individual change (Levin, 1993). From this perspective, even severe depression, if treated effectively, can have a positive aspect. Through a therapist, a depressed individual may gain the motivation to make profound changes in his or her life.

It is well known that creative people can suffer psychic disturbances including depression. But creative individuals are also problem-solvers who recognize the value of success, even in a conventional sense, if it gives them the opportunity to do what they really seek to do. The creative student who exceeds the deadline and becomes a late bloomer may therefore be a compromiser—someone who recognizes that he or she can accomplish his idiosyncratic objectives only by becoming more sensitive to conventional standards.

Of course, many miserable people, whether or not creative, remain miserable, even when they are motivated to change. In order to be successful, they need a positive influence: a mentor, a peer group, or a role model that serves to supply them with the encouragement and support they need. Once a creative person decides to succeed in any conventional sense, then, the influence of instructors, advisers, and good friends becomes critical.

Some creative students reduce their achievements in high school, but many others are from an early age consistently thwarted. For such children, the roots of late blooming may be found in the early years of school. It has long been known that creative ability is stifled in the elementary schools and that creative students are, from an early age, labeled in derogatory ways (Holt, 1964; Kozol, 1967; Silberman, 1970).

Moreover, many creative children seem to operate under unusually high levels of anxiety. In combination with difficulty with details, they may easily be labeled as problem children or as emotionally disturbed. In more extreme cases, they may even be placed in special classes for emotionally disturbed youngsters or be given drug treatment for ADHD. The result is to suppress their creative impulses (Lynch, Scotti, and Rindler, 1973).

Creativity and Stages of Development

The notion of a fixed progression is deeply imbedded in the history of developmental psychology. For example, Piaget (1948) suggested that cognitive skills develop in a series of stages, each of which is a necessary condition for the next. From the Piagetian perspective, therefore, a child must first move through the concrete operational stage before he or she is cognitively ready to engage in formal reasoning and abstract thinking.

Extensive research conducted over the last two decades instead supports the view that cognitive development is much more uneven and unpredictable than the Piagetian version would suggest. Certain children progress in almost all areas at about the same rate, moving through the Piagetian stages of cognitive development as predicted. Other children make major advances in some respects, while they make very little in others. Some children are not ready for logical reasoning until they reach their adolescence, whereas other children exhibit patterns of logic when they enter the first grade. Piaget himself acknowledged that different children at various ages develop at different rates. There are some who develop in a direction that is not consistent with the Piagetian model (Swartz and Perkins, 1989).

Some research that supports the possible reversal in developmental stages for highly creative children comes from a study in which Lynch and Nottingham (1975) tested 160 children, 20 each in grades 1–8, with the Miniscat (1974) measure of creativity and the Draw a Person Test. Detail units were counted on the Draw a Person Test, and children were divided by grade levels into high and low creative groups using a median split at each grade level. Low as opposed to high creative children ages 6–8 were shown to use significantly more (twice as many) detail units in the Draw a Person Test. No difference in detail usage was shown for high and low creative children ages 9–11. High as opposed to low creative children ages 12–14 showed significantly more (twice as many) details on the Draw a Person Test. If one assumes that the extent of detail usage is directly related to the extent of focus on concrete operations, one may conclude that high as opposed to low creative children focused less on concrete operations during the normal developmental stage, ages 6–8, and more on concrete operations during the developmental stage of abstract processing, ages 12–14.

Based on Lynch and Nottingham's findings, it is possible to speculate that creative children reverse normal developmental patterns by focusing on the cognitive rules for abstract processing at the very time when their less creative counterparts are attending to concrete operations. Once they have mastered abstract reasoning, however, creative children are then ready to focus on the development of concrete operations. And they do so at a time when less creative children are just entering the abstract processing stage.

Creative children are particularly likely to deviate from any model that proposes uniformity in intellectual development. They are more typically different thinkers who, from an early age, have a predilection for complexity and a drive for deeper levels of understanding. Inherently, they tend to be experimenters, exploring meaning by playing with ideas and possibilities and constructing new ways of understanding based on the outcomes. In contrast to the notion of a set of mutually exclusive stages of development, these children travel concurrently within more than one stage. They are masters at alternating "childlike" thinking with more sophisticated levels of thought to produce unique ideas. As a result, they may be regarded as immature or even emotionally disturbed.

Encouraging Early as Opposed to Late Blooming in the Creative Child

As we have earlier suggested, many students who bloom in college may be creative individuals whose talents and abilities have never been recognized in any formal sense. Under different conditions, they might have succeeded far earlier—perhaps even in the elementary grades. Indeed, it may be possible to examine those characteristics of the college years that have encouraged creative students to become late bloomers for clues as to what could have been done to help them bloom at a much earlier age.

1. *The college curriculum recognizes and encourages specialized talents.* In some cases of late blooming, the college student really does not have to make profound changes; it is the learning environment that changes. In contrast to the broad range of abilities expected of students in elementary, middle, and high schools, the expectations for students at the college level tend to be much more specialized, based on their personal interests and talents. After taking a "thirteenth year of high school" consisting of a selection of basic courses in a variety of disciplines, most students are required to choose a major. From this point on, they may be able to avoid courses in the curriculum they consider irrelevant or too difficult and focus their energies on their favorite subjects—subjects that permit them to express their own particular forms of intelligence, as in social work (personal), music (musical), visual-spatial (graphic design), or bodily-kinesthetics (theater arts and dance).

According to Swartz and Perkins (1989), elementary school teachers should be cautious about accepting any approach that assumes that all children can or cannot do certain things at various ages. Instead, teachers should recognize the inconsistencies in students' intellectual development and teach to their students' areas of special concern. Also recognizing differences, they should not necessarily assume that all of their students are developmentally unprepared for instruction assuming patterns of logic. For example, the structure of scientific thinking can be taught to many creative students in grades K–8 who have developed an ability for abstract processing long before Piaget recognized that such abilities were present.

Creative children may also not pay enough attention to details to satisfy the requirements of an elementary teacher who lacks understanding of their personality style (Lynch, Scotti, & Rindler, 1973). Creative youngsters may lag behind their classmates in terms of psychomotor skills. As a result, they may not be able to stay within the lines when coloring or painting. Creative children often possess a perspective at odds with the aesthetic and artistic conventions shared by their teacher, and may be regarded as willful and disobedient students who refuse to cooperate. Creative youngsters may spend more of their time in the periphery of attentional focus. They may pay little attention to teacher demands for taking notes home to parents or bringing lunch money to school. Teachers who recognize and accommodate the idiosyncratic learning needs of all children tend to foster and encourage the development of creativity.

Gardner (1993b) emphasizes that we have incorrectly treated intelligence as a unitary concept reflecting the tremendous value that we have in Western society for verbal and mathematical skills. He proposes instead that intelligence comes in a variety of forms including musical, visual-spatial, interpersonal, and bodily-kinesthetic skills.

From the elementary school years on up, verbal and mathematical abilities are emphasized to the exclusion of the other varieties of intelligence. To be considered a success, it is necessary for a student to excel in these and related areas—for example, geography, science, social studies. As a result, creative youngsters who are brilliant musicians or exceptionally insightful in human relations may nevertheless be regarded as abject failures—unless they also achieve high marks in arithmetic, punctuation, and spelling.

2. *The college curriculum recognizes and encourages differences in learning styles.* A second aspect of the learning environment also tends to change from high school to college. From kindergarten on, the teaching-learning format tends to be structured hierarchically—that is, from the teacher on down to the student. In college, the hierarchically structured classroom continues to make its presence felt—for example, in the form of large introductory lectures—but there is also space for a wider range of teaching styles, including small discussion groups, constructionist learning, and the Socratic method. There is no reason why elementary school teachers should not also vary their pedagogy by recognizing that students differ considerably in terms of the circumstances under which they are effective learners.

3. *Colleges vary the pace of learning.* Another form of flexibility found more at the college level than in previous years of schooling involves the timing of requirements. In many college-level curricula, the pace of teaching and learning is also more variable and therefore more likely to be in sync with the orientation of creative students. Unlike most elementary, middle, and high schools, few colleges maintain a five-day-a-week, six-hour-a-day classroom schedule. A college student finds more opportunities for "time-out" periods during which he or she can reflect, interpret, and create.

In order to encourage their creative students, elementary schools might similarly operate within flexible schedules and timetables better suited to a creative inclination. Too often, just the opposite is now true. In many schools, there is an inordinate, even irrational, emphasis on the speed of students' responses, on their ability to give *the* right answer within a specified time period, and on their competence at finishing a task despite the need for more time to think it through and consider a range of possibilities. The degree to which elementary school children meet these criteria continues to be used as a determinant of success versus failure. Unfortunately, the quick-fix approach to learning and educational reform undercuts and reinforces anti-intellectual sentiment. It also retards and discourages the creative student.

Swimming against the Tide

Many creative children are so thoroughly discouraged from an early age that they never develop their considerable talents and abilities. Teachers are not always willing to take a flexible pedagogical approach in which the range of student needs and interests is represented. Not only does the potentially creative child suffer, but society at large is robbed of one of its most important assets—its source of innovation and discovery.

There are many important ways in which our institutions of higher learning could improve the quality of the learning climate they provide to their students. Overall, however, colleges have done a better job of reaching students whose creativity has long been suppressed as a result of ignorance, harassment, and inflexibility. Some creative children have waited to bloom until they reach early adulthood. Such late bloomers and the circumstances under which they finally succeed may provide us with clues as to how the elementary school classroom can be changed to accommodate and encourage creativity at an early age.

Teaching Creativity
in Special Groups

Mainstream creativity characteristics and those that are differentiated need to be viewed through specific attributes for appropriate development. Attention must be paid to developing creativity in special groups if all elements in our society are to be given voice, and if all human resources potential is to be realized. A pluralistic society that truly reflects its nature will encourage creativity in all ethnic groups and foster the development of creativity in the culturally different and in children with disabilities as well as in children from the mainstream.

This section seeks to provide insight into the process and problems involved in fostering creativity in special groups, with concentration on the African American child, the Asian-Pacific child, and the child with learning disabilities. Although other special groups deserve and need attention to fostering creativity, the scope of this book does not permit extension to all groups. The three chapters dealing with these special groups, however, have many useful suggestions that can be applied to other special groups.

In her chapter on teaching the creative African American child, Alexinia Baldwin delineates creative behaviors specific to African American children. She outlines strategies for fostering development of creative potential utilizing culturally specific attributes, with special attention to the African American child who has been hesitant to respond to traditional teaching.

Asian Americans whose creativity will remain untapped unless measures are instituted that take cultural attributes into account are discussed by Carole Ruth Harris. Because many Asian American children are recently arrived immigrants, identification and service provision for fostering creativity in these Asian Americans are frequently compounded by linguistic complications, cross-cultural stress, and intergenerational conflict. Effective strategies in the context of classroom practice are offered for application in the world of practice with a view to offering opportunities for the nurturance and development of creativity.

Instructional approaches to teaching the creative child with learning disabilities, addressed by Amy Phillips in her chapter, provide insight into the importance of creativity to this population. Creative children who are learning disabled are in danger of being misunderstood in both areas of disability and of creative behaviors. This chapter outlines the areas of difficulty and also provides principles and techniques for maximizing the creative potential of these children through research, the use of vignettes, and specific methodology.

Effective implementation of developing creativity potential requires innovation, flexibility, sensitivity, and understanding of the delicate and complex issues. These are inextricably bound to the values and ethical systems that educators must and should utilize to foster individuality and creativity. Attention to the variegated cultures that represent a diverse and dynamic society with burgeoning change, renewed capacity for discovery, and multiple sources for creative endeavor can presage a creative society, a society that can develop without limitation.

Teaching the Creative Child Who Is African American

ALEXINIA YOUNG BALDWIN

Abstract

Creativity and intelligence have been studied by many researchers in order to clarify the interdependence of these two constructs. For African American students, creative behaviors are often mistaken for lack of interest in the traditional school setting. Although common creative behaviors exist in all cultures, the environmental settings determine the manner in which these behaviors are exhibited and developed. Educators who understand and recognize these creative behaviors and use them as a catalyst for developing academic skills will help the child develop a positive self-concept and have a worthwhile school experience.

Teaching the Creative Child Who Is African American

Let me share with you the story of Larry Thomas, who was selected for a class for the gifted. He was in the fourth grade and one of several African American students who represented the first class in this southern town for gifted children of this ethnic group. Larry's unique quality was his creativity. All aspects of his academic work flourished through his ability to create ideas that were original and elaborate. I remember well my first reaction to an English assignment given to the class. Larry brought the assignment back carefully illustrated as a comic strip with the character's words and the environment properly colored and designed. His response to the assignment was quite different from what I had expected, and although it was basically correct in content, my first reaction was to give the paper back because it did not represent the "proper" format that I had assigned. His patient attitude with me as his teacher helped me to realize that giftedness could be exemplified in many ways. Larry was a creatively gifted student and, as a teacher, I needed to allow this creativity to flourish.

Much has been written about the relationship of giftedness to creativity and/or the quality of giftedness or creativity among children of African American heritage. Some of the behaviors that need to be recognized among students of African American descent—the behaviors and experiences related to creativity—overlap those of many other ethnic groups. As Banks (1988) has indicated, cultural behaviors can be distinct within the ethnic group, yet have an overlay of other cultures of the environment in which they exist. Also, Montage (1974) ". . . seriously questions the validity of the concept of race and believes that it has been a highly destructive factor in the history of humankind. . . . The fact is that all human beings are so . . . mixed with regard to origin, that between different groups of individuals . . . 'overlapping' of physical traits is the rule . . ."(p. 7).

Realities of Culture

Historical and societal precedents have noted the unique problem-solving skills used by African Americans to survive inequities in society. Little attention, however, has been paid to the relationship of these skills to creativity and to intelligence. This lack of understanding regarding creative behaviors and their relationship to intelligence has led to misconceptions regarding the intellectual ability of students of African American descent. Herrnstein and Murray's (1994) most recent book is an example of this misconception. These authors have used standardized tests to rank individuals of various ethnic groups hierarchically, grouping those persons of African American descent at the bottom. As indicated by Baldwin (1997), "The Bell Curve manuscript does not tell the whole story." In one example, it was noted that:

> *From the reports and tables listed, crimes; illegitimacy; poverty; school dropout; and divorce are highly correlated with the lower IQ scores. Conversely, their data show that high-paying jobs, long-term marriages, college graduation, etc., are highly correlated with high IQ scores of those they call the "cognitive elite." There are certainly exceptions to both of these categorizations which make these blanket generalizations dangerous. One only needs to note the cognitive elite loan executives who skillfully bankrupted the Savings and Loan institutions of America; or to look at a college dropout such as Bill Gates of Microsoft billions. Further, they can look at Alex Washington, my grandfather, the son of a slave, who successfully built a thriving farm and community business without the benefit or opportunity for a formal education in a segregated south, to see the inconsistencies of the assumptions regarding the relationship of certain human conditions and events to IQ scores. (p. 616)*

The term *minority* at one time referred mainly to African Americans; however, there are increasing numbers of ethnic groups being included under the umbrella of "minority." The terms *minority* and *African American* will be used interchangeably in this chapter, but concentration will be primarily on the African American child. With this in mind, Ogbu (1994) posits that there are two different groups of minorities—those who voluntarily became a part of the American population and those whose forebears involuntarily became a part of this population. African Americans who are a part of this *involuntary* group have found themselves being judged by the color of their skin rather than by the unique abilities they might have.

Some common characteristics and indicators that reflect creative traits, as listed by Baldwin (1985), include items such as:

1. Language rich in imagery, humor, symbolism, and persuasion.
2. Logical reasoning, planning ability, and pragmatic problem-solving ability.
3. Sensitivity and alertness to movement.
4. Resiliency to hardships encountered in the environment.

These traits are often exhibited in unusual and seemingly unacceptable classroom behaviors such as talking out of turn in order to express a new idea, using inventive terms to describe situations, challenging the teacher's authority, daydreaming, and so on. However, many teachers do not capitalize on these qualities to develop appropriate classroom activities that can (1) develop new ideas through many mediums, (2) become a catalyst for enhancing academic weaknesses, (3) be a means for developing leadership skills, and (4) promote a positive self-concept.

Torrance (1968) warns about discontinuity that can occur among children of minority groups when they lack a good self-concept or are not seen as having true potential. He refers to this as a disruption of a child's experiences, thus causing him or her to feel out of place and creative activities to cease or become diminished. "Minority status involves complex realities that affect the relationship between the culture and language of the minority and those of the dominant groups and thereby influences the school adjustment and learning of the minority" (Ogbu, 1994, p. 361).

Realities of Creativity

There has been a continuing discussion about the relationship between creativity and intelligence. This relationship was explored in preschoolers for the purpose of finding out how preschoolers could be included in programs for the gifted (Fuchs-Beauchamp, Karnes, & Johnson, 1993). Whereas the Fuchs-Beauchamp et al. study included flexibility and fluency concerns, other researchers have suggested that examination of originality and imagination, as well as other components of divergent thinking, should be included in this research area.

Vygotsky's (1978) writings have led psychologists to focus on the influence that environmental stimulation has on the language and intellectual development of children. If this is to be recognized as a valid theory, then helping disadvantaged students or African American students to develop their creativity should involve providing stimulating environments, the use of manipulative or other nonverbal materials, and a chance to work independently or in small groups.

Runco (1993) focused his article on creativity and the *disadvantaged* child. Whereas it is important that we not equate the term *disadvantaged* with African American students only, it is true that these students often find themselves in unique and disadvantaging situations. With this caveat, Runco's ideas are significant as we look at creativity and the African American student. He has stated that "there are several reasons to be optimistic about the creative potential of at-risk and disadvantaged students. One reason for optimism is simply that creative potential seems to be very widely distributed." Runco suggests further that educators should be careful not to undermine the intrinsic motivation of students and that they should work to value and appreciate the expressions of flexibility and originality and also encourage independent work.

Renzulli's triad model (1977), which is now incorporated in the Schoolwide Enrichment Model described in this book, provides an excellent format for designing activities that capitalize on the creative abilities of African American students. This model, as well as Feldhusen's (1993), also discussed in this book, which stresses multiple options for developing the talent of students, is focused on encouraging the development of new ideas through brainstorming activities, questioning, using higher levels of thought questions, and the creation of new products or ideas.

Practical and Theoretical Concerns

Chislett (1994) made comparisons of the Creative Problem Solving (CPS) model (Isaksen & Treffinger, 1985) and the Type III portion of Renzulli's Enrichment Triad Model (1977). According to Chislett, research has substantiated that ". . . training in CPS does increase the quality and quantity of the responses of children on creative tasks" (p. 4). She also found that each model has important components that will help children to develop their creative productivity. Each guides the child toward important processes such as identifying the problem, collecting data, formulating ideas, solving the problem, and deciding on solutions. The Type II portion of the Enrichment Triad Model helps students to use these same skills as they move toward the process of developing a product that is unique.

Davis (1973) theorizes that creativity equals self-actualization. He says that "Creative thinking is much more than using your imagination to invent lots of new ideas. Creative thinking is a lifestyle, a personality trait, a way of perceiving the world, a way of interacting with other people and a way of living and growing. . . . Being creative is developing a sensitivity to problems of others and problems of humankind" (p. 2).

Overall, the research of Clasen, Middleton, and Connell (1994) supported the idea of assessment of artistic and problem-solving performance in minority and nonminority students. They used a multidimensional approach that involved students in solving problems given in a scenario by the researchers. Through this process, it was found that fluency and flexibility were the two constructs of problem solving that needed to be identified. Other criteria used for assessing these abilities were the reports of peer identifications. A large number of male minorities were identified as having advanced skills in art. The researchers noted, "At a time when school dropout rates of minorities, especially minority males, is of national concern, it would seem that systematic recognition and development of diverse talents is one way of convincing students that education can be meaningful" (p. 31). A reflection of the attitudes acquired by students in this research project can be seen in the observations they made. Students made the point that art was fun but didn't matter and that the other items of school were considered work and more related to expected school answers.

Overall, the research of these authors supported the idea that attention to talent can raise the self-evaluation of students. Whereas the emphasis in this research was to find an effective process for identifying students using protocols other than the usual ones, using these techniques to surface these abilities in the classroom is invaluable. According to Clasen, et al. "The task is to have the will and perseverance to develop tools capable of revealing hidden abilities and programs designed to develop both talent and individual abilities across all ethnic, racial and gender lines."

The work of Torrance on the topic of creativity is well known throughout the world. His research and writings about creativity in minority children have been a guide and a significant exposure of the quality of creativity and the lack of understanding of its presence in minority students. Torrance (1971) used the statement of a young five-year-old black student as a title of his conference paper "I Was a Block and Nobody Builded Me!" From this title, Torrance built a case for providing the "disadvantaged" youth an educational program based on their creative *positives*. Torrance has called these traits *positives*, although he acknowledges that these same positives can be considered as deficits by some educators. They are:

1. Ability to express feeling and emotions
2. Ability to improvise with commonplace materials
3. Articulateness in role playing and story telling
4. Enjoyment and ability in visual art—drawing, painting, sculpture, etc.
5. Enjoyment of and ability in creative movement, dance, dramatics, etc.
6. Enjoyment of and ability in music, rhythm, etc.
7. Expressive speech
8. Fluency and flexibility in non-verbal media
9. Enjoyment of and skills in group activities, problem solving, etc.
10. Responsiveness to the concrete
11. Responsiveness to the kinesthetic

12. Expressiveness of gesture, "body language," etc.
13. Humor
14. Richness in imagery in informal language
15. Originality of ideas in problem solving
16. Problem-centeredness
17. Emotional responsiveness
18. Quickness of warm-up (p. 4).

The ability to express feelings and emotions might be shown in writings, poetry, drama, or drawings that depict violence and despair; however, the lives of these youth may be free of violence. The hostility expressed in these activities can easily be considered a threat or a lack of acceptable "school behavior." The ability to communicate a concept through kinesthetic or nonverbal media can be used as a vehicle to understand meanings. For example, having youngsters use these positives to illustrate—through movement, music, or drama—emotions such as peace, frustration, mistrust, and happiness helps them become able to articulate the concept of these words and transfer this creative activity to the structured content area of writing and reading. This type of activity can occur in grades K–8 using words that are appropriate for that grade level. Children can also invent words and recommend ones that can be used for illustrations.

Torrance's theories about the value of recognizing creative behavior among minority students have been on the forefront for nearly four decades. His theories have been passed on through the work of his students. Haley (1987) reanalyzed her dissertation, which was completed under the guidance of Dr. Torrance in 1979. She extended Torrance's research by looking at the effects on creativity among advantaged and disadvantaged black kindergartners who participated in socio-drama activities. The findings of her first question regarding the difference in response styles were:

> . . . that the differences are a function of creative response style rather than a substantial difference in overall ideational fluency and originality in divergent production. The differences in creativity expressed through verbal and kinetic modes are consistent with the results of earlier socio-economic studies: lower socioeconomic status subjects were more kinetically creative while middle-class subjects excelled verbally. . . .
>
> Middle-class black children were more successful in creative problem-solving using verbal expression. . . . Both advantaged and disadvantaged children were more successful in creative problem solving in different types of expression. . . . [this] has implications for the potential impact of environmental influences on hemisphericity and certain mental operations. . . . The advantaged may have learned not to use kinetic and integrative expression. . . . The disadvantaged, less traditionally schooled by age five, may retain creative strengths through kinetic and integrative expression. (p. 38)

While her research provides information on the roles community, home environments, and economic status play in the mental development of children, she has also provided a teaching strategy in sociodrama that can be effective in developing kinetic fluency and originality. Playing out a role to resolve conflicts such as fighting, family-related conflicts, or roles that are based on sympathetic feelings for others bring together the use of verbal and kinetic skills.

Much research has been done on the use of creativity in the identification of students with special abilities. Theories and research by Gardner (1993b) and Sternberg (1988a) have caused educators to observe more carefully the behaviors that might indicate creativity and to explore the correlation of these behaviors to intelligence measures. Perhaps, as Gardner has theorized, "a new approach to the study of creativity [is] necessary" (p. 299).

Classroom Activities and Ideas

The characteristics that are creative positives of African American students as listed by Torrance and the cognitive characteristics as listed by Starko (1995) go hand in hand with the planning necessary for creativity to flourish. Starko lists, along with others mentioned before, *metaphoric thinking*, which makes it possible for students to use one idea to express or explain another; *visualization*, in which students are able to visualize things they cannot see: they enjoy playing with mental images; and *finding order in chaos*, in which students prefer visual images that are complex over those that are simple.

Runco (1993) suggests that the following guidelines be used for enhancing creativity for "disadvantaged" students.

Avoid relying on verbal materials; use a variety of materials; tap various domains (e.g., music, crafts, mathematics, language arts, physical education).

Avoid relying on verbal rewards. Concrete reinforcers may be best for many disadvantaged students.

Avoid over-emphasizing structure and curricula with predictable outcomes.

Ask questions that allow students to follow their own (potentially divergent) logic and thinking, even if unpredictable.

Plan to follow students' own interests part of each day.

Avoid prejudging students who are nonconforming and students who find their own way of doing things.

Avoid suggesting (even implicitly) that your own way of doing something is the best or only way.

Avoid going overboard—strive for a balance between structured and unstructured tasks, between independence and working in small groups, between rich and open stimulus environments, and between convergent and divergent tasks.

Allow independent work, and not just where it is easy (e.g., while working on crafts or art projects).

Discuss creativity with students; tell them why it is valuable. Be explicit about how and when to be original, flexible, and independent.

Monitor your expectations; and be aware of potential halo effects.

Recognize the multifaceted nature of creativity.

Recognize that creativity is a sign of and contributor to psychological health.

Work to appreciate what children find for themselves.

Inform parents of what you are doing and why.

Read the creativity and education literature and work with others who study and value creativity (pp. 13–15).

In Meeker's (1990) handbook on stimulating creativity, she has listed for all students six keys to creativity. They are:

Key #1   You begin by doing. . . .
Key #2   Find quiet time so that you can experience inspiration. . . .
Key #3   Tap into your subconscious. Everything that you experience is stored in your memory. . . .
Key #4   No matter how foolish the exercises seem, keep in mind that to become creative you must re-establish contact with the child inside you. . . .
Key #5   Keep and use your sense of humor. Collect funny cartoons.
Key #6   Exercise . . . [it] oxygenates brain cells.

Some of her suggested activities include exercises in past lives, in which the student becomes someone in the past and imagines what it would have been like; writing different endings to the same story; creating mosaic tessellations; and many more that allow flexibility, fluency, and originality—the basic constructs of creativity—to flourish.

In addition, I would propose here that group activity, debating, logic, and historical literary comparisons can be used to enhance creative achievement. A *sensitivity enhancement model* to use in sensitizing all students within the classroom would be important in the process of developing a nonprejudicial, self-enhancing perspective of those persons who are different in culture or physical appearance. Role playing and game strategies in which students reverse roles are helpful activities that can be used to develop sensitivity to the feelings of others. The *information processing model* can be used to provide facts about various events (historical and contemporary). Library research, field trips, mentors, local historians, and time capsule planning can be effective activities. A *concept development model* can be used to involve students and teachers in the use of content from various cultures and ethnic information to teach a concept. Sociopolitical parallels, graphic and performing arts of the world, and language structures are just a few examples of the use of this model.

A Sample Lesson Design for Teachers Incorporating Ideas Listed Above

Ideas for classroom use should be designed to use themes, concept development, and problem-solving processes through materials that reflect the culture of the African American student. These plans are for all students; however, the inclusion of African American history and other aspects of African American culture is the first step toward unlocking the creativity of children who have been hesitant to respond to traditional materials.

An important first step in this process is to have a *belief* that creative potential exists in these children and that through this process their educational experiences can be enhanced. A sample belief statement and its application to the creative process follows:

> **BELIEF STATEMENT:** Concept development, which is enriched with a wide range of data from different cultural and ethnic experiences, creates a learning environment where students can become creative producers and effective consumers of information.

> From the belief statement, goals and objectives can be developed. An example of goal and objective statements are as follows:

> **GOAL:** Students will become more aware of the societal influences that affect their lives.

> **OBJECTIVE:** Students will be able to draw logical conclusions from data collected.

An example of a project that would involve students in creative thinking, that draws on culture, and that requires several cognitive skills is given here in skeletal form. The completed program would include additional belief statements, goals, and objectives.

Sample Unit Outline

Theme: Social and Political Parallels in History

Questions: Was the type of jazz played during decades beginning with the 1920s influenced by the political emphasis of the time? Were there parallels in the changes in politics and the changes in the presentation of jazz music?

Research Focus: (a) Library research on the politics and personalities of the various decades; (b) research on the history of jazz and the leading personalities in this area, the musical structure of jazz, and the vocabulary of jazz; and (c) listening to jazz recordings of the various periods.

Class Activities: Group planning and development of a time line of politics and characteristics of jazz, sharing of research and music, possible performance by mentor or video of same, and/or class discussions of the findings listed on the time line.

Evaluation of Activities: A review of the data collected with answers to unit questions answered with logical supporting rationale. The development of a school newsletter or article to the newspaper as a product would be a Type III product as suggested by the Renzulli triad model.

In this activity, the learning styles of students, the group planning, the logical reasoning, the development of ambiguities, as well as the use of materials from the African American culture will allow students to use their creative skills to solve a problem.

Concluding Thoughts

My student Larry was a diamond that might not have been discovered. His creative ideas that bubbled out over and over again would not have been considered appropriate in his regular class because his creative activities did not conform to the traditional content expectations of the teacher. Fortunately, he was part of my class for gifted students where teacher and students learned from each other. Larry wrote and directed class plays, designed a booklet for class use on the origin of words, and instituted several creative ideas for class participation. He completed his college career with studies at the Sorbonne in France and received a degree in International Studies from George Washington University in Washington, DC.

Too often, students of color are judged to be obstinate, irascible, and lazy when they exhibit behaviors that do not follow the traditional expectations of the class and curriculum. This lack of attention has allowed too many students, particularly African Americans, to "fall through the cracks." The research on creativity is significant for its importance in the identification and program adjustments for all students; however, there is a uniqueness in the representation of creativity in large segments of the African American population that must be recognized and made a part of the planned program for the development of the individual or all of society loses.

Torrance's early concerns in the 1960's, about creativity in minority students and his continuing concern in the 1990's about the lack of understanding and the manner in which creativity in minorities is recognized and enhanced, highlight the slow recognition of this aspect among African Americans. Hopefully during the next century, educational theories will include as a part of their facts and generalizations these creative positives that educational planners *must* recognize.

Chapter 8

Fostering Creativity in the Asian-Pacific Child K–8:

Identification, Strategies, Implications

CAROLE RUTH HARRIS

The problems of accurately identifying and servicing creativity are vastly compounded with children of Asian origin. Linguistic and cultural complications, economic and attitudinal factors, sociocultural peer-group expectations, cross-cultural stress, school system conflict, and intergenerational conflict frequently deflect efforts to recognize creativity. In addition, there may be difficulties connected with refugee problems, illegal immigration, and the fact that many of these new arrivals are from groups whose culture and language differ markedly from their resettlement situation.

Presented is an analysis of the problem areas and the underlying causes, followed by practical suggestions that address these areas and offer viable application of field-based coping techniques. An exploration of possible outcomes concludes with a discussion of the societal and educational implications of the identification of creativity in Asian American students.

Problems of Identification of Creativity in Asian American Students

Linguistic

Many Asian groups have difficulty with English because the native language has vastly different structures in spoken and written language, in grammatical structure, and in the alphabet (Harris, 1997). The strangeness of the alphabet provides a huge stumbling block to the acquisition of reading skills, creates an emotional barrier, and increases feelings of isolation (Sheehy, 1986; Wei, 1983). As a result, Asian American students are often hesitant to express original concepts verbally and may mask unusual perceptions and original ideas that emanate from imagination rather than from classroom expectations (Plucker, 1996). At home, there is often limited or, in the case of immigrants and refugees, sometimes no use of English with home/school interface minimal, thus further limiting language skills (Bermudez, 1993). Asian students are frequently perceived as "not ready" for the exercise of verbal and written assignments associated with creative activity, with the result that few are encouraged to exercise this aspect of themselves.

Cultural

Cultural problems are concentrated largely in the area of social customs, and may seem strange to the classroom teacher, or perceived as insulting, rude, or laughable. Among these are voice tone, eye contact, and body contact or gesture. Patting a child on the head, for example, is perceived as insulting in Thai culture, but when given by an American the gesture is one of affection. A Thai child is likely to shrink away if patted on the head and is unlikely to manifest thereafter an original idea in the classroom setting. Sex-role problems also emerge here, with sex-role response a strong factor in creating barriers to adaptation and acceptance of different cultural mores (Goffin, 1988, Harris, 1995b; Sheehy, 1986). Many Asian cultural groups have very specific behavioral expectations for what is appropriate for boys and for girls. Recent immigrants do not instantaneously adopt the blurring of gender lines that is encouraged in modern society, particularly in American society, and the child may be perceived by caretakers as not being a "proper boy" or "proper girl." The areas of drama, dance, and field activities, such as sports, are particularly susceptible to sex-role conflict (Harris, 1995b).

There are cultural differences in listening behavior (Trueba, 1983) that may be negatively perceived by the teacher and in response behavior (Harris, 1988; Cohen, 1988), like lowering of the eyes when addressed, passive, seemingly unresponsive staring, or behavior that is interpreted by American teachers as aggressive or discourteous. If an Asian American child is reprimanded publicly for these behaviors, confusion and embarrassment can ensue and block out articulation and may even block any creative response at all.

Economic

Many new Asian immigrants are below the poverty line. In the United States as many as 80 percent are from Third World countries and arrive with few financial resources (Harris, 1997). Some support multiple households, both here and in the land of origin (National Coalition of Advocates for Students, 1988). In addition, the families are large, and older students work after school, with the result that some perform poorly. This is all too often reflected in poor response to creative activities, which further excludes them from exercising their creative potential.

A hidden factor in this area is poor health, with limited access to health care through lack of knowledge or accessibility. The latter is frequently the result of illegal status, a problem that sometimes results in neglect of basic prevention, including immunization procedures (Clark, 1988). Added to this are physical problems, such as poor vision and hearing loss, and psychological problems, some caused by torture, as with the Cambodian children now living in Massachusetts (National Coalition of Advocates for Students, 1988). Authorities are aware of the problem, but no data is available, according to the report by National Coalition of Advocates for Students (1988). The impetus for further exploration of creative challenge is largely absent in Asian American children who manifest these types of barriers to mental play and creative productivity.

Attitudinal

Reasons for immigration play an important part in the attitudes of immigrants and refugees (Harris, 1995a). An Asian immigrant who comes to the United States for economic betterment, or as a result of leaving an untenable political situation, has a vastly different attitude from one who is a refugee and comes to escape from danger. The attitude is a reflection of the originating status, yet all immigrants have an area of social murkiness in that they do not know what to expect or the expectations of others, a murkiness that deepens according to fear, present or residual (Kuwuhara, 1997; Sheehy, 1986).

Many feel they do not truly belong in their new country, and sometimes give testimony to this in interviews (National Coalition of Advocates for Students, 1988). Emotional problems, including symptoms of "depression, impaired memory, panic, severe insomnia, periods of disorientation and confusion, reliving of war experiences, separation anxiety, family conflicts, isolation, and suicide" (National Coalition of Advocates for Students, 1988, p. 24), are heightened by guilt over survival when members of the family have been killed, and by family separations when members remain in the endangered area. This is a difficult area for many Asian American students and their teachers, whether the students are immigrants or second generation, because family history frequently carries with it emotional baggage with an associated propensity for conformity rather than originality in the school setting.

Barrier-type attitudes are erected by a fear of authority, either residual or because the child or a near relative is an illegal immigrant (Gratz & Pulley, 1984; Portes, McCleod, & Parker, 1978; Vasquez, 1988), thus preventing close relationships with teachers. This mistrust of authority results in a syndrome associated with exhaustion of coping behavior (Clark, 1988).

The National Coalition of Advocates for Students (1988) reports a poor self-image among Asian immigrant children as a common attitude, citing the testimony of one who ostensibly "made it" finally, as a paraprofessional in the United

States, because he found the inner strength. He asserts that this was despite school personnel who "tried to destroy . . . motivation. But many of my classmates didn't make it" (National Coalition of Advocates for Students, 1988, p. 51). According to this report, frustration often turns to self-hatred and extends to hatred of school and family, constantly aggravated by a feeling of not belonging. Encouraging creativity becomes extremely difficult for the classroom teacher because the student is guarded and fearful of the experimentation and risk-taking that must of necessity accompany creative endeavor (Feng, 1997).

Sociocultural and Peer-Group Expectations

A growing problem in this area is racial conflict along with a fear of personal safety associated with the formation of youth gangs. Research among groups in the United States (National Coalition of Advocates for Students, 1988) indicates that ethnic, racial, and racially aligned gangs can be seen in Lowell, Massachusetts (Cambodians versus Puerto Ricans), Providence, Rhode Island (Hispanics versus Southeast Asians), and Boston (blacks versus Chinese), all of which lead to new forms of self-hatred as internalization of racial prejudice.

There is a dividing line between the aspirations of illegal immigrants and other groups, including refugees (Portes, McLeod, & Parker, 1978; Trueba, 1988), and differing expectations economically, psychologically, and politically (Verna, 1998). Desire to investigate alternative thinking strategies is curtailed by the status of both the family and the child, and many Asian students will contain themselves within perceived boundaries according to family ethos.

Cross-Cultural Stress

Vasquez (1988) reports that the sex-role related problems as a factor in cross-cultural stress are exacerbated by "feminization of the classroom" (p. 245), particularly in the lower grades. Cross-cultural stress is not a new but a continuing problem, and as long as there are differences, it will be there, with tension between newer ethnic groups, no matter what the origin (McWilliams, 1973).

This is not to say that the continuation of this widespread problem should give rise to acceptance, but rather that it is time to seek ways of dealing with it through appropriate preparation. Encouragement of self-expression and the stimulation of creative thinking are essential to the well-being of every child. If Asian American students manifest special problems in accepting new modes of thinking and are inattentive to their originality through neglect of their special problems, everyone will lose by it.

Intergenerational Conflict

This extends from the placing of responsibility on young children who act as interpreters for their families to a shift in cultural values within generations. In the one case the newly acculturated children and youth may resent the dependence of the elders, and in the other the younger generation is seen as disassociating itself from the old traditions.

This produces a double stress, resulting in coping strategies that have a negative effect both on self-concept and on family relationships (Harris, 1988). Certainly it blocks creative productivity in that new ideas may seem offensive to traditional cultural values and place the Asian American child in an untenable position.

School System Conflict

Misplacement in schools, with the placements made according to chronological age rather than level of education, is one of the more severe problems in identification of creativity for this population. Asian immigrant students may have had little or sporadic schooling, possibly even *no* schooling, prior to coming to the new country. Such misplacement is aggravated by the lack of school records, and nothing on which to base information. Wei (1983) reports the frequency of the wrong date of birth in school records. The problem is often not solely attributable to school authorities, because many children hide facts about years spent in the former school to save face (Center for Educational Research and Innovation, 1987; Vuong, 1988).

Poor motivation for creative endeavor in school and clashes with school personnel can be attributed to low sensitivity of teaching personnel coupled with misconceptions about the originating culture (Feng, 1997). Goldberg (National Coalition of Advocates for Students, 1988) relates the practice of superficial treatment of the originating culture, "two foods and three old heroes" (p. 52), as a source of conflict.

Overcrowded classrooms and schools, combined with opposition from staff to curricular alteration and overuse of results of standardized tests, may preclude entrance to any available enrichment activities that might stimulate creativity in this population. According to testimony by Steinberg and Halsted (National Coalition of Advocates for Students, 1988), Asian American children are frequently tracked into English as a second language classes and then encouraged to take vocational courses or to study academic subjects that do not require verbal skills, frequently to the complete neglect of the arts, which the Asian family might perceive as nonserious study. Misplacement also occurs when handicapped are classified only in terms of handicaps (Poplin & Wright, 1983), a problem not confined to Asian American students, as Phillips tells us in her informative chapter in this book.

Absurdities result in ethnocentric misplacement, giving rise to learning problems and blockage of creative characteristics, such as placing a rigorously trained Japanese 14-year-old in need of calculus with a Laotian 14-year-old who had but two years of schooling because they were both Asian (Vuong, 1988). In both cases, creative activities were eliminated from learning trajectories entirely. On the other side of the coin may be seen a very high barrier to the exercise of creative potential erected by the parents of Asian American children who mistrust any kind of enrichment and regard it, by and large, as trivial (Wei, 1980).

Sugai and Maheady (1988) report a disproportionate number of Asian immigrants as referred for psychological services. Research by Trueba (1988) reveals that teachers identify behaviors in terms of adjustment and/or achievement problems. Further, field-dependent learning styles are frequently open to misunderstanding, as many Asian cultures do not foster independent work but emphasize group cooperation, team effort, and obedience.

A Widespread Problem

In terms of identification of creative Asian immigrants on a broad scale, the Center for Educational Research and Innovation (1987) asserts that most children of immigrants are disadvantaged in countries of employment and are frequently inappropriately assigned to special education in Western Europe, Canada, and Australia as well as the United States. That this is a fact is cold comfort. Recognition of the problem is but an initial step, and means must be sought for solution.

Strategies for Aiding Creative Development

Effective strategies that are directed to the problem areas offer applications for positive action in the world of practice. Renzulli's three-stage model using exploratory activities followed by cognitive skill development, culminating in concrete products (Renzulli, 1977; see also the chapter by Reis and Renzulli in this book) applicable to a real-world situation, is well suited to Asian American children for the simple reason that it encourages them to develop and utilize areas in which they may already excel as the basis for creative productivity. Guidelines for brainstorming and webbing techniques (Renzulli & Reis, 1997) and support of authentic learning experiences (Renzulli, 1997) are excellent techniques to utilize with Asian American students with regard to respecting individual learning style and attaining confidence as skill areas develop.

The effort to defuse anxiety supports Feldhusen's research (Feldhusen, 1995; Feldhusen & Wood, 1997) in the area of the relationship of anxiety and creativity, the fact that high expectations in specific areas increase performance standards (Dai & Feldhusen, 1996), and that early recognition is essential for implementation of growth plans and long-term commitment to talent development (Feldhusen, 1995). Feldhusen also suggests options (Feldhusen & Wood, 1997) for growth plans that derive from learning style. With this in mind, the following suggestions are directed to developing creativity of Asian students, according to the problem identification areas previously outlined.

Linguistic

Target limited language-proficient students who are perceived as "not ready" for creative work in verbal areas, and give some form of enrichment to sustain them until their language skills show sufficient progress. Institute independent or small research projects with books that reflect creativity in the native language and have artwork that will prove familiar to the family setting, such as the composite king-peacock-Buddha that depicts artistic synthesis and creates "something of new and spectacular beauty—a harmonious union from which peace, relaxation, activity and composure, and rhythm and balance emerge" (Arieti, 1976, p. 217). Couple this with a presentation to the immediate group or the class. This gives responsibility, respects the learning style, and opens the way to expression of creativity within and beyond the Asian culture that can be shared and understood.

Cultivate an awareness of code-switching to increase linguistic sensitivity on the part of the staff (Trueba, 1983). Play with it, utilizing Asian words in poetry, drama, or collage to release creativity and encourage experimentation.

Explain the concept of creativity to parents in their own language, verbally or via a simple publication like a photocopied booklet so that the home is receptive to nonacademic endeavor. Provide focus on the objective ability to speak the new language, the demonstrated desire to learn it (Kuwuhara, 1997; Portes, McLeod, & Parker, 1978), and the ways in which the new language may be used to express creative ideas (also see Harris on poetry in this book). Emphasize that linguistic "mistakes" may sometimes lead to unexpected discoveries (see Lynch, Harris, & Williams chapter in this book; also Robinson chapter in this book). Watch for the higher achiever in his or her native language and encourage creative language arts products in the native language, such as *Happy Days* (Schulkind, 1979), a bilingual poetry book written by Marshallese children.

Cultural

Use the informal approach to allay the fears of the parent and of the child. Conduct parent interviews in the native language whenever possible, perhaps with the assistance of a community volunteer, using culturally sensitive questioning. Become familiar with the nuances of social customs, with particular emphasis on interaction between adults and children (Feng, 1997). Become very familiar with sex-role expectations in the country of origin. Examples are expectations in play patterns, particularly those involving body contact, and expectations with respect to modesty in clothing, regardless of the season or practicality. Avoid public commentary about individual behavior, whether complimentary or uncomplimentary (Feng, 1997). Avoid public reprimand; instead, refer to the situation obliquely so that the child can "save face."

Economic

Take into account the aspirations of the family, with attention to parental status variables such as occupation, education, and so on (Portes, McLeod, & Parker, 1978). Assume nothing about the economic status or economic perceptions of Asian American students, including the "model minority" stereotype or extended family obligation of any Asian ethnic group. Work from facts only. Be sensitive to any special projects that involve extra expense for the family, no matter how small. An Asian American student may opt out of such an activity without giving the real reason.

Attitudinal

Work to increase home/school interface (Harris, 1988). This frequently results in lowered conflict and higher achievement (Plucker, 1996). Cultivate an awareness that most Asian children possess extraordinary resiliency, are optimistic, are well-balanced, and have a strong desire to overcome shyness and have an outlet for self-expression.

Tap the sense of self-reliance by utilizing a biographical approach that concentrates on the positive aspects without the embarrassment of seeming to boast of accomplishments. Recognize the ego strength, achievement motivation, and tolerance of ambiguity (Portes, McLeod, & Parker, 1978). This would suggest that the Torrance Tests of Creative Thinking (Torrance, 1997), even with the new and expanded scoring system, might not be suited to Asian American children who have a different concept of art and value balance. An example is one 9-year-old Micronesian-Japanese child who created a picture using the first shape in the TTCT Figural B with a sun and a lone tree where the use of space was the aesthetic standard. Her elaboration score was very low, but the concept was exquisite in its application.

Encourage empowerment through expression, such as publications or journals containing writings like those of *MOSAIC*, from South Boston High School. Give the message, "You are valued, your culture is valued, and you have much to contribute." Encourage journal writing, which is therapeutic—for example, the loneliness and healing power of writing described by Bulosan (1973).

Encourage the writing of stories and poems. It helps them "to get the darkness out," as Lakhana, a teenager from Cambodia, who was adopted by an American, says in her poem:

> *—I'm in the darkness of pain.*
> *It's hurt, and hurt so much I*
>   *couldn't describe*
> *Couldn't show, couldn't talk,*
> *Worse than a handicap who*
>   *uses a crutch but I don't*
>   *have a scar or a mark.*
>   (Sheehy, 1986, p. 335)

Sociocultural and Peer-Group Expectations

Use of narratives, role playing, and bibliotherapy (Ramirez, 1988; Torrance, Goff, & Satterfield, 1998) will help open a pathway for creative expression and diffuse conflict in this sensitive area. In conjunction with these activities, identify weakness in locus of control (Vasquez, 1988), ascertain the causes, and provide specific intervention through creative product completion. Be alert for signs of racial conflict, with special attention to racially disparaging commentary. Present alternative thinking strategies using ethnic examples wherever possible to encourage emulation of role models. Many ethnic folk tales emphasize alternative thinking or new solutions to old problems, and illustrations are often culturally appropriate.

Cross-Cultural Stress

Increase the motivation for self-identification as creative, softening the cultural difficulty of self-proclamation by reference to self-expression as an opportunity to contribute special perceptions from the Asian cultures and to provide enrichment for the class. Use care in selecting any special staff for identification of creative potential, with specific attention to the sending cultures and ethnocentric attitudes.

Bicultural Effectiveness Training (Szapocznik, Santisteban, Kurtines, Perez-Vidal, & Hervis, 1983) used as a model may ameliorate behavioral problems stemming from cultural conflict. Keep in mind that experimentation and creative expression may temporarily increase cross-cultural difficulties or intergenerational conflict in some cases.

Intergenerational Conflict

Utilize situational problems to provide avenues for the exercise of creative problem-solving potential—for instance: "What would you do if you were: a) locked out of the house, or b) had no heat on a cold day?" These are real-life situations and tap the reservoir of resourcefulness that many socially reticent creative Asian American children possess. Stress independence and self-responsibility in an effort to uncover ability and potential.

Use of fantasy and/or nonverbal expression such as music, dance, or drawing brings the parent or family into the product execution and assessment. At the same time, utilize peer referral both within and outside of the culture as an additional source of identification of creativity. Involve outreach workers here, as some parents of immigrant Asian children are illiterate and/or fearful of school authority. Utilize electronic media, audio, and videotape in the native language to accommodate parents who are not literate or cannot speak or understand English so that creativity assignments can be welcomed as appropriate for school achievement. These services are usually available through local agencies that serve specific cultural groups.

School System Conflict

Place or identify students according to creative potential background and not simply according to chronological age. If an Asian American child requires advanced work, such as art, music, or experimental biology, make arrangements for the child to learn at a higher level by sitting in on an advanced class or procuring a mentor. Monitor the progress of creative students after curricular intervention and enrichment placement. Include the activity setting—that is, the classroom, playground, or gymnasium (Trueba, 1988)—in observations for identification of creativity and for refinement of curricula. Utilize a flexible central theme curriculum rather than a more usual scope and sequence outline and observe behavioral response to facilitate curricular refinement.

Interpret bizarre behavior in the light of the child's experience (Ramirez, 1988), like intolerance for or fear reaction to colors, especially red (National Coalition of Advocates for Students, 1988). In one case, the child was a refugee. The color red reminded the child of blood, and she would hide if another child used red paint on a picture (National Coalition of Advocates for Students, 1988). Colors representing mourning or celebration are different in many Asian cultures, and awareness of their applications are useful when planning for art-related projects. Symptoms of post-traumatic stress disorder should not influence identification of potential but should be taken into account within the learning environment. Utilize extracurricular activities for input to creative projects, and encourage incorporation of these activities into the learning goals. Be on the alert for contradictory behavior or passive behavior that may be masking creativity (Vasquez, 1988). Eliminate the medical model and the focus on inadequacies.

Utilize problem-solving, hands-on experiments and manipulatives to test ability and potential for flexible thinking. Ensure that any selection personnel for activities such as theater and art exhibits have cultural knowledge of creative production and/or performance, and include representative community members in the final decision. Focus on cause-and-effect teaching and testing (Vasquez, 1988).

Avoid stereotyping Asian American children in castelike groups (Harris, 1995a; Ogbu, 1978). Focus on the "zone of proximal development," which

> *defines those functions that have not yet matured but are in the process of maturation, functions that will mature tomorrow but are currently in an embryonic state. This concept permits psychologists to understand the developmental processes that are forming, and that will constitute future accomplishments*
> (Trueba, 1988, p. 281)

Avoid the superimposition of past records when planning for individual children who may be concerned with doing the "correct" thing. Assess from the perspective of field-dependent and individual learning styles, such as that used by Ramirez and Casteneda (1974). Place the child in a minimal-stress, "culturally congruent" (Trueba, 1983, p. 412) environment and observe for a period of time before designing individualized curricular intervention to increase creative productivity. Utilize computers, which are nonthreatening, and observe progress and concentration span.

Identify creative potential within an instructional context, relating specific examples to the planned topic, such as those suggested by Sugai and Maheady (1988), according to the quality and quantity of instruction received. Assess the teacher attitudes periodically. Utilize the developmental (Reyes, 1988) rather than a crisis-oriented model, or a view that the students are coming with liabilities. Utilize curriculum-based assessment, which provides diagnostic information and allows teachers to accommodate instruction with the regular classroom (National

Coalition of Advocates for Students, 1988). Last, but not least, apply the *Framework for Meeting the Educational Needs of the Immigrant Student* as outlined on pages 152–153 of *New Voices* (National Coalition of Advocates for Students, 1988), with specific applications to the diversity of Asian cultures. This framework—available from the National Coalition of Advocates for Students, 100 Boylston Street, Suite 737, Boston, MA 02116—lists questions "that should be asked by a school-based team of professionals who are knowledgeable about the student's language and culture" and provides strategies according to whether the answer is "yes" or "no." It gives specific steps that involve plans for instructional services and problem identification, among other concrete guidelines, and is a valuable resource for maximizing both cognitive and creative learning response.

Implications

The Asian American student has a profound impact on local areas and on a nation's future. Cultural sensitivity programs merely produce a benign atmosphere and do not of themselves assist the school to maximize each student's creative potential.

It devolves on the schools to understand the process of change and to employ that process in the interests of both the Asian American student and the nation. It is perhaps appropriate to examine Menlo (1987) in the light of change in the student, in the family, in the school, and in the larger national and international picture, with concentration on the problems of identifying and serving the creative Asian American child:

> *My notion has been that all living systems have an inherent drive for change— and activeness, curiosity and a search for betterment—and that daily life is comprised of a multitude of receptive responses to requests for action and change initiated by self and others. (pp. 29–30)*

Societal change is always to be expected, but in the interest of the society within which that change takes place, provision must be made for, not denied to, those who would infuse it with new life, from the rich perspective of cultural diversity. Creative contributions of Asian American children are important to their individual fulfillment, and provide life satisfaction over and above academic expectation or achievement.

Conclusion

When the Asian population is tapped for talent potential, then both society and the individual benefit. Problem areas must first be accurately defined in the light of the specific Asian culture and cultural conflict, taking great care not to consider all Asian cultures as identical or even similar. They are not. Only their creative potential is similar to that of children the world over. Attention must then be directed to problem-specific techniques to ensure identification, placement, and appropriately differentiated learning experiences for the creative Asian American child.

If Asian American children are to be included in the creative life of this country, then they must also be included in a vision of education that speaks to the fulfillment of each child's capabilities rather than molded images or stereotypical expectations. As Iaian Chrichton Smith (1976) says so eloquently in his poem:

Two Girls Singing

It neither was the words nor yet the tune,
Any tune would have done and any words.
Any listener or no listener at all.

As nightingales in rocks or a child crooning
in its own world of strange awakening
or larks for no reason but themselves.

So on the bus through late November running
by yellow lights tormented, darkness falling,
the two girls sang for miles and miles together

and it wasn't the words or tune. It was the singing.
It was the human sweetness in that yellow,
the unpredicted voices of our kind.

Instructional Principles for the Creative Child with Learning Disabilities

AMY L. PHILLIPS

<table>
<tr><td>

THE CLAOD
ARE FULOFY
I WANT WON

by Anna, age 6
</td><td>

????

by Hernando, age 13
</td></tr>
</table>

Introduction: Two Creative Children, from K to 8

Anna's poem is now in print. She is an ardent and meticulous poet, rightfully proud of her appreciative audience of family, teachers, and friends. By all indications, Anne is a creative youngster without any particular learning challenges. For the purposes of this chapter, creative children are those who delight in the exploration and expression of nuance, and who do so at least a bit differently, and often surprisingly well. Anna reflects on her creative endeavor in this way:

I saw how cuddly and fluffy the clouds were and thought how people might want one. I wanted to write as "mostly" as I could. I didn't want to write about real life. Then I would have to say "I want one, but I know I can't have one" and of course I already know that. So that's why I wrote a haiku. A good haiku must say a large, a humongous thing, but in only three short lines.

Anna has always been possessed of a graceful kinestheism. Her recent discovery of syntax and semantics has given her much greater scope to express her full nature: "I like to dans. I like to ruite hikoe. I like to here hikoe. I like to ruiete. I like to rede. I like to cudul."

Hernando is another creative youngster. The poem I would have liked to include, above, I remembered as also rich in nuance, deeper than is usual for his age. Unfortunately, it will never be printed here as unmistakable proof of his talent, and he can't talk about it like Anna can about hers. He seems to have lost it. When I asked Hernando for a copy of the poem, he looked blank. His father had a thought, "Was that the only copy that you walked over for weeks on the floor of your room?" Hernando allowed as perhaps it was, although he still couldn't recall it, and, most poignant of all, couldn't even recall that others had ever been impressed with it and with him.

Discovery of the loss of Hernando's poem came at a conference I attended at the request of his parents and long-time tutor to discuss his creation of a portfolio record of his many accomplishments. The tutor felt that Hernando's creativity was obscured to himself and to others due to his significant learning challenges in reading and writing, organization, and attention. As with the poem, he tended to simply lose things, to forget he had done things, to not connect the value of his work to a larger picture of work the world values, and to have to move so quickly from one struggle to the next that his accomplishments went undervalued, trampled and forgotten.

This became the object lesson for this chapter on creative children with learning disabilities (C/LD). What can we do as teachers so that children like Hernando's poems are not lost, so their lives find the fullest expression? How can we help them to grow confident and competent and to believe it enough to preserve and share the evidence?

Five instructional principles will be explored for these children:

- understanding for effective practice;
- building facilitative learning communities;
- crafting congenial instructional systems;
- crafting congenial curriculum; and
- personalizing instruction.

The foundation principle is to listen to people who are both creative and who experience significant learning challenges and to those most close to them. This allows us to take an "inside-out approach" as author Donna Williams suggests "carers and professionals" try to do (Williams, 1996). Without this vital orientation, Williams says that we can assume someone belongs to a general category and roughly match approaches in unsubtle and even damaging ways. She gives an example of "sensorily and emotionally hypersensitive people" she has known "who are already suffering from extreme information overload who have been put through the emotional and sensory bombardment of 'hug therapy' " (Williams, 1996, p. 49). She says that what was often "missing [from carers and professionals in cases like this] was a proper understanding of what these 'autistic' people were dealing with and enough humility for carers and professionals to admit when they weren't sure or didn't know how to help a particular person" (Williams, 1996, p. 49). Williams, a person with autism herself, warns that each person has unique, subtle, dynamic challenges and needs equally subtle matches of support and instruction. Her advice is humbling and instructive for those working to support anyone else's particular version of the human condition, and reminds us to listen to them first if we want to get the most direct advice.

Ideas of people who are both creative and who experience significant learning challenges deeply inform this text. I interviewed five such individuals in depth about their elementary and middle school years: two adults, two young adults, and one adolescent. All five individuals have demonstrated their creativity through work and school. Each has been diagnosed as having specific learning disabilities (SLD) and/or attention deficit disorder (ADD). Close family also give essential perspective: I interviewed two parents of such youngsters; one was a parent of an adolescent interviewed; the other was a parent whose son I did not speak with (he is nine years old and just being evaluated). All have been given pseudonyms, and some identifying details have been changed to preserve confidentiality. I refer to all the interviews throughout the text and include four vignettes.

Insights derived from my experience teaching and doing psychoeducational therapies with students and partnering with their families, teachers, and specialists also inform these suggestions for practice. Five years' work with student teachers in inclusive settings has also enriched my understanding. Kate Frank, whose work focuses on children with learning differences, and who emphasizes school-family systems solutions, was extremely generous in sharing her wisdom. Her ideas are referenced throughout (although if they are misrepresented, it is entirely of my own doing).

Principle One: Understanding for Effective Practice

A Note on Nomenclature

Readers may be familiar with the gifted/learning disabled (G/LD) designation. The focus here is on the *creative* aspect of giftedness and on the *learning challenges* some of these children may have in the area of academic performance, including attentional issues. I will use the shorthand creative/learning disabled or C/LD when appropriate.

C/LD students are a varied group. They range from children with extraordinary creativity and severe learning disabilities to children who have some evidence of creative ability along with one or two mild or subtle challenges in attention or academics, with every combination in between. Readers should mainly think of creative children with so-called *specific learning disabilities* (SLD) "identified on the basis of a significant discrepancy between ability and achievement in one or more of 7 areas of academic functioning" (Gresham & MacMillan, 1997, p. 383); and with *attention deficit disorder* (ADD) in the inattentive or hyper-active-impulsive or mixed groupings.

A noncategorical lens on creative youngsters challenged in school achievement reveals a much larger pool than children with SLD and ADD. Some creative children will simply underachieve if assignments don't match their gifts. Some learning disabled children who are not particularly creative can become quite ingenious in finding alternative learning pathways, and many can increase their productivity when they are encouraged to use their ingenuity and imagination to solve problems they face. Teachers should also consider if creative abilities coexist in children demonstrating facets of behavior disorder (BD); conduct disorder (CD); emotional disturbance and serious emotional disturbance (ED, SED); affective disorders such as depression or anxiety, or mixtures (often co-associated with creativity); adjustment disorders; social difficulties such as shyness or isolation; challenging temperaments (Greenspan, 1995); post-traumatic stress disorders (PTSD); and particularly autism and Asperger's disorder (who may have visual-spatial and symbolic strengths). And whether or not they evidence heightened creativity, many children coping with these challenges seem also to benefit from the kinds of scaffolding and support for their own ingenuity that creative, well-planned creative environments can confer.

Caution in Labeling: Seeing Children Whole

Creative and learning disabled children may be misunderstood on both fronts. One should not assume people know what is meant by either the creative or the learning disabled part of the moniker. For instance, in an informal poll of eighteen college-educated adults, I found that a majority mistakenly felt children with learning disabilities (LD) had deficits in basic intelligence (Phillips, 1997b). Some did not think of ADD as a learning disability, and many did not realize it need not include hyperactive features, or that hyperactivity was often associated with impulsivity. This perhaps reflected complicated debates within the field. The term *learning disability* tends to connote a deficits model and to be overdetermined and imprecise.

The single most important thing we as teachers may be able to do for children with these sorts of advantages and challenges is to see them clear and whole. This may be anticipated through interviews. The present chapter reports on such interview data. A threat ran through the interviews: how much it hurts to be unseen, and how great it feels to be recognized. Silvie, an adult with high creativity and what she terms "100% dyslexia," remembered best the one teacher who saw her clearly:

> *Mrs. Driver is the one I remember. She had a warm smile and sparkly eyes. She really liked children and she really liked her job—she wanted to be doing it with us. And she thought I was just terrific just the way I was.*

Helen's voice is shadowed as she describes the conflicting picture of her son, Clay, painted by his classroom and art teachers and strong when she expresses her demand that he be seen in the round (see Vignette 9–1).

VIGNETTE 9–1   Helen and Clay

Helen speaks here about her son, Clay, who had never had trouble before in school. This year, however, he is in third grade, and seems to be hitting some sort of wall, and getting frustrated. He even has gotten in trouble on the playground, which he had never done before. Clay is being tested for "learning and behavior" problems. This vignette features Helen using her deep knowledge of her son to advocate for a fair testing approach that sees him whole. Says Helen:

Clay never had trouble before this year. I am not saying there isn't something . . . a few of our other family had problems in school, too. So I'm OK with an evaluation—knowledge is power. But I also think it's not just him. His teacher says, "He has his head on the desk all the time," but she also says "He talks all the time." How you can do both is beyond me. I asked him what he was thinking about when his head was down and he said he was bored. I told her, and she says, "I don't think he's bored. I think he's just not paying attention." I asked him again—it's not that he isn't paying attention—it is that he didn't *get* the directions.

Once I asked him how much time she spends on directions and corrections and he said most of it. That concerns me, and I certainly don't think that is the way he needs it. I know he does better with transitions or new ideas if you prep him first—if you plant an idea, then come back to it every once in a while and revisit it. I don't think she does that.

I did tell him to pay really careful attention when she gives directions. But I don't know if it will work. Sometimes by far the safest thing to do is to do nothing so you won't be judged too harshly if you get it wrong. He has to know the teacher cares—if he doesn't think she likes him, he hesitates to ask her for the help he needs, because he figures—why would she want to spend the time on me? If he knows she cares, he'll do anything for her because he wants to please her—including being sure he understands what she wants him to do. . . .

After my conference with her, I saw the art teacher. She tells me he's doing great and to check out the "awesome" jaguar he drew. "But doesn't he talk all the time?" I say a bit disingenuously. "What do you mean? There's no such problems here," [sic] she says. And he *is* very creative and sensitive to his surroundings. Two years ago he was assigned a Christmas tree and he worked for hours making it all colors in stripes, with a big smiling star and smiling tree. Then, suddenly, every other tree he brought home was green. I asked why, and he said, "That's how we do it in school." I think this new art teacher understands him and appreciates his originality.

So I decided: You can test him all right, but you have to have everyone he works with fill out reports: his art teacher, his first and second grade teachers who say he was great, staff at recess and on the bus, adults who know him outside of school. He's got a lot of skills that may not show up in this classroom and a lot of good adult friends (the teacher insists he is disrespectful of adults . . .). I want the full picture and I won't quit until we get it. . . .

It is also poignant when Jewel talks of the "basically wasted years" when she wrote wonderful stories in her head that no one ever heard and was forced to stand still in a corner when she needed so much to move and interact (see Vignette 9–2).

VIGNETTE 9–2   Jewel

Jewel is a college graduate with a degree in music and education. She works successfully with children with severe psychological needs. Jewel's story features her memory of what school was like for her from early on as she was being steered into special education programs while her creative interests went underdeveloped. Says Jewel:

When I was trying to remember what school was like for me as a child, I went over some of the reports. Basically, they said repeatedly I just would not pay attention (and there were some pretty weird writing samples, I must say). I really tried to remember what school was like and how I dealt with it all, and you know I don't remember much—and I think maybe that's how I dealt with it. . . . I was off in my imagination world; I basically ignored a lot of stuff, spent a lot of time in fantasy land. If I could have written, there'd have been some great stories. I'd have written a ton of books with all the things I was making up. . . .

When I think about teaching now, I think you really have to keep the pace going, and have real things to do, you know—not filling in worksheets like I always had to do. Let kids express things in real words, not fill in the blanks. The major reason I went into teaching was to prevent any child ever having to go through what I did—somewhere in the back of my mind I knew there were other ways to do it. . . .

My first memory of school was having my nose taped to the wall for being out of control. A lot of what I remember was being put places for doing things I wasn't supposed to, then missing a lot. In first grade I remember the teacher always sat *behind* us and gave us sheets to fill in, and I think I was talking when I wasn't supposed to be. I don't ever remember ever seeing her in front of me . . . but she put *me* in front on this one blue square. I can still see it perfectly—I had to stand on it many times right by the door, and I missed a lot of what was going on. One time I was talking to this little boy and I ended up there but he never got in trouble. . . . My sister had her too, and she didn't get in trouble either (she was an overachiever, real polished, and she'd do exactly what the teacher asked).

By fifth grade I was out a lot for reading and math. Being out was a really fun time; we got read to a lot and played computer games. But I was expected to do all the other work in the actual class too. . . . And one day, I must have been out on vacation, but when I got back I was really behind in all the work and I remember the teacher yelling and screaming at me and the resource teacher and hearing basically how I would never ever have recess again for the whole year it seemed to me. I just remember feeling really sad and sobbing in the hall. It was basically a wasted year.

By sixth grade we had a substitute all year or something and I barely made it into seventh grade. Another basically wasted year. In seventh grade it all basically stopped and I was tested and they couldn't find anything really wrong but they said I had a low attention span so they just put me in Level II track for everything and sat me in the front of all the classes, and then I had to fill out these weekly sheets for monitoring, like conduct and homework and quizzes and grades. There was some improvement because I wasn't pulled out, but not much. I only enjoyed one class when we read these really awesome Dostoevsky books. Otherwise I was totally bored.

And "you" just got put in place and were expected to stay there—it was real male-dominated, like a hierarchy all set up . . . like I was a better field hockey player than most of the girls on the field but I somehow never really got out there much. . . . When I entered ninth grade I wanted art class but they said kids like me had to take typing. So I took neither. At least I discovered my great passion for music—I played in the marching band for a good while—we were great—#1 on the whole West Coast. . . . I couldn't memorize which notes went to what, but it was a very strong, empowering beat we were famous for and real deep, jazzy stuff. Then they made me stop because my grades weren't keeping up. I was absolutely happiest when I was playing.

Another thread that runs through the interviews is how *difficult* it can be to see C/LD children whole. For instance, I know Hernando (of the lost poem) is creative, but readers of this chapter might never be sure. And he has quite a history of being misunderstood and underserved. Despite his above-average intelligence, he tested in kindergarten at much lower because he answered "I haven't the vaguest idea" to any question about which he thought he did not have the perfect answer. (The tester apparently did not seem to notice the hallmarks of perfectionism and love of irony common to many children with C/LD.) Over the years, if one looked closely, Hernando's demonstrations of understanding (Gardner, 1998) have allowed some to see around his more problematic struggles. Examples include the poem many admired despite its loss; his second-degree brown belt in karate despite his avoidance of team sports; his deep grasp of abstract concepts despite his difficulty retrieving facts; his command of a sophisticated array of computer programs and his struggles in math class. Through the expressions of his talents, Hernando is recognized by many close to him as highly creative, someone with much more than the "vaguest idea." The next task is to help others see him whole as well.

Regarding the Paradox

Like Hernando, many children with C/LD are paradoxes and have even been called "paradoxical learners" (Tannenbaum & Baldwin, 1983). For instance, they may tend to be both profound and scattered; to be perfectionistic and apt to lose things; to have penetrating insights and a tendency to daydream; to have restricted or nontraditional interests and extreme curiosity and an open, questioning attitude; to see the "big picture" and have difficulty getting to the point; to perform well on complex tasks but to avoid simple ones (summarized from Table 3, Gehret, 1997a, p. 2); and to need both "intellectual stimulation and remediation" (Gehret,

1997b, p. 2). Not surprisingly, many of these gifted students also have strong feelings of ineptness, and perceive themselves as failures (Baum & Owen, 1988, p. 324). They may have "a very poor self-image" and tendencies to high-risk behavior and even to suicide (Gehret, 1997b, p. 2). And despite creative abilities that can help them to break out of such constrictions, "frustration is a trademark of G/LD students, particularly those that elude identification" (Gehret, 1997a, p. 2).

Overlooked and Underserved

C/LD students' gifts can be obscured by their disabilities; their disabilities can be obscured by their gifts. A good rule of thumb might be to consider that puzzling children may be gifted, and that gifted children who are not achieving may be in need of special support. Silvie, for example, was so bright that she figured out how to get around her "100% dyslexia" by crafting her own reading method as well as a way to fool others into thinking she was doing it like everybody else. This worked well when she could work alone and take the time she needed to use her own approach. It tended to be less effective when she had to work with a group or when she was asked to produce material to order. Had Silvie's teachers noticed her atypical working pattern, they might have realized that she had developed her own brilliant, if semi-functional, coping strategies, and could have begun to help her to become even more effective within more typical constraints.

We tend to let our misconceptions affect our identification of C/LD children. Winner (1997) speaks of many myths we have about gifted children, including that we tend to think that they must be gifted in only linguistic and logico-mathematical realms. She clarifies that many gifted children will be quite variable in their profiles and can certainly be learning disabled. C/LD children have tended historically to be excluded from gifted programs on two counts, because both special education children and children with intelligence in areas such as in high artistic creativity have both tended to be excluded. "These youngsters are often disqualified from gifted programs" (Gehret, 1997a, p. 2), or from thinking of themselves as gifted. As Jewel says, "If I could have written, there'd have been some great stories. I'd have written a ton of books with all the things I was making up . . ." (see Vignette 9–2). Silverman (1989) reviewed the literature to demonstrate that gifted learning disabled children share many of the same characteristics as gifted "underachievers" and are often labeled as such (if their gifts are noticed at all).

Looking for the Big Picture

Silverman (1989) enumerates ways teachers can help to identify gifts in learning disabled children. We need, she says, to make it a habit to always search for special abilities as part of every special education (SPED) evaluation protocol, just as Helen insisted be done for her son, Clay (see Vignette 9–1). Silverman says that evaluations for gifted LD students should be done with large assessment batteries in a variety of contexts, such as through timed and untimed tests, judgment of student responses to multiple presentation strategies, and multiple student-presentation options. She suggests trusting higher scores, teasing out the meaning of scatter in such items as comprehension versus mechanics, or high achievement in harder levels and low in easier levels of a subtest. I would add that we should look for high creativity versus low basic skills scores.

Creative detective work is needed when viewing puzzling, cloudy, and suggestive results of assessments. Continuous, accurate, broad-based assessment spirals among assessment, planning, and implementation as learning evolves and demands change is, of course, the state of the art for all children. It is particularly vital for children with C/LD, so much more likely to be understood in patches and taught without taking the full picture into account. We as teachers must advocate for long-term, team-based assets mapping for these children and those we suspect may fit this designation.

Family and Community Experts as Advocates

Jewel frequently referred to her mother as an advocate during her interview, saying "my mother told me to review my file. . . . My mother says I should. . . ." Helen insists that each adult pool their views of her son Clay before she will be satisfied that an accurate picture is seen by all. Angel attributed some of his self-knowledge to his parents: "I'm grateful to my parents for keeping after it and for insisting everyone try to understand me and work with me" (see Vignette 9–3). Reis, Neu, and McGuire (1995) found that parent-advocates who know their children well are vital to LD students' success. They say that high-achieving LD students develop a sense of efficacy through identification and exploration of their "special talents or interests" out of school or within school in extracurricular areas, which then helps them and their parents to see their real potential and work to fulfill it:

> *Most excelled in spatial areas that were not rewarded or paid particular attention by schools. . . . A child does poorly in school and his or her parents, sensing that their child is bright and talented, look for alternative ways in which the talent can be manifested. This, in turn, causes the parent to invest time and capital into looking for ways to nurture talents. Once this occurs, the child begins to feel better about his/her talents and begins to think that achievement might be possible in other areas, such as school. (p. xvii)*

Feldhusen suggests that creatively gifted children need a wide array of experiences in courses, extracurricular events, and the community. This allows a "self identification process [to develop] to understand better their special aptitudes and talents, grow in knowledge in the fields related to their talents and increasingly commit themselves to the full development of their talents" (Feldhusen, 1997, p. 189). Kate Frank also stresses that all LD children need to be recognized for their talents by objective outside standards (personal communication, January 7, 1998). This, she feels, can offset their tendency to fail to recognize, value, and build on their own achievements, and to undervalue the positive opinions of their closest

---

VIGNETTE 9–3   Angel

Angel designs Internet sites for companies all over the United States. He speaks here about his educational and psychological theories and offers suggestions for the schooling of students like himself (he qualified for special education services due to ADHD during his early elementary school years). Angel says:

Anything new interested me; otherwise it simply couldn't capture my attention. If I'd never heard it before I was at least curious. My Dad says the first half hour he'd try to work with me on homework, I'd do absolutely anything I could to get out of it—it seemed like going over the same thing again. Once I realized fighting it would keep me from doing new things even longer, and there was absolutely—and I mean absolutely—no other alternative, I'd finally buckle down and get through it so I could get on with other things. I'm always inquisitive because my mind leads the way. . . .

I have what I call a Swiss cheese mind—the cheese is the system holding things together. There are lots of holes (all the details—I never remember details), but there's more and more cheese the older I get. Now I see how things work in a big way—like now I totally get quantum mechanics. Science made total sense as soon as I knew there was a system. I forget most anything particular, but I know I can find what I need again if I know the system. I think this is an advantage over the other way around, because it is much harder to get the big picture if you don't have it than it is to find details about things. So I'm glad I'm me and have this way of thinking.

That's why I like my work. HTML programming code [HyperText Markup Language] is the bones—I don't have to remember any of the details—things just go where they have to. It's like making a salad—I have all the tools for this task, the carrots and lettuce and tomatoes . . . yet I end up with a new salad every time—because I know what makes a salad work. . . .

I have the perfect solution for the education of children like me: Start with the very beginning of time and work up from there. That way everything would be new by definition, and yet there would be a lot of order to it so you wouldn't get lost. Everything could build on everything else. You could get in all the subjects that way—science and history and art and how people built things and farmed and made their way over the world. Don't give me American history twelve different times. My way, our minds could construct the full picture of what came from what came before. The ring of a bell doesn't signal another subject. . . . There must be some structure built in to draw the links between. . . . Now it's all discontinuous—one teacher, one grade, one class . . . all cut up.

---

supporters. She says these children need to learn early that there are adult analogues to what they love to do and to see adults doing these things at expert levels. For the C/LD child, a careful self-identification process like the ones that Feldhusen and Frank describe is particularly critical as we have seen that these children tend to develop distorted pictures of their own capacities and tend also to be seen by others as puzzling and sometimes highly problematic. Careful scaffolding may be needed to support the identity explorations of these students as they develop confidence and expertise in the larger world.

Principle Two: Building Facilitative Learning Communities: A Reverie on Superinclusion

As teachers, we each need repertoires of special and creative/gifted education approaches that can be crafted to meet individual student needs. But no one teacher can or should provide the array of supports that is optimal for all children. As a general rule, children who are both creative and learning challenged will benefit from an integrated team approach rather than an array of unconnected special supports. Individual scaffolding, such as can be achieved through coaching, organization plans, personalized study skills strategies, compacted curriculum, and creative mentorship—can be integrated by the team into the learning community system. Let's imagine an ideal environment to see how we might encompass all of these strategies, which I term *superinclusive*.

Let us imagine that Clay's school transformed into a superinclusive community learning center (CLC) just before his special education evaluation was completed (see Vignette 9–1). Full inclusion in small classes is collaboratively facilitated by teachers with expertise in subject areas, creative education, and special education, and with specialists such as play, occupational, and speech and language therapists supporting all developmental domains. Community-based management offers an extended day schedule, 7 A.M. to 10 P.M., integrating on-site full health and social services. Classes for all ages, citizens projects, zero to five, and pre- and after-care programs are distributed throughout the school, multimedia center and library, technology labs, health club, and arts center with studios, practice rooms, and performance spaces. The CLC has formal partnerships with business, arts institutions, universities, libraries, and the judicial system, which both share the center's resources and offer their own, extending the campus into the city and the city into the campus. Mentorship, intern, and apprentice arrangements are common. Such a superinclusive center is described in Freihage, Murrell, and Phillips (1995), based on research into the infrastructure needs of Boston's public schools for the Mayor's Blue Ribbon Commission.

Let us imagine that it has been determined that Clay is eligible for special education services because of mild learning disabilities. Helen will be in charge of the planning process for Clay as the primary expert on her child and the manager of his education. The CLC partners with her by arranging for a meeting with all staff who know him or might work with him and for anyone else that she wishes to attend. Helen schedules the three-hour meeting for one of the many times dedicated each week for team planning. A core evaluation will occur and an individual education plan (IEP) will be developed after this meeting. The core evaluation is meant to be enriched but not replaced by the IEP.

The great day arrives. Present are Helen and Clay, several close adult and child friends and family members, and his current teachers. The classroom teacher now teams with a specialist in extending and compacting curriculum for gifted children and a SPED learning specialist. Also present are the psychologist who did most of the testing, and all who filled out the observation forms Helen had insisted on, including bus driver, recess monitor, librarian, school secretary, a community administrator, Clay's pediatrician, and a representative of the museum school for children.

Helen runs the meeting, partnered with a facilitator trained in using a process called MAPs (making action plans) developed to support full inclusion (Pearpoint, Forest, & O'Brien, 1996). She welcomes all and asks each attendee to explain how they are related to Clay's life. She explains that the meeting has been called to address the question "What do the child and family want?" and to make a map that provides directions to meet their goals. Her co-facilitator is skilled in taking notes on very large paper with clear words, symbols, and images and will include all voices in summaries.

All consider a series of questions, making sure the voices of Clay and family are fully heard and that all present feel included. First they ask, "What is Clay's story from the time he was born?" Next, they respond to, "What is the dream for Clay?" cost not considered; and, "What is the nightmare/greatest fears?" They ask, "Who is Clay?" listing honest, personal terms, adding a list of things heard earlier, such as any labels he'd received or insults he has heard, grouped to contrast with the team's descriptions. Next the group asks, "What are Clay's strengths and unique gifts, what does he like to do and is good at, and what does he need to make the dreams happen?" Concrete plans of action include agreeing to immediate next steps, a formative evaluation process of both Clay and the team's progress, and setting times for multiple future meetings when all can attend (see Pearpoint et al., 1996, pp. 68–71).

Let's imagine what might have happened after the meeting. Everyone agreed that it was a pleasure to focus such positive attention on this fine youngster. Clay's interesting life story was fully heard, including several moves and much adventure. Hopes for his great potential and fears that it would be thwarted were eloquently specified. Many vivid descriptions captured his essence like "strong, clever, imaginative, will stand up for himself if he thinks things are not fair, fun to be with, quick to help others, funny, talented in a lot of things"; and some of the earlier phrases he had heard like "poor with adults, inattentive" were seen in this larger context.

It was arranged with the museum-school staff member present that Clay would attend the after-school studio sessions with artists held both at the CLC arts center and the partnering museum. These would alternate with one-to-one tutorial sessions designed to establish an array of strategies for Clay to use in various learning contexts. These would be practiced throughout the day with the learning specialist's help, and faded out, added to, or refined as necessary. Clay's classmates volunteered to check in with him periodically to be sure he was on track with assignments. The learning specialist volunteered to lead ten-minute coaching sessions in the beginning, middle, and end of the day that would include updates on the strategies she and Clay were developing. She suggested that Clay's peers could collaborate in these sessions and might eventually partner with Clay on their own. Clay's grandfather decided to take music classes at the CLC so that he and Clay could meet for supper a few days a week in the international food court. At the end of the meeting, everyone wrote down precisely what they would do and made a few plans for how they would keep track of progress.

Many children with C/LD would benefit from the sort of superinclusion possible in such a CLC. Until our more typical settings transform in this direction, teacher-leaders can advocate for this type of collaborative planning with the child's nature, interests, needs, family, and community at the center of the process. This planning can be supported by constituting a team around the individual to do creative problem-solving and to implement a systematic plan based on formative evaluation.

How vital the participation and coordination of those connected with a student is cannot be overstated. Only then can the child be said to have a true support team. In reality, Clay's mother, Helen, has called for just such a team approach to Clay's evaluation and program planning. She says that institutional barriers have been great, in that it took months to get the full array of observers to fill out the forms she wanted and then it seemed logistically impossible to get all to the table. Jewel seems to have been valued for her strengths while in band and in her fifth grade resource room and undervalued just about everywhere else during her school years. Hernando has had many meetings with involved adults present, but never one where all were at the table at the same time. This year, for example, a math teacher marked him down on several assignments because he was using the computer mandated in his IEP because she had missed the only team meeting and apparently not reviewed the paperwork. Once she finally came to the table, she responded quite appropriately.

Learning to Plan as a Team

Meeting the C/LD student's needs can enrich the whole group and bring cohesiveness to the learning community team. An example of this is modeled in an exercise in which our Wheelock undergraduate early childhood student-teachers participate while teaching in kindergarten to third grade classes. The exercise begins as a simulation of a team planning meeting, and ends with student-teachers thinking about how to work in such a way with their own students (Phillips, 1997a). In the first round, a particular learning community (LC) planning team is asked to design experiences for a pool of students with highly varied profiles, including a C/LD child. The team must pool their resources and craft collaborative supports for whatever activity they design. The team is made up of lead teacher, psychologist, paraprofessional, art teacher, computer specialist, administrator, social worker/family, group and play therapist, two parent representatives, behavior specialist, learning specialist, and speech, language, and occupational therapists.

Student-teachers often voice surprise at how exhilarated they are by what is usually an unfamiliar experience. They report how each team's temperament affected its deliberations, but tend to say that they grew to trust one another's perspectives and "expertise" as they "felt each other out" as individuals and felt the power of the group as it began to work. They often seem to feel that the team finds surprisingly effective, creative solutions to what at first seem like impossible tasks. Most say that, even when feeling overwhelmed, stuck, or confused about their roles and rights, great things resulted when they started to focus on the same wavelength; for example, the children's strengths, loves, and motivators; their most pressing needs as a group, such as needs for activity, to learn social skills together, or to strengthen writing and reading for everyone.

After the full team meeting, student-teachers distribute their own students into randomly mixed groups, replay the game with the new group and take turns simulating the actual support systems at their sites. They have been developing individual profile cards (IPCs) for their own students since the beginning of the practicum (Phillips, 1995). In this second round, student-teachers see how they as team members might work with an idealized deck of resources, and then explore how to be constructive within the real world of typical opportunities and constraints. This often results in future teacher-leaders stating that they will work to advocate for more time and resources to pull together their own learning community teams. Some say they particularly look forward to creating and working in teams when they become teachers because they have learned that the collaborative approach makes the design of individually responsive, diverse, challenging, and creative experiences much more efficient and possible.

Principle Three: Crafting Congenial Instructional System

Every learner needs structure, and every learner needs freedom. Every learner tends to need the discipline of structure and the spontaneity of freedom in his or her own rhythms, intensities, and proportions over the course of his/her own particular hour, day, week, and school year. Think of an infant's day with its balance of rest and wakefulness; the caretaker learns to engage when it is alert and ready to play, experiment, and learn, to soothe when it is overwhelmed and ready to rest. But as my student-teachers sometimes lament, "Must we then just individualize everything, spending endless hours crafting a set of systems to fit each person's rhythms?"

Because this sort of supersystem is impossible, it is lucky that it is not the ideal. The infant does not become maverick master of its own personal system; it learns to adjust to the world and the human connections that constitute key parts of it. The sooner it finds a balance between its internal sensations and external constraints and delectations, the better it feels. In fact, finding this balance among one's own rhythms and those of others is the story of society, and we all know every classroom is a microcosmic society. The trick then is to accustom, let us say, this particular group of learners this particular year to one another's learning rhythms and intensities at the same time that they are learning to accommodate the expectations and rewards of responsible social membership common to any year—to get students to buy into creating a learning ecosystem that works for each and works for all.

Creative children with LD are the ideal candidates for such a model and some of the most telling challenges to it. These children tend to need maximum structure and maximum freedom simultaneously. They stretch the limits of our ingenuity and of their own. They require us to craft and individualize an accessible palette of learning strategies while providing systems that allow their best application.

Frank (1998, personal communication) says the best teachers for her creative clients with LD have attained such a level of mastery that they can be spontaneous and emergent at the same time that they communicate organization, consistency, and clarity. In this setting, she says, C/LD children do not have to spend too much time trying to figure out what is expected of them and can concentrate on acquiring knowledge and skills. One such model is described by student-teacher S. Clark (personal communication, February 1, 1998) after her first few days with master teacher Judith Richards and her bilingual Haitian-English third-fourth grade class, in which 50 percent of the students have been designated as having special needs:

> *Everything has a system—there are systems for systems—every detail has a place somewhere. But kids have it all down—they run it with her—I wish I'd been there in the beginning of the year because that's when they planned most of it together. The first day I was there, something had come up, and the kids called a meeting, led it, worked it out, got it all settled, and started back to work all on their own. Judith didn't even appear to be monitoring things or checking what had happened (although I knew she knew pretty much everything). I'd thought I'd have to take a part, but as I saw it unfold I sat there in awe.*

In Judith Richards' class, there are rhythms for individuals threaded within the whole song. For instance, children each have certain days on which they can use a cozy, private loft. But if someone else really needs the loft, they get first "dibs" and a listed occupier misses for that round. Clark says that children seem to understand this fully and do not even ask to get their turn back. They seem to know that someday they can ask for the loft if they need it and will be assured of getting it without an uncomfortable negotiation.

The principle of the loft can carry over to many other adaptations of traditional space and time usage. Does each classroom have space to be alone or to be in quiet conversation; to move away from the group to a pleasant place when overstimulated and to return when ready to learn; to be working at one's own pace while still keeping pace with all that is required? As can be seen in the vignettes, students who may have difficulty tolerating some aspect of the group ambience often then find themselves excluded in overt and subtle ways, and therefore frustrated as they learn even less. For instance, Jewel's hours spent standing on the blue square for various infractions are deeply regretted to this day because she missed so much she could have learned. Clay, who, the teacher claims, spent most of class with his head on his desk or talking, might be signaling his need to be active or quiet at times not in rhythm with the milieu (one might look to his art class to see what a more congenial match might be).

For these sorts of students, a sense of quiet purpose and order is explicitly maintained *for the purposes of setting the conditions* for creative action. Frank suggests we create environments that make lucid thinking likely (personal communication, January 7, 1998). Is there a sense of undifferentiated mass in sound or on crowded walls? Do teachers and students review assignments, maintain homework systems, keep up with record keeping, and check in with one another frequently? Are systematic plans made to help students who need to stay organized and in control, and are they linked to symbolic communications that are most congenial to them? And most importantly, do these systems not only maintain compliance, but also foster experimentation in the service of creative expression? For Jewel, the rigor of the marching band freed her jazz spirit. For Clay, permission to draw his most beloved thing kept him focused until he was satisfied his jaguar was perfect. For Angel, learning HyperText Markup Language (HTML) for Web pages gave him a channel to express all the new ideas he desired.

Principle Four: Crafting Congenial Curriculum

When Wheelock student-teachers play the team-planning game, they are asked to develop a focus and a learning scaffold for a highly creative, learning disabled child; a gifted, socially awkward child; a developmentally delayed child; and three more typical children, also unique. (They receive model individual profile cards on each student.) What seems to make sense to most teams are multifaceted long-term projects that feature students' shared interests. Team members can then collaborate to support the emerging project. Projects that teams think these students might enjoy have included: an around-the-world discovery game in multiple learning centers; the co-creation of child- and family-focused after-school programs and family centers; a variety show; an obstacle course based on a classic journey story that children build themselves; and a video production or a multimedia magazine exploring and explaining the nature of their shared world.

Silverman indicates that "learning disabled gifted children generally thrive on abstract concepts, inductive learning strategies, multidisciplinary studies, holistic methods, and activities requiring synthesis" just as in gifted programs (1989, p. 41). She cautions, however, that they require specific strategies for success crafted to their particular challenges. Suggestions include keeping in mind that these students tend to "remember what they see and forget what they hear," so that one should always couple talk and demonstration and build in much observation of competence. Other tips include remembering to keep hands-on, to limit directions, and to avoid distractions (1989, p. 41). Renzulli and Reis (1991) describe provisions useful for gifted students in regular classrooms such as learning centers; small group work on self-selected interests, respecting individual learning styles; and differentiated, compacted, or modified curriculum (see Figure 2, p. 33, for complete information). Typical students can also benefit from these methods to "develop gifted behaviors" (Renzulli & Reis, 1991, p. 34).

Baum and Owen (1988) say, "it is important for bright students who have problems with decoding written information to have information-gathering options that do not insult their intelligence" (p. 92). Some of the compensation strategies they suggest include using "inquiry methods and primary sources," field trips, "visual aids such as films, television documentaries, live drama and computer software packages, taped interviews and tapes of books" (1991, pp. 92–93). They remind us that books with pictures are available in all subject areas for both children and adults who are visual learners (see Baum et al., p. 93, for a list of some good ones). They indicate that G/LD students tend to prefer to reverse the typical order of reading/lecture/interesting activity: "With GLD students, a more motivating approach is to challenge them first with a creative project relating to the topic. Their reading and research is directed toward a specific goal that is more meaningful than doing well on a test" (Baum, Owen, & Dixon, 1991, p. 98).

Froebel's famous "Gifts" such as blocks, balls, paper, drawing, sewing, parquetry, rings, and sticks (Brosterman, 1997) are found incarnate in many classrooms today. Gifts were to be used to create things that fit "loosely into three fundamental categories: forms of nature (or life), forms of knowledge (or science), and forms of beauty (or art)" (Brosterman, 1997, p. 37). Angel's educational advice seems to support the notion that systematic exploration of the essence of matter and action might be helpful indeed for children with ADD. Says Von Marenholtz, in her *Reminiscences of Freidrich Froebel,* of her mentor's approach, prefiguring Angel's theory:

> *If the child's mind, through his own outward creative activity, imitates in a measure the building up and development of the universe . . . if he learns to see the connection of all things, and nothing comes broken and isolated before his senses; if things, from the simplest to the most complex, appear to him fixedly arranged in their natural, logical succession, from unity up to manifoldness or plurality, and his own handling of materials leads to plastic formation . . . the child's mind must, in later stages of development, arrive at the consciousness of the organic life imitated by his own hand, and will find it again in nature in its most original state of existence. And thus he recognizes the agreement between the intellectually organic linking of his own being with that of the material world (Brosterman, 1997, p. 36).*

C/LD children may excel in fields like the computer sciences, arts, and architecture because these fields are congenial to the inductive, abstract, synthetic, multidisciplinary, and holistic thinking on which they thrive (Silverman, 1989, p. 41), and C/LD children simultaneously are drawn to the metacognitive support within these systems as the scaffold upon which they can construct meaningful work. For example, Angel feels he can create Web pages with ease because HTML is a fundamental building block that he can know without needing to use easily overlooked detail. He feels that he becomes more fully capable of understanding the world as his "Swiss cheese mind" grows to have enough "cheese," or systems of ideas, that they become unavoidable (no matter what else may be capturing his attention). "Now I see how things work in a big way—like now I totally get quantum mechanics. Science made total sense as soon as I knew there was a system." Silverman says that many such children are late bloomers. She indicates that they frequently use metaphors such as "It was as if my brain woke up when I was a sophomore in college and I could do things I couldn't do before" (1989, p. 39). Certainly, environments rich in Gifts like those Froebel found so metaphysically satisfying, and rich in systems that elucidate them, may be just what C/LC individuals are seeking and tend to turn to as they mature.

Exemplars for the Creative Student

Mature exemplars who have mastered a system, whether it be carpentry or law, can bring C/LD students to understandings faster than when they are left to find their own way with less congruent models. Communities offer great adult analogues for student modeling. The proficient artist offers one example particularly congenial to some C/LD students. I often think of the young author of an "All About Me" form I saw posted on a school wall. The form said, among other things: religious background: *god*/ most favorite thing to do: *draw*/ least favorite subject in school: *art*. What was missing at this child's school that might have provided the adult models he seemed ready to savor? What do artists do in their work that we might learn to better employ in school?

Many an artist's greatest asset is the ability to act with expressive force while exploiting the properties of materials with intense discipline. This parallels the maximum structure and maximum freedom equation earlier indicated as congenial for C/LC students. And the best artists tend to be masters of technique—whether classic, invented, or eclectic—and practice, practice, practice on multiple versions before gleaning acceptable results (Feinburg & Mindness, 1994). Many use a series format that allows them to range widely but to return to the focusing structure whenever they wish (akin to Angel's HTML). Many are fascinated with excellence and originality in the disciplines, ever curious about how different types of people make tangible their own thinking and feeling. When planning schedules, space, and curriculum that support creative experimentation and rigorous practice, the model of the atelier with its rhythm of reflective and creative hard work is a rich analogue.

The following gives one illustration of how an artistic child with learning disabilities might blossom in a superinclusive environment where real people share real projects. It is an expansion of our vision of an ideal CLC first presented in the Elementary Education Committee's report to the Boston Mayor's Blue Ribbon Commission for Community Learning Centers (Freihage et al., 1995). (Clay's MAPs process, could be said to have been held at the "same" site.)

Imagine that a student guides a visitor through the center. Highly intelligent and talented in art, with serious challenges in reading and writing, Beatricia is a 12-year-old who has been a part of the CLC since she was an infant. The following contains her description of her art that has been linked to the CLC's multiyear, multidiscipline action-study of animals in the urban environment:

"What are you working on?" I ask my guide, Beatricia.

"Well, we keep investigating our city's animals. Some of our projects will tour the 200 CLCs nationwide later in the year. In a way, we've been doing it since we were little kids. It all started when we couldn't have pets in my building and we decided to keep some in the CLC. Let me show you where it all began."

She takes me to a blooming and buzzing early childhood center where I see a giant ocean-sand box with what seems like a vast collection of tiny animals and people. Several children seem to be playing out some chapter of a story that they have been telling in many forms, many times before. Says Beatricia, "We always

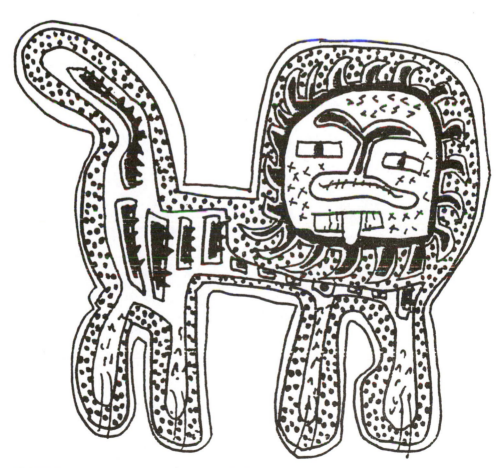

FIGURE 9–1 Teacher's Drawing of a Lion

FIGURE 9–2   Teacher's Drawing of an Animal Cluster

play with that collection, and we just keep adding to it . . . and I know most of these little guys as well as I know my own name. When I was really confused about how to write, my teacher had me do portraits of all my favorite little animals. . . . I made it into a book." She steers me to a laminated big book illustrated in an early version of her distinctive style. "I adored the fonts on the word processor, so I really got into writing that way." She next indicates many beautiful volumes laced throughout the area and tempting computer displays: "Aesop's fables, haiku, world folk tales, and myths from all the continents. . . . I love the creation and naming stories. We have the biggest collection of illustrated books, CD-ROMs and picture histories, visual encyclopedias, and videos in the CLC system. Of course, we use the museum's photography and print archives when we need to. We get trained in proper use, and they have certain supervised hours for us."

FIGURE 9–3   Teacher's Drawing of a Cat and Dog

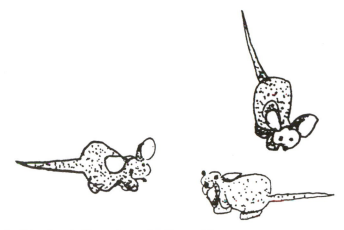

FIGURE 9–4   Teacher's Drawing of Mice at Play

We go to the art center, where an array of vivid tempera paintings gleam in one studio. "My series for the traveling show are portraits of all three types of animals in this neighborhood. Did you know there are some in captivity, some domestic, some wild? I do paintings of each of them where they live.

"The zoo (an old city trooper in the park at the top of the hill) has all my favorite wild ones from Africa and South America and Canada. I usually do them in their cage setting, with their natural habitat around the edges.

"Neighbors show me the pets' favorite spots, and I paint 'a domestic scene.' A lot of the pets actually like to pose for me. I'm doing an iguana and a parrot who are friends now.

"The wild city animals are the most interesting. I usually do them with just glimpses of the beasts—I paint them the way I can see them, which is real fast when I'm real lucky. I have been working with a naturalist who is into photography, and together we go scouting for spores and tracks. She's taught me where most of the wild birds and rodents hang out, and we even think we saw a fox one day over by the old city-hospital grounds. There's several families of raccoons who have moved in over there, and they scout through the adjacent neighborhoods. Many people think the cities are all barren now, and I hope this will show them they are missing a lot.

"Part of my series is on unwelcome half-wild, half-domesticated beasts we have whether we like it or not. It will be linked in the traveling show with our research on illegal dumping in the vacant lots and the impact of the pests that move in to next-door buildings—like the rats and mice and cockroaches and mosquitoes who love the water pooled in the old tires and containers. The health-action team is looking at absentee rates and medical costs associated with high asthma rates that can be set off big time by cockroaches and dust and mold blowing off the lots. My paintings illustrated our report to the mayor and the governor and state and federal legislatures when the legislation team spearheaded a drive to shut down the dumping."

Principle Five: Personalizing Instruction

Creating Individual Profiles

Wheelock early childhood student-teachers in inclusive classrooms create individual profile cards (IPCs) for every student in their classrooms. IPCs ask students to discover what the child loves and is motivated by; to describe learning strengths and challenges; to generate goal statements in the four main developmental domains (cognitive, physical, social-emotional, and language); and to write an instructional profile similar to those found on IEPs. To do this, student-teachers are encouraged to use their own qualitative judgments of children combined with any other assessment data, including IEPs.

The student-teachers first see models of these IPCs for the six diverse students featured in the team-planning game. They then each contribute a few of their own cards and play the game again with a random group of new peers. They are often pleasantly surprised with how well they have come to know and to be able to advocate for their own students. After the team-planning practice, as student-teachers work with their students and learning community team on emergent curricula, these IPCs become tools for matching small and large groups, for keeping track of progress on goals, for reminders about what motivates individual students, and so on. They have even been used for developing actual IEPs (for example, one student's IPC goals were used to refine the more generic goals that had been on the previous year's IEP).

We do not expect that these cards should be exhaustive or can be perfectly accurate. We assign them in order to underscore the importance of getting to know one's students through the power of close observation, reflection, and description. And we find that they can help student-teachers to see what *kinds* of information they know about *which* children, and to think about what this implies about their own characteristic ways of relating to and planning for individuals within a group. At first, many student-teachers seem convinced that developing these cards will be a huge and impossible task. But when comparing notes on their first submission of the sets three short weeks into the semester, they tend to be impressed by the depth and breadth of their own knowledge and return to school motivated to fill in the blanks of things they had tended to overlook systematically .

Student-teachers have interesting insights. For instance, a student-teacher may comment that her IPCs of typical children are sparser, while atypical children are much more likely to have made themselves known. But she may also note that certain of her atypical profiles feature dense challenge sections, while more typical student IPCs are rich in strengths detail. Another may realize that students who require a great deal of limit-setting have skimpy loves/motivators information, and return to the classroom determined to find out more about these things to be more effective in limit-setting.

The C/LD child is a great candidate for the IPC card, as the process can bring these often paradoxical youngsters into stronger relief. For instance, analysis of his cards helped one student-teacher to note that two students he knew to have learning disabilities in reading and writing both loved drawing, cartoons, and sociodramatic play, and that their activities in this area revealed a breadth of knowledge and depth of insight he had not seen in their halting writing samples. He was moved to state that he would never teach without some process of systematically regarding his students because their talents "are too precious to overlook."

Final reports often indicate that this assignment, at first the source of considerable trepidation, has given teachers-to-be a way to develop and demonstrate competencies that they have come to value enormously. Some vow to pay more attention to children they had not even realized they were overlooking. Others state that they will have more faith in their own impressions of children as they found them borne out over the semester. Many claim they will create their own comprehensive IPC system when they have their own classrooms, one saying "they can be the basis for individual education plans for all the students."

Balancing Individuals' Interests and Challenges

Team-planning game players often deduce that the diverse group will be much less able to work together unless the focus contains elements of personal interest to each child. They also conclude that children's challenges can best be addressed while motivation is high. Individuals who know C/LD children very well can be excellent sources of information on the child's preferred activities and how they can best be utilized to motivate work on more difficult tasks. Frank's tutorial model is based on intimate knowledge of what makes her clients want to work hard (personal communication, January 7, 1998). It offers many tips for classroom teachers.

While Frank makes sure that every session revolves around reading, writing, and study skills, she also finds many ways to convey the message that this will always be done through respecting and valuing client interests. For instance, it is made to be important that the students find their preferred type of writing paper (for example, lined, unlined, make one's own lines; hold long or tall?) and favorite pencil and pens (sharp-point or blunt, soft lead or hard; ball point or felt tip or roller ball?). Further support for the balance of preferences and needs comes from the assignment for the first session. Clients are asked to bring three things. They bring something familiar they feel they can do easily. They bring something they want to hear read to them but can't read. (This will tend to reveal something about the level of language complexity they enjoy, and with C/LD children may well be something far above "age-appropriate" levels.) She asks clients to also bring something they would like to be able to do in the near future that is a little too hard.

At least the first whole month is kept in the comfort zone around things the client can do successfully. At no point are they pushed so that it feels unsafe to fail. If parents question her, Frank explains that this kind of redundancy allows automaticity with basic skills upon which fluency and eloquence are built. She moves to working on the challenging items chosen by the clients as they get to know her and feel comfortable stretching to meet their own goals. They can also then co-design strategies to meet challenges that will continually arise in school, building a repertoire of tools and experimenting with their use and refinement.

The continuous, systematic experimentation and support that an expert like Frank can provide is ideal for many rapidly developing C/LD students in the kindergarten to eighth grade years. Her model suggests four general principles that the LC team can keep in mind. First, build long-term relationships across many years of schooling and connect observations across many settings so the whole student is supported. Second, be attuned to when the student is likely to come up against his or her particular challenges. Times to be alert include when new demands are made, when many demands pile up, when demands are too high on one cognitive system (for example, much memory load, reading, or writing), when the child must process many different instructional styles or presentational formats, and when several tests are given in the same period or tests are widely spaced with little feedback in between. Third, design a tool box the student will find useful in real life. Find sustainable, efficient, relatively unobtrusive methods; experiment with new approaches; identify new demands that need new tools; refine methods that lose their effectiveness. Fourth, make it a habit to use creative techniques in facing challenges, particularly those that employ the student's own creative strengths. Identify where boundaries are and push or break them, cultivating a tinkering mentality, and deliberately look at things from unfamiliar perspectives. Ada eloquently describes the labor-intensive process of creative and systematic experimentation based on deep knowledge of the individual (see Vignette 9–4, below). She arrives at a refutational process that seems particularly effective (see Lynch, Harris, & Williams chapter in this book).

VIGNETTE 9–4   Samuel and Ada

Samuel was selected for special services beginning in kindergarten. He is talented in music, creative writing, computer sciences, and individual sports. He has just left junior high school and is coping with the intense demands of the high school years. This vignette features the labor-intensive experimental processes he and his mother must undertake to find workable study strategies congenial to his learning style. His mother, Ada, is speaking:

He has to find some way to engage with the material—he can't just sit there and absorb it. When he was very little, way, way before school age—maybe 3 of 4 at the most, he'd take the book away—like *Where the Wild Things Are* or *Green Eggs and Ham*, and he had this phenomenal memory—he'd read the whole thing to you with perfect inflection, turning the pages just right. If he hadn't been so little, you'd have sworn he was reading it.

But most of the books they read in school didn't even engage him. In fourth grade he decided he wanted to read *Lord of the Flies* and then *Do Androids Dream of Electric Sheep*. They tried to discourage him, but he plowed through and really pushed himself—I think he got fascinated with the strength of the language, the pictures it made in his head. . . .

But with regular schoolbooks, we are still experimenting all the time with how to study. He can read and basically grasp the story, but if you ask him he can't recognize the names of any of the characters or tell you particular facts. To some teachers this means he can't know anything, and he flunks the type of tests that ask for that kind of knowledge.

What works to learn what is never obvious—you have to get real creative and careful at the same time, because even the littlest thing might be getting in the way and you'd never even know it. Like highlighting doesn't work but underlining sometimes does . . . and if you mix highlighting with something else that might have worked alone you might never know it.

Our latest experiments have to do with matrices. He reads along, and when he gets to a new character or a new place or thing or word he doesn't get, he just underlines it or types it in with the page number and keeps going. Then he goes back later and fills in on the matrix what the thing was and why it is important to the story. It takes a long time to get the matrix design just right . . . lines in the wrong place and he gets distracted. I think it works in part because he needs several times of doing something to the material.

And then we still have to experiment with ways to get stuff into long-term memory and how he can be as independent as possible. The more creative we get, the better. I remember the expressive way he'd read as a tiny little guy, and it reminds me to put some fun into it . . . like when we use the matrices to study for a test. At first, we experimented with folding them in half so he could flip from one side to another like in "Jeopardy" so he could study himself, but that didn't seem to work. He'd still get a sort of resistance and get it wrong somewhere between flips of the paper. . . . But what seems to really work best right now is where we can flip back and forth between us asking and answering one another. It especially seems good now to have him ask me. It is nonconfrontational, and he can avoid the hot seat. As he listens to me muddle through and struggle with the answer (often getting it wrong), he realizes he can fill in what he knows differently.

Individualizing Adaptations to Preserve Creative Thinking

As Ada exemplifies, children who are creative benefit from supporters who are creative. Possibilities are infinite. The following offers an example in which a teacher's sensitivity to a creative style is blended with skill in helping a student design her own information-organizing scaffold. It is adapted from a technique Frank developed with one of her clients (personal communication, January 16, 1998).

A new requirement in seventh grade is to learn to take notes from lectures. Louise does so on her own and finds them unhelpful when a quiz occurs. The teacher notices that there has been a new demand without a personalized strategy developed, and they agree to craft a note-taking approach together.

Teacher and student analyze the original notes. They see that they consist of prematurely truncated phrases, single words whose relevance Louise can't remember, clusters of half-thoughts spaced seemingly randomly over the page. The teacher asks, "What were you trying to do here?" Louise thinks and points, "Here I was trying to get down something that seemed important . . . but then this came up, so I tried to get it down, but there wasn't time . . . and this sparked an idea for my current project, so I tried to put that down too but there wasn't space. . . . Then I think something else reminded me of the video game I'm designing so I got into that, and I guess I lost the next part of the lecture (indicating a complex doodle on the left-hand page of the open notebook). The teacher reframes; "Some of the facts and some of the creative associations are now present in a jumble—the notes didn't keep track of basics or allow you to develop your creative directions. How can we capture key facts in a useful order and find a way to capture interesting associations so that you can develop them later but are not distracted from recording vital new information?"

Louise is happy to hear she doesn't have to leave out her associated thoughts. As teacher and student hold the page open, they notice both pages were used. They sketch out a system that begins to work quite well after some trial and error. Now Louise always uses two pages to take notes, holding the book open. She tracks key facts on the right page, sometimes circling them if she'll need to ask for clarification or more information later, and jots or quick-sketches interesting associations on the left page that she knows she can also elaborate on at a later date. The sense of spaciousness and order gives her freedom to imagine while developing concrete knowledge to support her vision.

Analyzing Creative but Dysfunctional Patterns for Useful Strategies

Dysfunctional coping strategies can be transformed into useful approaches. Louise's jumbled notes held clues that allowed her to construct a note-taking system that could be both linear and associative. In the following scenario, Aaron, a child with ADD, learns to monitor his own attention by first following its chaotic path and then being encouraged to flow along it into a more constructive trajectory. The following "star" scenario is compounded from several strategies I have used:

During free choice time in kindergarten, Aaron would always bounce around from interesting moment to tempting thing. If one could have drawn his trajectory, it would have looked like a jumble of angled and crisscrossing lines. The teacher noticed he was fascinated by many things but never really got time to focus on any one of them.

She did not want to force Aaron into acting like a different child. She respected his curiosity about anything new. She had just read Goldhaber (1997) and knew that "multitasking," a buzzword of the '90s, was a skill today's children would find useful in the New Economy based in cyberspace and informa-

tion. At the same time, she remembered he had written that awareness of one's attention patterns, and the ability to attract attention to one's own ideas, is also vital to becoming effective in a complex world. Multiple task demands call for skill in prioritizing, in choosing a path that becomes creative and not just reflexive. She was reminded vividly of Aaron when she read Goldhaber quoting from Howard Rheingold's online book Virtual Community *(www.rheingold.com/vc/book/), saying that he laid out two guidelines on connecting to the community of cyberspace: "Rule Number One is to pay attention. Rule Number Two might be: Attention is a limited resource, so pay attention to where you pay attention" (Goldhaber, 1997, p. 184).*

To help herself and Aaron to pay attention to his attention, the teacher and Aaron drew the jagged pattern of Aaron's morning, labeling the thing that had caught his interest at each turn of the line. From this, they made a list of things Aaron seemed to like to do. Then they made a deal. Aaron could continue to choose from these sorts of things, but he was to keep track of himself using a star pattern. Whenever he moved to a new thing he had to go to a clipboard in the middle of the room where a page with a circle was laid out with room for him to draw a many-pointed star. He then had to make a check mark in the middle of the circle, and draw a point on the star tipped by a picture of where he was going. Each time he changed—back to the center, make the check, the star point, the picture.

The teacher could always check to see if he was where he had said he would be. At the end of each day, he would analyze what he had done and why. He learned over time to create a beautiful and ordered star pattern moving back through a center point of decision each time his attention shifted. Still active and quick to prefer the new, Aaron learned better how to pay attention to his own attention and became more able to get himself organized and focused.

Crafting Creative Organizing Plans

Aaron became a star in his own classroom by learning to make a star out of his own learning pattern. The following example features another creative child who learns to make and use a creative system. It is a synthesized version of some work I was closely involved with as the individual therapist and art teacher. Here, people from varied perspectives, paying sustained attention and calling on their combined creative ingenuity, help Mark to design his own creative behavioral plan.

Mark's team included his art teacher, psychotherapist, occupational therapist, behavior specialist, special education teachers, and parents. They recognized that his great cartoons revealed his storytelling flair, his uncanny ability to crystallize symbolic representations, and his visual-spatial competence (as seen in his ability to draw cartoon boxes freehand in any configuration). They also knew that he struggled with reading and writing far below grade level and with compelling impulses to "do his own thing" despite explicit school requirements that he pay attention, remain seated, relate in reality, and remain calm. All understood that his frequent difficulties in these areas caused him to "get in big trouble again," as he would put it. Using the principle of looking for functional directions in dys-functional coping strategies, the team decided that a symbolic, narrative-based organizing plan would help Mark act like a director of his own life instead of a fol-lower of his own whims.

Mark kept a clipboard nearby at all times. A top page was crowned by a clever, prescription-type label Mark had designed, and lettered "To Use When Trouble Is Brewing." A set of "organizing to learn" rules Mark had co-written was on the back of the clipboard, each paired with an easily recognizable symbol he'd also generated. At any time, Mark could volunteer, or a teacher could ask him to pick a rule with which he needed to better comply. He would then redraw the symbol for the rule ten dots across the page (which he would do freehand in perfect spacing). This would tend to focus and relax him, at which point he would use the scale he had just created to judge for himself what portion of "100 percent on target" he was at that moment. He was then required to draw a quick cartoon to show how to get back on track.

The system was very effective—not to mention a joy to use and see. The cre-ative strategy and its revisions supported Mark's learning for several years. New team members could look at the delightful records and learn about Mark's strengths as they were revealed in his own depictions of positive ways to solve his particular problems. Elements from the system became part of his IEP. The fol-lowing compound objective encapsulates how the organizing plan and its adapta-tions were framed over the years:

> *Given immediate access to and support in choosing a range of expres-sive and constructive alternatives (follow-through with self-designed organizing plan; take a five-minute art break; create an explanatory car-toon; translate feelings into symbolic representations; ask to see art teacher for special moment; and other ideas to be co-designed as needed by Mark and team), Mark will increase voluntary choice of these constructive alter-natives over destructive actions, from X percent of the time to X percent of the time.*

Mark's imagistic and narrative understandings of how the world is organized made it possible to construct a scaffold that fostered his ability to concentrate on learning and avoid "brewing trouble." Each child with C/LD can craft such meth-ods with their team to keep in shape, in touch, and on track.

Conclusion: Millions of Stars

The claod/ are fulofy/ I want won. Anna knows she can't have one, but writes about it anyway. An era of widespread appropriate education for creative learning disabled students sometimes seems far away, but we want that too, and choose to write about it. The stars/ are twinkly/ we want them.

The exploration here of five instructional principles was framed to consider how we can encourage youngsters like Hernando to keep track of their poems—to value their talent and skills enough to share them as Anna was able to do. And the foundation principle, of learning from the people most involved and most affected, seems borne out in the wisdom offered by Hernando and Jewel and Angel and Silvie, Samuel and Ada, Helen and Clay, as they gave us their vision from the "inside-out" (Williams, 1996).

As the generous sharing of their stories makes clear, students who are both creative and learning challenged are a gift to educators. Benefiting most from subtle understanding and highly particular learning profiles, excelling when teams use nuanced methods crafted with them and with those who know them best or who think as they do, these children also give us a chance to enjoy the fullest exercise of our own skills. They also help us to consider how to actualize our knowledge or educational excellence, such as perhaps through a vision of super-inclusion. For, although their needs are varied and particular, their potential is great. What may be best for them helps us to think of an inclusive environment for all children, bigger than any one classroom or school, continuous over a lifetime of development and learning, active at all hours of the day and evening, and embedded in and created by a community of citizens whose priority is their youngest members.

Stimulating Creativity in Subject Areas

How can creativity be stimulated within subject areas? This section deals with a variety of subject areas and offers specific suggestions for stimulating creativity through the disciplines.

In their chapter on creativity and invention in science, Jonathan Plucker and Jeffrey Nowak address the question of whether creativity in science is different from creativity in other areas. The authors review pertinent research and debunk the inspiration, chance, and luck myth by illustrating methodological approaches to fostering creativity in science through problem-based learning and offering advice on implementation of skill-development techniques based on solid scientific knowledge, simulation, and content mastery.

In her chapter on teaching reading for creativity, Joyce McPeake Robinson cuts across the various schools of methodological approaches and demonstrates the components of a structural framework for combining teaching reading with stimulating creativity. The chapter divides reading activities by grade level, addressing each area through goals such as directionality, sequencing, and visual and auditory discrimination while providing the stimulation and excitement needed to foster independent creative thought.

By connecting sensitivity, imagination, originality, and verbal fluency to the multifaceted nature of poetic expression, Carole Ruth Harris illustrates approaches of fostering creativity through poetry. Beginning with exposure to good poetry, skill development is explored through multidisciplinary approaches, including sense-training, emotional involvement, structure, and the tools used by poets to create understanding, insight, and connection.

In performing arts, Carole Ruth Harris concentrates on drama, structuring learning so that it supports creative production that concludes in successful stage production and good theater, providing structure without stricture. Showing the process of building performance through a problem-solving framework, the chapter on performing arts guides the instructor through the stages of process dynamics from the intuitive stage through the rational, conscious stage until the process culminates in the performance apex.

Fostering creativity through music is represented in the chapter by Laura M. Schulkind. In this chapter, the reader is guided through the systems that children develop that contribute to their aesthetic evolution and connect these systems to the sound-symbol relationship in music that acts as the gateway to the development of different areas of creativity. Utilizing applications of music as a form of communication, the author provides concrete examples of activities for the classroom, along with examples illustrating their outcomes in practice.

In the chapter on art talent development, Gilbert Clark and Enid Zimmerman formulate the meaning of creativity in the visual arts and provide understanding of what constitutes artistic talent. By providing examples of educational interventions, illustrated by case examples, the authors show how enrichment activities in visual arts can support and enhance other subject areas while providing a means of aesthetic understanding, skill development, and sophistication and encouraging originality.

The chapter by Robert Kaplan introduces the Math Circle, an innovative concept geared to providing stimulating activities in creative productivity through mathematics. The author, in describing creative approaches to mathematical learning, illustrates how to guide children through mathematics by appreciation of its beauty, discovery of its adventure, and immersion in its awe and wonder.

The reader who goes through these content areas needs to keep in mind that there are myriad approaches to creativity, and that creative potential knows no limits as long as the right doors are opened. Represented by experts in the various fields, these suggestions will enable the practitioner to set off the sparks that ignite ideas for invention, for discovery, and for knowing in the possible that is creativity, the possible that begins in childhood.

Creativity in Science for K–8 Practitioners

Problem-Based Approaches to Discovery and Invention

JONATHAN A. PLUCKER   *JEFFREY A. NOWAK*

Prior to the early 1950s, interest in scientific creativity was sporadic. Few theorists concerned themselves with it, little if any research was being conducted on scientific creativity, and educators had few places to turn if they needed support in their efforts to enhance students' creativity in science. But the coincidence of several separate events helped to change this situation. First and foremost, the launching of Sputnik by the Soviet Union helped create an environment in which a greater emphasis was placed on scientific innovation.

A lesser known event that also had large repercussions was an address at the 1950 American Psychological Association (APA) convention. J. P. Guilford, the APA president, decried the lack of creativity and problem-solving research in the social sciences, especially psychology and education. Sputnik, Guilford's speech, and other related events created a climate in which people were much more interested in creativity than they had been previously, especially as it was applied to science, mathematics, and engineering.

Creativity soon became a popular topic in journal articles, at research symposia and conferences, and among researchers and educators. The famous Utah conferences on creativity featured a Who's Who of American scientists, engineers, and creativity researchers (Taylor & Barron, 1963; Taylor & Williams, 1966). MacKinnon (1978a) and his colleagues at the Institute of Personality Assessment and Research (IPAR) conducted many studies on people in different professions, including architects, scientists, and mathematicians. The psychological study of creativity, including the application of creativity to education, also became widespread through the work of Guilford (1967), Torrance (1962, 1966), Wallach (Wallach & Kogan, 1965; Wallach & Wing, 1969), and their colleagues.

This burst of energy dissipated by the late 1970s (Sternberg, 1988b). Interest in creativity waned, and few educational fields outside of arts education and the education of gifted students were marked by a significant concern about creativity. But this trend again reversed itself by the mid-1980s, and we are currently in the middle of the second golden age of creativity theory, research, and education. Books and articles on creativity are published regularly, and conferences in diverse disciplines address creativity and its applications and enhancement as a method for improving quality and efficiency in business, education, families, medicine, the arts, literature, engineering, science, the military, and most other areas of human endeavor.

Can Scientific Creativity Be Enhanced?

Given the two periods of strong interest in creativity in the latter half of the twentieth century, one could reasonably assume that creativity can be taught. However, Torrance (1972) acknowledged that many people believed that creativity was a natural, inborn trait as recently as the 1970s. Although educators' and laypeople's perceptions have changed slightly over the past thirty years, a great deal of controversy still surrounds the nature/nurture issue as applied to creativity.

People on both sides of this issue generally agree that we are each born with a genetically determined range of creative ability (that is, creative potential) that can be enhanced and fostered. Efforts to enhance creativity will not expand one's capabilities but may help students reach their creative potentials (Plucker & Runco, 1999).

Important Issues in Scientific Creativity

Before effective strategies are discussed, three questions need to be examined. First, is creativity in science different from creativity in other content areas? Second, is creativity in science usually the result of serendipity? Third, does a teacher need to have a comprehensive and complex understanding of science in order to foster scientific creativity?

Creativity in Science versus Other Content Areas

The issue of whether creativity is similar across content areas (creative generality) or applied differently to specific content areas such as mathematics, science, and the fine arts (creative specificity) is one of the most controversial issues in creativity education (see Baer, 1998; Plucker, 1999). A few researchers have gone so far as to conclude that creativity is *task* specific *within* each content area (Baer, 1993a, 1993b). For example, a child's creativity on a biology task involving dissection is assumed to be independent of a child's creative performance on a biology task involving the water cycle. This position is an application of learning theory often called *situation cognition,* which will be described in detail later in this chapter.

But other recent research on creativity (Plucker, 1998) and on cognition in general (Pressley, Borkowski, & Schneider, 1989; Sternberg, 1989) suggests that creativity has both general and subject-specific components. This observation has critically important implications for the enhancement of scientific creativity. For example, any effort to foster a child's creativity in science should acknowledge the importance of general creative skills and personality characteristics (divergent thinking, risk-taking) *and* content-specific procedural and creative skills (ability to operate a microscope in microbiology, ability to compare and contrast in comparative biology). A good example of a program designed with these areas in mind is the Purdue Three-Stage Enrichment Program (Feldhusen & Britton-Kolloff, 1986), which accents the development of self-concept and creative skills through the use of guided and independent problem solving.

A related issue involves defining the difference between discovery and invention. Are they essentially the same, or do they represent distinct processes and products? Boorstin (1983) defines a discovery as a "need to *know*—to know what is out there" (p. xvi, emphasis in original), whereas invention is the creation of something that did not exist before. This distinction is used frequently, but its relevance to teaching children is open to question. The processes involved in inventing and discovering are treated similarly in our discussion of strategies and techniques.

The Myth of "Scientific Chance"

A widespread misconception (and frequent obstacle to teaching scientific creativity) is the belief that creative discoveries and inventions in science and technology happen purely as matters of chance. There are two problems with this myth. First, many famous examples of "lucky" discoveries simply are not true. After countless retellings, accounts of scientific creativity often incorrectly lead the listener to believe that the discovery or invention "just happened" by pure chance. Second, this misconception deemphasizes the importance of preparation in creative and scientific processes. Edison's famous quote about success resulting from perspiration much more than inspiration is a classic example of this, especially considering his well-documented experiments related to his invention of the electric lightbulb (Friedel & Israel, 1986). For our purposes, it seems reasonable to assume that unexpected discoveries result from the incidence of preparation and opportunity (that is, serendipity = preparation + opportunity).

How Much Content Knowledge Should the Teacher Have?

Perhaps the greatest obstacle preventing many K–8 teachers from fostering new scientific understanding within the walls of their classrooms is not knowing where to start. Many teachers were not science majors in college, and it is safe to say some even have a fear of science with some of its mathematical equations and its own set of terminology. True science and discovery, however, can occur without the use of technical terminology. Often the teacher needs to look no further than the children in his or her own classroom for constructive scientific strategies in applications of problem-based approaches to enhance creative productivity.

Fostering Creativity in Science

Science inherently fosters creativity. Based on discovery through experimentation, science seeks to uncover the wonders of the world around us. Hence, science at its very core is a field in which creative thinking, excitement, and creative achievement form the framework upon which impassioned individuals build innovative new approaches to heighten creativity. Science education—when openly approached —aims not to limit a child to one right answer but rather to push the envelope of possibility and foster expanded realms of understanding. Described are a specific set of techniques, often referred to as *problem-based learning* (PBL), that can be used by science educators to introduce creative skills and provide students with the opportunity to apply those skills to science content, along with general strategies and resources for enhancing creativity in science.

The discussion begins with students' scientific misconceptions, which can be the building blocks for learning and creativity in science (see Lynch, Harris, & Williams chapter in this book). Problem-based learning and related issues will be examined, including group work, the role of field and museum trips, and examples of the use of technology, with particular reference to the Schoolwide Enrichment Model (Renzulli, 1994; Renzulli & Reis, 1985, 1986).

Addressing Student Misconceptions

A student's scientific misconceptions can be a driving force for his or her personal discovery. Traditional approaches to student misconceptions usually involve correcting the student's mistake and providing the correct answer. Newer strategies (for example, the refutational process; Lynch et al., 1997), influenced by constructivism (Brooks & Brooks, 1993; Duffy, Lowyck, Jonassen, & Welch, 1993) and sociocultural theory (Moll, 1990; Van Der Veer & Valsiner, 1994), emphasize the role of the *student* in correcting his or her own misconceptions.

Conceptual Change Teaching

One such approach is *conceptual change teaching,* in which students are challenged to modify, extend, or exchange their misconceptions for the appropriate scientific conceptions (Hausfather, 1992). Consider the following example: A student remarks that the back of a metal chair "feels" colder than a wooden bookshelf. A teacher could easily inform the student that he or she is wrong and point out that the temperature of the objects is identical because the room temperature is constant. Although this approach saves time, there is no guarantee that the student will remember the relevant scientific principle. An alternative approach would be to hand the student a thermometer and let him or her discover that the temperatures are similar. The ensuing discussion among students in an attempt to explain this observation can be guided by the teacher to a point where students have constructed an understanding of the scientific principle. The latter approach models the process of discovery that actual scientists undertake daily. Renzulli and Reis (1985, 1986) have referred to this creative learning strategy as a Type II and 1/2 activity, in which the teacher guides a group of students to the construction of new knowledge through the pursuit of real-life problem solving. Even if a teacher cannot explain every phenomenon that arises in the classroom, learning can still occur through an open-minded pursuit of understanding.

The Learning Cycle

Another technique for modifying student misconceptions in science is *The Learning Cycle,* in which students' current conceptions are examined during hands-on science activities *before* covering any related text material (Barman & Kotar, 1989). Through the stages of exploration, concept introduction, and concept application, students and teachers work together to explore their current understandings and create new understandings. The teacher is a facilitator, posing questions, organizing students into groups, leading large-group discussions as necessary, and providing opportunities for students to apply their conceptions.

Problem-Based Learning

Conceptual change teaching and the learning cycle require students to construct new knowledge of science content and skills. A related but more complex approach is often referred to as problem-based learning (PBL), a strategy based on theories of situated cognition. These theories posit that *learning outside of school* is a product of interaction with the individual's environment (Lave, 1988), yet *school learning* accents "general, widely usable skills and theoretical principles" (Resnick, 1987, p. 15). School learning occurs on the assumption that these skills transfer to a wide range of situations, whereas situated cognition posits that transfer occurs infrequently and that learning requires situation-specific competence (Brown, Collins, & Duguid, 1989; Resnick, 1987). Rather than present students with information that they may or may not be able to use to solve problems, situated cognition stresses that knowledge should be presented in context, preferably in a problem-solving scenario.

Although several authors have raised questions about the claims of situated cognition proponents (Anderson, Reder, & Simon, 1996; Plucker, 1999), the criticisms are generally cautionary. In the following paragraphs, we describe key features of problem-based learning when it is used to enhance scientific creativity, draw parallels to the Schoolwide Enrichment Model, and suggest strategies for overcoming many of the problems mentioned by Anderson et al. (1996).

Rather than provide a detailed, cookbook-like list of steps to take during the design of PBL activities, we have summarized the suggestions of several authors (Gallagher & Stepien, 1996; Gorman, Plucker, & Callahan, 1998; Savery & Duffy, 1995; Savoie & Hughes, 1994) into the following recommendations (detailed examples are included in subsequent sections):

Role of the Problem
The learning activities should be anchored to a larger task or problem. This problem should be authentic in order to capitalize on students' intrinsic motivation to identify useful solutions to real problems. Research suggests that PBL is most effective when students encounter an ill-structured or ill-defined problem (that is, the type of problem most often faced by students outside of school). This reliance on ill-defined situations allows students to develop problem-finding skills that are key components of scientific creativity.

Ill-structured problems have several characteristics. First, the information that is readily available to the students is not sufficient to solve the problem. Indeed, much of the information may not even be useful to the students. Second, a single, correct process for solving the problem is not readily apparent or does not exist. Third, the nature of the problem may change as the students attempt to solve it. Assigned problems with these characteristics have several advantages, including a more accurate reflection of the complex environments in which students will need to apply their newly constructed knowledge, and require students to consider alternative points of view and strategies when attempting to solve the problem.

Several authors (for example, Gallagher & Stepien, 1996) recommend structuring the subject-matter content around the problem and not around the discipline being covered. Although this recommendation is reasonable, teachers may be better served by creating a complex, realistic problem with an eventual solution that will require students to learn the procedural and factual knowledge that is the focus of a particular lesson or unit.

Role of the Teacher
In PBL, the teacher serves as a facilitator or "metacognitive coach" (Gallagher & Stepien, 1996, p. 261). Rather than provide information during a lecture, the teacher monitors each group's and student's progress during the PBL activity. At various stages in each group's problem-solving process, the teacher may interject with a mini-lecture or provide students with additional resources that will help them to solve the problem.

This is admittedly difficult for many teachers, because our automatic response to a student misconception is to correct it. Over time, most teachers become comfortable with a role that allows them to facilitate learning by playing "devil's advocate," helping students locate resources, and maintaining accountability for each group and student.

Role of the Student

Most authors recommend that the student be given the ownership for completing the task. In principle, this sounds great, but how can this be accomplished? For the most part, the authentic, ill-structured problem and restriction of the teacher to a facilitator's role encourage student ownership and responsibility. Allowing students to create and choose their own solutions further enables ownership, especially if students are held accountable for their efforts and solutions. For example, students should be required to present their solution to their peers and possibly community members. This public presentation of their work, which is strongly encouraged for Type III products in the Schoolwide Enrichment Model, creates student ownership of their learning and further develops thinking and interpersonal skills.

Role of Thinking Skills

Several different models of problem solving are available to educators. Basic steps that are included in these models are problem finding, data gathering, divergent thinking or idea generation, evaluating solutions, and applying a solution to the problem. Of course, these steps do not necessarily proceed in a given, linear order, but the basic steps can be introduced to students either separate from the problem or during their efforts to solve the problem, much in the manner that Renzulli and Reis (1985) recommend that thinking skills be taught as Type II learning activities.

A related strategy is to teach students research skills. Several excellent resources for teaching children the basic concepts needed to conduct legitimate research are included at the end of this chapter. Countless examples of how students can use research methods as part of the problem-solving process are found in the work of Renzulli and Reis (1985), as manifest in the Schoolwide Enrichment Model.

The PBL activity should be designed to encourage critical thinking. By exposing children to problems without an easily identifiable solution and encouraging students to consider alternative perspectives, teachers help students develop thinking skills within the context of the problem being solved. One thinking skill that is often mentioned in the literature is the student's ability to reflect on the content that he or she has learned and on the creative process that he or she used to construct the new content or product. As described in the invention example below, teaching reflection is not as easy as it sounds.

Role of Social Interaction

A key facet of many PBL activities is social interaction. Collaboration forces students to reflect on their peers' and their own problem solving, further enhancing creative learning of content and skills. Our experiences also lead us to believe that interaction among groups is also helpful. Each group will develop its own culture of learning, and allowing students to interact with other groups further encourages the consideration of alternative perspectives.

Example I: Identifying minerals. Traditional methods for teaching students how to identify minerals involve providing students with several tools (for example, mineral key, pictures of crystal shapes, a streak plate, glass plate, nail, penny, weak acid, hand lens), a step-by-step demonstration about how to use the tools, and an activity in which students identify the minerals based on the demonstrated procedure. Instead, suppose that students are told that they are playing the roles of geologists. Their task is to identify the minerals at a couple of local sites in order to facilitate the modification of local zoning ordinances. All of the above-mentioned tools and various minerals are made available to students working in small groups and asked to identify the minerals. Student curiosity becomes engaged, and the freedom to explore eliminates student fears of not using the "correct" method. After preliminary attempts to identify the materials, the instructor encourages students to discuss the various methods they employed (such as, comparing similarities and differences, classifying the various characteristics). At this point, the teacher introduces the standard method of mineral identification and has students probe the method's strengths and weaknesses. Students are then given the opportunity to apply and expand their knowledge by identifying a new group of minerals. Then, near the end of the unit on minerals, the students are brought to a local quarry and a wilderness area and told to identify as many different minerals as possible. Finally, a debriefing discussion during the next class meeting in which individual students and small groups reflect on and share their experiences with the rest of the class helps students to compare and contrast the creative skills employed.

Example II: Teaching invention. Many educators have lamented that our schools do not do a good job in teaching inventive skills to students. In response to this need for better preparation in scientific creativity, Michael Gorman and his colleagues at the University of Virginia created several problem-based invention units for college students and middle/high school students (see Gorman & Plucker, in press; Gorman, Plucker, & Callahan, 1998; Plucker & Gorman, 1995, 1996, 1999). The unit described here has been used at both educational levels, and interested educators are encouraged to both visit the related Web site (http://jefferson.village.virginia.edu/~meg3c/id/id_sep/id_sep.html) and also read the various publications on the project.

At the beginning of the module, students were presented with the following problem: It is 1876, and Alexander Graham Bell is about to patent his telephone. Students were required to design a variation of the telephone, build a working prototype, write a patent application, and present and defend their design and prototype to a person acting the role of a patent examiner (in one iteration of this unit, the patent examiner was an inventor from AT&T).

Students had access to a variety of materials, most of which would have been available to inventors around the time of the Bell patent. They were also provided with copies of the various patents, notebooks, and paperwork from many of the inventors working on telephone projects, and were given a packet that contained a detailed description of the problem and suggestions for beginning the project. Student packets, lesson plans, and examples of student work are available at the invention Web site.

Many of the students had little knowledge of circuit design, the physics of sound, and other important content. The instructor, an experienced physics teacher, circulated among the groups and delivered mini-lectures on these topics to those students who appeared to need the information. The teacher occasionally stopped all of the groups and delivered a 20- to 30-minute lecture on content with which most of the class was having difficulty. These whole class lectures were very infrequent, and the teacher usually imbedded the content in a historical context that added further to the real-life application of the creative skills and content. For example, rather than deliver a straightforward lecture on circuit design, the instructor described that most inventors were actually trying to invent the multiple telegraph, through which multiple telegraph messages could be sent simultaneously, as opposed to the telephone. By comparing the circuitry of a multiple telegraph to that of a telephone, the students obtained the necessary information within the context of the simulation.

Additional Issues in the Use of PBL

Teachers who attempt to use PBL to foster creativity in science tend to have similar questions. In this section, we discuss issues such as transfer of knowledge, the role of field and museum trips, and the possible uses of technology during PBL.

Transfer of knowledge.   Even the most thorough understanding of specific content is useless unless it can be applied to problems set in different contexts. For example, the crew of the HMS *Titanic* was by all accounts an experienced and knowledgeable group of seamen. After the *Titanic* hit an iceberg and began to sink, the crew made few attempts to save the ship, and many people lost their lives. But if the crew had looked beyond their experiences, the familiar ending to the *Titanic* story may have been much different. For example, by flooding the rear bulkheads of the ship, the bow of the boat may have slipped into the water at a much slower rate. This "found time" may have been long enough to allow the nearest ship to reach the *Titanic* before it sank. Although this solution seems obvious now, why did the captain and crew not consider it? One possibility is that their entire seagoing experience reinforced the need to keep water on the *outside* of the ship. The inability of the crew to overcome the bias introduced by prior experience is referred to as functional fixedness by psychologists (Benjafield, 1997; Matlin, 1998).

Many critics of PBL believe that it can encourage functional fixedness. After all, by introducing skills and content within specific contexts, students may not be able to transfer their newly acquired procedural and factual knowledge to different contexts. For example, if specific physics skills are introduced through an activity in which students learn basic engineering principles by constructing bridges out of toothpicks or dried spaghetti, any creative knowledge constructed by the students may not be readily transferred to other relevant problems. A solution to the transfer problem is to provide students with a variety of different situations in which to practice applying the knowledge they develop in a PBL activity. Following up the bridge activity with a lesson that requires students to develop a cage to protect an egg dropped from the school roof would require students to transfer the knowledge from the previous activity. In the telephone invention project described earlier, transfer of the inventive skills was encouraged through a solar energy scenario in which students had to create inventions that would introduce electricity into a rainforest village. Allowing diverse application opportunities also capitalizes on individual preferences and interests and promotes diversity in problem finding and solving.

Field and museum trips.   PBL can be facilitated by field and museum trips. Traditionally, these great educational tools are often the most abused. Many of us have witnessed school-sponsored trips that take children to fascinating places where little formal assessment of student learning is attempted. The trips are sometimes viewed as a "day off" rather than a special opportunity to learn. One possible strategy is to provide students with prearranged tasks. For example, if going to an aquarium, students can identify different species of fish that start with each letter of the alphabet. To enhance divergent thinking skills, students can be told to find a marine species "that no one else will be able to find or think of." This strategy, taken from research on divergent thinking tests (Runco & Okuda, 1991), should prevent each child or group from listing common sea creatures (for example, octopus for "O," whale for "W") and force them to expand their thinking. Another exercise to use, especially with younger children, is to have them draw pictures of the interesting items they see. Nothing makes a venture to a new place more worthwhile than an activity that capitalizes on its wonders.

An amazing realization of this fact was seen firsthand from a trip to a well-known amusement park. A booklet of assignments related to science and the uniqueness of the theme park itself was passed out to the pupils to be completed while there. For example, students were asked to draw a picture and describe the scientific laws and principles at work on one of the roller coasters. As might be expected, this assignment initially brought about a less than excited response. Once at the site, however, students became completely enveloped in attempting to exhaustively illustrate how the roller coaster worked. After having gone through the experience, most of the students related that they had never before given thought to how science applied to amusement parks, expressed considerable enthusiasm, and were truly appreciative of the work given them! These PBL modifications are less logistically intensive than full-blown problem-based learning activities, yet still allow students the freedom to assume a more active role in the teaching of science knowledge.

Comprehensive PBL activities should not be ruled out on field or museum trips. Near the end of a recent geology unit with upper elementary children, Nowak took students to some geologically interesting sites. On arrival, each group was given a field notebook with data collection sheets having places for filling in discovered minerals, rocks, fossils, stratigraphic pictures, notes, and so forth. As was pointed out to the students, the notebooks were not unlike those used by professional geologists. Not only did the children attempt the task at hand, but they continually consulted one another in an attempt to glean as much data from this outdoor experience as possible. Even after a few hours of fieldwork, the children were so engaged in the task that they complained of not having enough time and wanted to continue working!

Technology. A person does not need a highly specialized degree to observe that technology can have both positive and negative impacts on student creativity in science. The explosive growth of the Internet—and the increasing ease of access to e-mail, the Web, and other Internet resources—provides educators and students with an information tool of unprecedented power, size, and speed. But few checks and balances exist regarding the quality of information that is downloaded, and concerns over inappropriate content have been well publicized.

A major problem with the use of technology in our classrooms is the over-emphasis on "the latest hardware" at the expense of content. A classic example is the use of temperature probes during science lessons. The use of temperature probes was very popular when the technology entered the market in the 1980s, but the probes frequently malfunctioned, needed to be constantly recalibrated, and took a great deal of time to prepare for a lab or lesson. In the end, students and teachers saved time and money by taking temperature readings with a standard thermometer!

Any use of technology to foster scientific creativity should first focus on procedural skills and then be strongly linked to content. These procedural skills are essentially Type II skills in the Schoolwide Enrichment Model and should be introduced when appropriate. For example, during Plucker's first year of teaching, he designed a problem-based lab experience in chemistry around the use of brand-new, state-of-the-art microscopes. However, he ignored the importance of procedural skills and merely instructed the students to "use the 'scopes.' " Not surprisingly, the students were unable to complete the project due to their lack of familiarity with the new technology. If proper microscope use had been described and modeled, the students would have been able to master the necessary procedural skills relatively quickly and then applied those skills to the complex problem that was the main focus of that lesson. In a similar vein, having students use global information satellite (GIS) systems to map an area in preparation for an outdoor education activity will be a frustrating experience if students are not comfortable with the technology (yes, another lesson learned the hard way by Plucker!).

Teachers may also use advanced technology to provide otherwise unattainable experiences to students. For example, creative students often have a penchant for realistic simulations (Davis, 1998; Plucker & Runco, 1999), and units on insects, ecosystems, or ecology can be complemented by the use of computer simulations such as SimAnt (in which the student participates in the activities of an ant colony from an ant's perspective) or SimEarth (in which students control a planet's environment in order to foster the development of diverse life-forms) or Internet-based simulations such as Maple Seed Science (see Web address in the resource list at the end of this chapter). These Internet activities, which require a great deal of scientific creativity and problem solving, would otherwise be impossible or very difficult for students to complete.

Conclusion

Scientific creativity is fostered by general creativity enhancement strategies in addition to the specific techniques described in this chapter. Recent research suggests that creativity has cognitive, affective or emotional, attitudinal, interpersonal, and environmental components (Plucker & Runco, 1999). With the ideal that all facets of creativity should be represented in enhancement efforts, Plucker and Runco recommend the following general guidelines.

Teachers should supply information about strategies that is both useful and interesting. Information on the difficulties in building a canal or on intricacies of Einstein's general theory of relativity may not appeal to students, but stories about Einstein's struggles to get his ideas accepted or about the political creativity involved with constructing skyscrapers may be appealing (and appear more pertinent) to this group.

Excessive evaluation and supervision should be eliminated from the learning environment. Micromanaging is just as disruptive to young students as it is to teachers and corporate managers. While the absence of evaluation and supervision can be just as debilitating to the enhancement of creativity, the middle ground—in which teachers serve as facilitators and provide constructive feedback to students—should be a goal of creativity education at the K–8 level.

Attempts to alter attitudes about creativity and encourage "creative confidence" (that is, creative self-efficacy) and risk-taking usually lead to increased creative performance. Similarly, educators should avoid making assumptions about student capabilities and learning preferences. Creativity also happens in surprising places at unexpected times, and preconceived judgments about students' creative capabilities are often proved to be wrong.

Finally, educators should consider the use of well-established programs that address multiple components of creativity, such as the Schoolwide Enrichment Model and the Purdue Three-Stage Enrichment Model. These programs have been field-tested and refined over several decades, which allows the teacher to focus more on the development of student creativity and less on logistical and administrative details.

The purpose of this chapter was to debunk common misconceptions about teaching scientific creativity and to describe effective strategies for enhancing creativity. The chapter stressed the creative value of allowing students to correct their scientific misconceptions rather than correcting the misconceptions as they arise. Problem-based learning, an effective and increasingly popular strategy in this area, allows students to learn scientific content and creative skills through the solving of real-life problems. By exposing children to multiple problems, adding realism to the problems through the use of field and museum trips, and encouraging students to facilitate their problem solving with technology, problem-based learning can be an effective technique for enhancing scientific creativity.

Resources for Fostering Scientific Creativity

Research Sources on Creativity and Science

Journals such as

Science Education, Journal for Research on Science Teaching, Journal of Creative Behavior, Creativity Research Journal, Gifted Child Quarterly, Journal for the Education of the Gifted, Roeper Review

Internet Sources

Maple Seed Rocket Page:
http://www.cs.indiana.edu/hyplan/jwmills/EDUCATION.NOTEBOOK/rocket/rocket.html
Journal of Maple Seed Science:
http://www.cs.indiana.edu/hyplan/jwmills/EDUCATION.NOTEBOOK/journal/journal
.html
TappedIn: http://moo.tappedin.sri.com:8000/
Invention Education Site at the University of Virginia
http://jefferson.village.virginia.edu/~meg3c/id/id_sep/id_sep.html
Invention Resources Site at the University of Virginia
http://jefferson.village.virginia.edu/~meg3c/id/id_home.html

Resources on Teaching Research Skills

Baum, S., Gable, R. K., & List, K. (1987). *Chi square, pie charts, and me*. Monroe, NY: Trillium Press.
Gonick, L., & Smith, W. (1993). *The cartoon guide to statistics*. New York: Harper Perennial.
Starko, A. J., & Schack, G. D. (1992). *Looking for data in all the right places: A guidebook for conducting original research with young investigators*. Mansfield Center, CT: Creative Learning Press.

Resources on Invention

Blond, G., & Spivack, D. (1991). *Invention and extensions: High-interest, creative-thinking activities*. Nashville, TN: Incentive Publications.

Goldfluss, K. J., & Sima, P. M. (1993). *Thematic unit: Inventions.* Huntington Beach, CA: Teacher Created Materials. (P.O. Box 1040, Huntington Beach, CA 92647)

Karnes, F. A., & Bean, S. M. (1995). *Girls and young women inventing: Twenty true stories about inventors plus how you can be one yourself.* Minneapolis, MN: Free Spirit.

Reid, S., & Fara, P. (1994). *The Usborne book of inventors: From Da Vinci to Biro.* Tulsa, OK: EDC Publishing.

Rowland, E., & Molotsky, L. (1994). *Resource of creative and inventive activities.* Richardson, TX: National Inventive Thinking Association. (P.O. Box 836202, Richardson, TX 75083)

Striker, S. (1983). *Build a better mousetrap: An anti-coloring book.* New York: Holt, Rinehart, and Winston.

Sylvester, D. (1993). *Inventions.* Santa Barbara, CA: The Learning Works. (P.O. Box 6187, Santa Barbara, CA 93160)

Organizations

American Creativity Association, P.O. Box 2029, Wilmington, DE 19899-2029

Center for Creative Learning, Inc. 4152 Independence Court, Ste. C-7, Sarasota, FL 34234-2147

Council for Exceptional Children, 1920 Association Drive, Reston, VA 20191-1589

National Association for Gifted Students, 1701 L St. NW, Ste. 550, Washington, DC 20036

National Association for Research on Science Teaching

National Science Teaching Association

Chapter *11*

Teaching Reading
for Creativity

JOYCE McPEAKE ROBINSON

Introduction and Overview

"I dwell in Possibility," Emily Dickinson writes about her role as a poet. Teachers of reading also live with opportunities to develop the unlimited possibilities in children, especially the creative child. It is the intent of this chapter to reach unmotivated children, often the most creative, with practical activities based on recent theoretical and instructional approaches (Feldhusen, 1991, 1993; Lynch, Harris & Williams, 1997; and Renzulli, 1977; also see the chapters by these authors in this book).

Picture this scene: A creative child sitting passively in a fifth grade classroom waits for the bell to ring while his teacher is presenting similes, figures of speech preceded by the word "like." The teacher stands in front of the class and gives a definition of a simile followed by a number of examples. She then asks students for their own similes, and only one hand goes up. The teacher firmly asks the rest of the class to pay attention and proceeds to discuss how poets often compare two things together as a way of showing how they feel about a subject. She has students open their anthologies to Eve Merriam's poem "Willow and Ginkgo," which uses similes to compare two types of trees. Several students volunteer to read stanzas and point out the similes when asked. This lesson may work for some intrinsically interested students but not for our creative child or a number of other unmotivated students.

Among the findings in recent research is that creative children respond favorably to a variety of unique learning experiences that adapt to their need for exposure to high-interest methods and materials (Feldhusen, 1991, 1993; Hennessey and Amabile, 1998a, 1998b; and Renzulli, 1977).

By changing the above lesson to include an unusual visual approach, the teacher can attract the attention of more students, especially the highly creative. The teacher writes "LIKE" in large letters on a thirty-six-inch sign. On the left side of "LIKE," a child holds a drawing or picture of a willow. On the right side of the sign, other children will pretend to "be" either "an etching fine-lined," a "soprano delicate and thin," a "velvet-nosed calf," or a "nymph with streaming hair." As the teacher reads the poem, she directs the students to "play" their parts.

A refutational version of this lesson is based on research by Lynch, Harris, and Williams (1997). The teacher mixes up what is on the right side of "LIKE." "The willow is LIKE stubby rough wool" just does not fit the willow. Creative children will see humor in the wrong information and become interested in correcting the error. Lynch, Harris, and Williams (1997) found that refutation stimulates creative children to be highly productive. A teacher's giving misinformation as fact sets up an active and exciting learning situation because students feel compelled to state what they know is true. They become alert and motivated and feel confident to be "correcting" the teacher.

Lynch, Harris, and Williams (1997) reported that the refutational approach improved performance in mathematics, science, and social studies and overall produced higher levels of student interest and intrinsic engagement. Burton (1998) found a marked growth of second graders' performance on informal reading and writing assessments after reacting to incorrect teacher-made story line presentations.

The key ingredients of the refutational approach have support from other research. Recent brain-based learning studies (Pool, 1997) found that challenging learners in different enriching ways produces better performance than providing simple, step-by-step, predictable tasks. Also, teaching reading with the refutational approach has its own significant reasons for potential success. The reading process is inherently linked to error detection and correction, with 90 percent of successful early readers rejecting error responses quickly and trying again (Clay, 1990).

Classroom experiences that promote creativity in teaching reading cut across the various schools of reading thought and need not address what Chall (1983) calls "the great debate" over which type of reading instruction is best. The history of teaching reading reveals steady debates since the early decades of this century, well before the whole-language movement. Yet generations of children have learned to read because of teachers who have sifted through the discourse to find successful strategies for their students.

Framework

Twenty activities follow as suggestions for combining the teaching of selected reading skills with stimulating creativity. They correspond with three developmental stages that serve as a guide for teachers: Level I, beginning reading; Level

II, grades 1–4; and Level III, grades 5–8. A brief introduction to the reading skills covered at each level precedes the corresponding activities. Each activity includes a learning focus, an enrichment activity, and a refutational component, along with relating how creativity is stimulated. It is expected that teachers will modify the sample of activities presented here as well as create new ones to suit their many personal, student, and curriculum expectations.

Level I: Beginning Reading

Children at this time should engage in a variety of experiences to help prepare for the formal reading process. Key skills needed are directionality, sequencing, visual sensitivity to letter and word forms, and matching oral and written language.

Until beginning to read, the young children's world was theirs to examine from every vantage point. Even for adults, the natural visual process involves random eye movements, such as when looking at a picture. To follow sequences in texts, children learn to move their eyes from left to right across the printed page and from book cover to cover.

The ability to discriminate visually has high priority in beginning reading. Children need to practice looking for distinguishing word and letter characteristics. Learning goes from letter-by-letter to units, increasing progressively in length.

By learning that written symbols match what they hear, beginning readers acquire the basis for reading and writing. When children enter school, they usually know approximately 2,500 words that they have heard spoken, but not the relationships between the sounds and their representational letters.

Activity 1: Moving to the Right Goal: Directionality

Discuss the need to go from left to right while following the text in a book, and explain that this activity is a practice. Ask children to draw a picture of a duck on the left side of the paper and on the right side a picture of water. Then say, "Look across the paper, imagining the duck going to the water." Other combinations follow, such as "bird to birdhouse" and "child to swing." Repeat at the chalkboard with children taking turns leading the class to make left-to-right eye movements. Children like using their imagination and leading the class as opposed to imitating patterns that a teacher controls.

For a refutation, say, "The water must go to the duck" and "Isn't that so?" This contradiction to what is known encourages creative children to want to prove themselves right. They will find the error humorous and become excited to show the duck's correct motion.

Activity 2: Comic Strip Jumble Goal: Sequencing

Sequencing meaningful material represents a good way to develop the pattern of story movement. Use a simple comic strip, such as "Peanuts" or "Calvin and

Hobbes," and then cut up the comic strip frames. Ask children to sequence the frames from left to right to make sense. This activity lets them imagine and discover their own meaningful pattern of frames instead of learning the meaning of sequences as a result of directed teaching.

A refutational approach increases the need to analyze the comic strip's organization: Put the frames in a wrong order and tell children, "This is the correct order." Creative children find humor in things out of place, setting up a relaxed learning situation. They become motivated to correct the frames and feel confident about being able to prove the teacher's sequencing wrong.

Activity 3: Paper Bag Words Goal: Visual and Auditory Discrimination

Ask children to label a small brown paper bag with "beginning" letters such as "d," or with an ending group of letters, like "end," "op," or "ill." Dr. Seuss books, such as *Hop on Pop,* are easily adapted. On blank note cards, children write as many words as they can find and then share their labeled bags with members of the class. The paper bags become part of the classroom's resources to use whenever needed. The open-ended responses for this activity rely on the child's own observing and categorizing. Also, using the common paper bag as a learning aid encourages children to think beyond using things such as the bag in narrowly prescribed ways.

A refutational extension: Add note cards with incorrect beginning letters combined with -end, -op, -ill, and so on to the paper bags of highly creative children, who enjoy the challenge of proving what they know to the "uninformed" teacher.

Activity 4: What Is Missing? Goal: Visual Discrimination

Choose a list of words, preferably those that can be called "sight words," or those that do not fit typical word patterns, such as "through." Have children keep the words on either note cards or on paper in front of them. Select children to go to the board to rewrite the word with one or more letters missing—for example, "nigt" for "night." The class checks to find the difference between what is on the board and what is in front of them. Children develop their own process of evaluating, comparing, and analyzing words to discriminate letters, instead of simply memorizing correct patterns.

A refutational activity brings about additional stimulation to discriminate visually. Present either one or more of the above words that have missing letters and replace with incorrect letters, such as "nigt" for "night." After the teacher says that the misspelled words are correct, creative children will be motivated to focus on deciding which letters do belong.

Activity 5: Storybook Labels Goal: Visual and Auditory Discrimination

Any book that has simple words for scenery and characters will work with this activity. An example is *Goodnight Moon* by Margaret Wise Brown. Ask children to make labels for such words as "moon" and "fireplace." Members of the class wear the labels, which also can include matching pictures they have drawn. While a child reads the text, a classmate points at appropriate times to the children wearing the labels in front of the class. Children enjoy the humor found in the unexpected way of dealing with characters and scenery, as classmates become everyday things. Also, they delight in creating individual drawings and word labels as part of the learning experience.

Mislabeling scenery as part of a refutational extension takes humor even further and stimulates children to come up with their own reasons for matching symbols and words. Point to the wrong scenery and characters while reading the text. Creative children find this situation entertaining, and it motivates them to make corrections.

Activity 6: Sound or Word Homes Goal: Visual and Auditory Discrimination

Ask children to draw individual houses according to a model, with a square at the base and a triangle on top. Each house represents a particular category, such as rhyming words (cat, bat, hat), as well as names, action words, animals, matching words, favorite stories, and words relating to school. Write the category in the triangle, or "roof" of the house, such as the "ill" ending words. Matching rhyming words go in the square: "till," "pill," and "fill." (See Figure 11–1.) Children are motivated to search for original responses in an inviting framework, while also developing their own ways for checking visual and auditory accuracy.

The teacher mismatches words and categories in a refutational component. Ask the class or individuals to add incorrect words to a house. Creative children enjoy correcting the teacher by finding the words that do not rhyme with the sound in the "roof."

Activity 7: Verbal Tennis Goal: Auditory Discrimination

Students form two lines that face each other and pretend they have tennis rackets in their hands. Allow enough space between children in each line. Say a word like "house." The first child at the beginning of one line does a pretend swing and says a word that rhymes with "mouse." The next child across "hits" another rhyming word with his or her racket. Continue the routine until possibilities are exhausted, and then add other rhymes. A good source for words is *The Reading Teacher's Book*

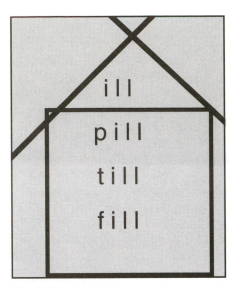

FIGURE 11–1   Example of Sound Home

of Lists by Fry, Polk, and Fountoukidis (1984). Children find humor in experiencing the blending of two seemingly unrelated behaviors, swinging a tennis racket and rhyming words. Also, combining rhyming with kinesthetic movement helps reduce tensions for more fluent expression.

For a refutation, during the "tennis game" stand in one line, and from time to time, give an incorrect response, such as "bright" following "train." The unexpected incongruent, nonrhyming responses break the rhyming routine, bringing about additional humor. Creative children become more alert, listening to correct the rhyming errors.

Level II: Grades 1–4

At this stage, children gain confidence in their increasing ability to learn meaning from unfamiliar print. They move from literal reading to inferential meanings as well as to critical reading. This period for children serves as a time for growth in reading maturity—a time for building what psychologists call individual schemata, or a store of background knowledge that helps create meaning from texts. To strengthen this effective reading power base, children need to continue improving oral and written language links and vocabulary.

Children are in the process of refining their understanding of organizational patterns and cohesive ties in texts, leading to self-monitoring of thinking, also known as metacognition. Knowing how ideas fit together represents a large measure of comprehension. Understandable parts help frame information and act as cues to meaning. Typical cues are time order, numbering, cause and effect, and comparing and contrasting. Graphic aids clarify meanings in texts across the disciplines, proving valuable for learning English, science, mathematics, social studies, and the various arts.

"Reading between the lines," commonly known as inferential reading, follows the ability to acquire surface or literal meanings. It involves forming and testing hypotheses to predict outcomes and draw conclusions. The reader learns to think along with the writer to help fill in any gaps in understanding the text.

Activity 8: Handicapped Scrabble Goal: Visual and Auditory Discrimination

A more sophisticated way to develop decoding skills is using a Scrabble game board in an unconventional way. Have available only certain letters that form desired teaching combinations, such as the consonants that can precede the endings "ough" or "ight." Children can be asked to make up either words or syllables. The activity appeals to children's developing sense of independence. They enjoy breaking from the established rules of the Scrabble game and also doing their own visual and auditory searches.

In a refutational variation, give children incorrect letters to complete a specified assignment. The highly creative become animated about solving the problem because they have "caught" the teacher's error of not including appropriate letters.

Activity 9: Breaking the Code Goal: Visual and Auditory Discrimination

Write simple sentences or paragraphs that omit vowels or other letters. Ask children to complete the sentence, such as: Wh–n w–nt–r c–m–s, c–n spr–ng b– f–r b–h–n–d? Children prefer puzzle work to study vowels over directed teaching lessons. They work out their own auditory and visual processes to find meaning in the given group of words.

A refutational version is to use the above sentence, or a similar one with omitted vowels, letters, or letter combinations. Tell children to read the sentence as if no errors exist. The garbled sounds of the readers cause laughter and punctuate the need for vowels in English words. Besides adding humor as motivational, children reportedly respond better to correcting inserted answers in blank spaces than to filling in their own answers in blank spaces (see Lynch, Harris, & Williams chapter in this book).

Activity 10: Twisted Tongues Goal: Auditory Discrimination

Using tongue twisters can help listening for learning alliteration, a way to reinforce auditory discrimination and the use of sounds in poetry. Start out with, "Listen to six sick sheep." Then ask the children what was unusual. Give the definition of a tongue twister as a phrase or sentence that is difficult to speak fast usually because of alliteration, or a sequence of nearly identical sounds. Ask students to come up with their own twisters to share. Here are several challenging twisters from *Games to Improve Your Child's English* by Hurwitz and Goddard (1969).

Wicked witches switch wishes
Which wicked witches swish wicket switches?
Which witch swishes?
Which witches wish wicked wishes?
Which witch wishes?
Wish a witch; switch a witch;
Swish a witch; switch witches.
A witch's a witch; a swish's a swish; a wish's a wish
Which witch switch a witch?
Which witch's which?

She's so selfish
She should sell shellfish,
But shellfish shells
Seldom sell.

This snail's stale.
His tail's stale.
This snail's tail's stale.
This snail's tail's still stale.
This snail tale's stale.

Children see humor in the alliteration of tongue twisters, and especially when they speak them quickly. They think through ways to hear similar sounds by carefully listening for like sounds and have fun coming up with their own twisters.

For a refutation component, children become motivated to challenge the incorrect twisters: Give the definition of a tongue twister; then modify one, changing several of the words to make a nontwister, and say it is indeed another tongue twister. An example: Change "She sells seashells by the seashore" to "He buys clamshells by the edge of the lake." Creative children find this experience amusing and become anxious to make the teacher's incorrect twisters have alliteration.

Activity 11: Ice Cream Words Goal: Word Analysis

Ask children to use saved round cardboard ice cream containers. Label containers with different categories, such as types of words, synonyms, antonyms, homonyms, or other distinctions, such as animals or two-, three-, four-, or five-syllable words. Children find appropriate words from their various texts, and the teacher can make additions to the class's submissions. Possibilities abound from literature, science, and social studies. *The Reading Teacher's Book of Lists* (Fry et al., 1984) is a good source. Pass assorted containers around for group work, which can include partner quizzing of differently labeled containers in preparation for vocabulary bees (similar to spelling bees, except word meanings replace spelling).

Using the learning aid of ice cream containers encourages flexible thinking about the use of other items. Children essentially feel that they have created their own lessons, leading to their feeling more empowered and confident.

A refutational approach: Put incorrect words into the containers, but tell the class that all words in the containers fit their categories. Have partners quiz each other; in the process, they discover the words that are mismatched with the categories. They discuss why certain words do not fit and decide if the words can be part of other categories. Creative children become excited to learn the terms' meanings more completely because of their desire to feel mastery in a contrary situation that needs correcting.

Activity 12: Paper Plate "Brief" Goal: Comprehension Improvement

Use uncoated paper plates for children to graph the organization of paragraphs or longer selections. Paragraphs can be "briefed." This activity is closely allied to outlining and similar to mapping and webbing. In the center of the paper plate, ask children to write a main idea from the text. From the center, they are to draw lines that branch out with written details found in the text. A good variation is adding a visual activity, such as drawing or pasting pictures, to accompany the writing. Also, allow for a wide range of paper plate substitutions, round or otherwise, such as poster-size Post-it® paper, cut-to-order hexagons, and trapezoids. The choice of paper plates as learning aids incorporates ways to have children think in different ways about what they see around them. Their "personal touch" in the "brief" shows each child's unique mental patterning and style. A wall display of the class's briefs will punctuate the individual differences.

Using refutation, pass out paper plates with incorrect details about a main idea or topic written in the center of the plate. Tell the class that these "briefs" are correct. This approach will encourage creativity by motivating children to analyze and correct the information and create a correct "brief" on unwritten plates.

Activity 13: "Six O'Clock News" Goal: Predicting Outcomes

After reading from one to four chapters in a book, such as Roald Dahl's *James and the Giant Peach,* ask children to act as news reporters for selected scenes. They are to make predictions to the rest of the class, who are playing a live television audience. Based on the information they have obtained so far, each "reporter" explains a prediction, backed up by evidence from the text. This activity amuses, motivates, and encourages original predictions.

One way to use a refutational approach with this activity is to create a humorous situation by playing a news reporter and making bizarre predictions. The motivating factor of humor helps put children in relaxed learning states, and the incorrect reporting causes them to more intensely need to analyze the text for accuracy.

Activity 14: The Author's "I" Talk Show Goal: Drawing Conclusions

Children "become" the author of a selected text and follow the thinking of the writer. Ask for conclusions about the author's ideas as interpreted from the reading as well as topics not even discussed; these may even be out of place and time. For example, after reading Abraham Lincoln's "Gettysburg Address," select a student to act as "Abraham Lincoln" to be interviewed on a "talk show." Another member of the class acts as host. "Lincoln" may be asked about his ideas on civil rights today. Answers must be supported by evidence read aloud from the text. The activity requires heightened imaginative and original expressive skills to go along with a clear understanding of content.

For refutation, act as an interviewer. Ask questions that do not relate to the text, such as asking "Abraham Lincoln" what life was like in 1975; or how did he like flying on the Concorde to Gettysburg. The outrageous will lead to humor, which stimulates creative thinking to prove the "interviewer's" questions are off base.

Level III: Grades 5–8

In the middle grades, children usually move from class to class and have different subject area teachers. More independence in and out of the classroom accompanies the expectation for unassisted reading in a wide range of content areas. Reading abilities can vary several grade levels within the same classroom, resulting in special challenges for teachers.

Mature readers at this stage are helped to develop literal and inferential reading ability through practice and guided experiences. They benefit from recycling the kinds of language activities mentioned earlier in this chapter but adapted to more diverse student needs.

Reading critically becomes an important expectation. Evaluating language requires complex thinking processes—holding more than one thought at a time to compare, contrast, and relate information. It means judging accuracy and scrutinizing language carefully.

Activity 15: Nothing But the Truth Goal: Distinguishing Fact from Fiction

Assign reading historical narratives, such as "Between the Devil and the Sea" by Brenda A. Johnston. Ask students to work in groups to research the story's historical facts, and make two lists, one for historical facts and the other for the fiction by the author. Members of each group take turns leading the class. They read their lists and have a question-and-answer session with classmates, who can challenge by making the sound of a buzzer or using a sounding device. Each group's goal is to have the least number of "challenges." This activity motivates children because of the game factor and their taking an active role in creating learning materials to help teach the lesson.

A refutational component uses the competitive challenge but also the excitement of refuting conclusive statements. Reverse the information of the "fact" and "fiction" lists, and read the incorrect information to a class that will be quick to want to set the record straight.

Activity 16: Keeping Score Goal: Distinguishing Fact from Opinion

Ask children to keep a double-entry journal to judge facts and opinions in selections from newspapers, magazines, the Internet, or nonfiction material. On the left page of the journal, they write the heading "Facts," and on the right side "Opinions." After scrutinizing the reading selections, they write their findings and add up the number of "Facts" and "Opinions." They must be ready to defend their choices in either small or large group work. Children develop a sense of authority and resulting confidence as they achieve the ability to sift language for facts and opinions.

More excitement to do this critical analysis occurs in a refutational approach. Present facts and opinions reversed from a teacher's journal, kept in the same manner as those of the students. On an overhead projector, show the journal pages, stating that the "Facts" and "Opinions" entries are accurate. Creativity is stretched when children enjoy analyzing and correcting the teacher's wrong statements.

Activity 17: "What Is "and "What Is Not" Goal: Comparing and Contrasting

Choose a concept such as "love," and randomly assign one of two paragraph choices: One paragraph begins with "Love is . . ." and the second begins with "Love is not . . . ." Have a prewriting brainstorming session about how comparisons and contrasts help define meanings. Ask if "love" can be understood without comparing and contrasting. Or can they know "hot" without "cold"? Put students' answers on the board under the appropriate headings, "Love is" and "Love is not." After children write paragraphs, have the "is" group move to one side of the room and the "is not" group to the other side for group sharing sessions. Brainstorming allows children to relax and share a flow of original thoughts. They gain confidence from coming up with their own concepts as opposed to learning from a teacher or text. This activity leads easily into analogy work (Activity 18).

For refutation, collect paragraphs from children before they have a chance to share them with the class, and read an opposite title for a selected paragraph. This approach causes creative and other children to become excited about proving what they know, and they develop greater mastery and self-confidence.

Activity 18: Singing or Chanting Analogy-Grams
Goal: Analyzing Word Relationships

Use a cardboard box that children decorate for "analogy-grams." What goes into the box are analogies that children create with one part missing, as in "building: tall :: train: _____." They write out the three parts of the analogy on the front of notecards entitled "analogy-gram"; on the back, they write their name and put the notecard in an envelope addressed to a classmate. Interoffice mail envelopes work well because the envelopes can be used over and over again, crossing out each name after the "gram" is delivered. At selected times, "analogy-grams" are passed out, and the receiver writes in an answer along with a written explanation of the relationship in the analogy. The author then corrects, and the analogy becomes part of a file of classroom analogies. One way to tie this activity with literature is to ask children to use a word from a novel or other work they have read. An example from *Call It Courage* by Armstrong Sperry: "courage: bravery :: honesty: _____."

Children become motivated because they take the leading role in making up their own learning materials. In effect, they teach each other and gain empowerment and confidence. Also, using analogy is a critical process (Gordon, 1960).

Refutation leads to increased interest and involvement by using a Socratic questioning approach. Take opposing views of analogies, for example, and challenge the children's answers. Creative children become highly motivated to disagree and state clearly each analogy's relationships.

Activity 19: Signpost Survey Goal: Prereading
and Letter and Sound Recognition

Explain that a book chapter is like a highway; signs in the text, as on the highway, show the direction of the author's mind and what to expect. A typical road sign gives a specified location and distance, such as "Boston 22 miles." Texts give direction with titles, section headings, illustrations, and marginal titles.

Choose one guide, such as section headings. A chapter on paragraphs from a grammar book might have the following section headings: "Good Paragraphs," "Making Up Topic Sentences," "Putting Things in Order," "Keeping to One Idea," and "Assignments." Each child creates a different "roadside sign" by copying the paragraph section headings on construction paper and taping them to the end of a ruler. Then children hold up and read the signs, followed by their prediction of each section's content. Children become motivated to individualize their visual and oral responses. They create their own guides while learning and sharing what they know about prereading skills.

For refutation, hold up a sign of section headings and relate erroneous information about one or more headings, such as "'Keeping to One Idea" that would include how paragraphs need to have one new idea in each sentence. Creative children find humor in the outrageous comments and become motivated to give corrected predictions of the chapter's section headings.

Activity 20: Book Shows Goal: Summarizing and Evaluating

Students write summaries, as either an individual or a group effort, and present them in the format of a television show, patterned after popular movie reviewers Siskel and Ebert. Material can draw from fiction and nonfiction as well as content areas. Presentations include condensed important information and readings with illustrations from the text, or student-prepared visuals, in place of the movie clips shown on the television show. Children prefer this whole-class involvement that serves as entertainment to traditional class discussions about literature. They are motivated to use their imagination for interpretations and to interact with the "talk show hosts," who help teach the class in a relaxed, enjoyable manner.

Adding a refutational component, take details of a selection like Hemingway's *The Old Man and the Sea* and present an incorrect summary, by focusing on less relevant information than what is required for a summary. For example, the "program" could focus on the color of the sea. Creative children especially enjoy this unique multisensory presentation along with the opportunity to take charge of correcting the teacher's "misinformed" teaching material.

Summary and Conclusions

This chapter presents activities that are based on research showing that stimulating children's creativity requires clever, interesting, and challenging experiences. Teachers of reading can intertwine various approaches to stimulating creativity with the teaching of reading. The refutational model receives special attention because of its unique contradictory approach and success in stimulating analytic, relational, and creative thinking.

C h a p t e r *12*

Teaching Poetry to the Creative Child K–8

CAROLE RUTH HARRIS

Poetry is a natural tool for creative expression. It is especially appropriate for the creative child who exhibits strengths in sensitivity, imagination, originality, and verbal fluency. Its flexible, multifaceted nature provides unique opportunities for individuality of expression, linguistic precision, and discipline (Schulkind & Baskin, 1973). Skill development is integral to the creative process (Feldhusen, Treffinger, & Elias, 1970) and assists the creative child to exercise discipline along with higher thinking skills, training in descriptive analysis, balance, and refinement while reaching for excellence (Harris, 1985; Schulkind, 1978b). A published poetry anthology, such as that described by Renzulli (1977) and by Harris (1985, 1991b), serves Type III enrichment (Renzulli, 1977; see Ries & Renzulli chapter in this book), and involves judgments of internal and external evidence, interpretations of attitudes and feelings, abstract relationships, composition, and balance. It includes a process of refinement that provides meaningful fulfillment in creative productivity combined with excellence while encompassing the affective domain and reaching for breadth and depth (Harris, 1985).

In order to implement these objectives, it is necessary to incorporate reading truly good poetry with substance and beauty, poetry that is crafted, poetry in which the words are like good carvings or sculpture that gives the recipient dimension and deep aesthetic fulfillment (Hirshfield, 1997). Children with creative potential should never be subjected to bad poetry. They deserve better treatment by the pedagogical establishment.

Teaching poetry to creative children includes exploration of different approaches and building activities that include a wide spectrum of experiences along with content, teaching strategies, assignments, and evaluation methods (Collin, 1997). A multidisciplinary approach that provides balance among skills and concept areas to culminate in a concrete real-world product (Durham, 1997) should also include investigational techniques such as research or concentrated reading in a specific subject area (Harris, 1985; Renzulli, 1977) to accomplish goals that include the affective domain along with stimulation of divergent thinking patterns (Schulkind, 1974; Statman, 1998).

The most appropriate ways of teaching poetry to creative children are those that take individual differences into account and combine to provide maximum flexibility to reach down into inner thoughts and feelings and reach up to true expression with skill as the vehicle for poetic articulation and meaningful verbal artistry. Ideally, poetry instruction for the creative child begins with sense training, combines sense-aware writing with the disciplines (McCue, 1997; Swiniarski & Halpern, 1998), such as mathematics, science, social studies, art, and music, and promotes linguistic discipline as it intensifies perceptual awareness (Schulkind, 1974).

Reading Aloud

Good poetry instruction begins with reading aloud, listening to the human voice, because poetry is sound. The atmosphere should first of all be conducive to understanding the poem's meaning. When reading Poe's "The Raven," for example, the shades can be drawn, the lights put out, and a candle placed near the reader to create an atmosphere of mystery. Wordsworth's "Strange Fits of Passion Have I Known," with its hesitant, closed, lonely sounds, can be read to the class outside under a tree, in a quiet place, or in the classroom as the students sit in a circle on the floor, *feel* the key words "strange—passion—near—dreams—dead," and relate to the concept in the way Ashton-Warner (1963) uses love, hate, fear, and sex words to open the passage that leads from the child's inner image to the written word (Schulkind, 1974). If the teacher feels unequal to the task of reading the way the poet meant the poem to sound, there are many recordings of poetry being read by actors or by the poets themselves that can substitute. Poems should be read aloud and discussed on a regular basis, whether instituting sense-training, connecting poetry with the disciplines, or providing students with the tools of poetry, such as metaphor, simile, alliteration, pathetic fallacy, hyperbole, synecdoche, and onomatopoeia, rhythm, rhyme, form, and meter (Dykstra & Dykstra, 1997; Selman, 1997).

Constructive Criticism and Excellence

The teacher should not evaluate students' poems, but should provide a vehicle for other students to have input (Harris, 1985) with constructive criticism so that everyone learns (Robertson, 1997). This can be done using computers, with several students gathered around one screen while one student-written poem is critiqued, refined, and polished. A student poem should never be given a grade, only commentary by the teacher and the class, so that standards of excellence can be met. The way this can be done is for the whole class to list standards of excellence on a chart, agree on them, and post them in the classroom so that these standards can be achieved (Harris, 1985). Discussion should precede any critiquing and subsequent refinement; that is, "I like" cannot be a criteria for excellence, but rather "It creates a lonely mood" or "It needs another word to make you feel that you really walked along that beach."

Sense-Training

The creative child who experiences sense-training will blossom as a poet. Sense-training finds its wellspring in the response to heightened awareness of the self and the environment and synthesis through precise descriptive analysis (Harris, 1985; Schulkind & Baskin, 1973). All of the senses should be tapped, with specific lessons devoted to each sense, followed by writing, and then turning the writing into poems, with attention to rhythm, tone, cadence, and poetic structure until the poem is polished and says what the young poet wants to convey.

Sense-training can be employed with any age and any developmental stage. It should always be experiential and hands-on, and can be modified and adapted as appropriate. Sense-training is not neat, but neither is creativity neat, so the teacher should be prepared to put up with a messy classroom and seeming disorder, and should also be prepared to facilitate rather than direct, as many responses will be unexpected.

Because vision is the most powerful sense, most sense-training begins with sound, with students wearing blindfolds so that there are no distractions (Schulkind & Baskin, 1973). Sound sense-training should begin with external noises such as gongs, paper crackling, and water flowing, and go on to internal sound, such as hearing the blood flow, the saliva swallowed, and listening for "inner voices." Students should be encouraged to describe sounds *exactly*, using very accurate diction. Student examples from poetry units include: "My inner voice is thin and stretchy," "My inner voice is hollow. It sounds round. It reverberates," "My inner voice is tinny and tiny. It just fell down my ear canal" (Schulkind & Baskin, 1973, pp. 1209–1210). Following is a sample of a sound sense-training workshop originally utilized with a highly creative sixth grade student. The basic structure and suggestions can be adapted to any age and individual child or group (Harris, 1996):

Description of Sound Exercise

1. Reading.
2. Experiential introduction to the auditory sense.
3. Creative writing.

Assignment

1. Read "The Bells" by Edgar Allan Poe and "At Sea in a Circle of Sound" by Patience Wales. Tell which tools of writing the authors use, and where. Make copies and highlight for alliteration, onomatopoeia, and other tools, using a color key. Keep it handy for later study.
2. Add to your previous collection of objects: aluminum foil, bells and gongs, coins, straws, rice, sandpaper, and two jars half filled with water. Prepare a blindfold and a tape recorder. Working with at least one other person, describe the sounds made as your partner pours water, jingles coins, and combines sounds, at random. Describe the sounds into the tape recorder in sound terms as you hear them, blindfolded. Do not name the object, but use sound words like swish, crackly, high whine thud, burble. Cover your ears and imagine and describe internal sounds, such as the blood flowing, hair growing, your "inner voice," and other internal sounds.
3. Write a scene with concentration on sound descriptive phrases. Close your eyes and make the sound again as needed.

Rationale

Initiates sound awareness.

Assists linguistic productivity.

Reinforces creative writing skills.

The next sense to be explored can be vision. A sample curricular segment, designed for a student in eighth grade, is as follows:

Description of Vision Exercise

1. Reading.
2. Experiential introduction to the visual sense.
3. Creative writing.

Assignment

1. Read "Giraffes," by Sy Kahn in *Reflections on a Gift of Watermelon Pickel . . . and other Modern Verse*, compiled by Stephen Dunning, Edward Lueders, and Hugh Smith, and "Pigeons," by Richard Kell, in *Zero Makes Me Hungry*, by Edward Lueders and Primus St. John. Review the visual descriptions in *Anne*

of Green Gables, by L. M. Montgomery. Read the description of the drive ("the drive twisted and turned as a serpent—no space to hold a house") on page 64 in *Rebecca,* by Daphne du Maurier. Discuss the tools the authors use to create visual imagery. As you progress through the unit, continue reading the rest of *Rebecca,* paying special attention to the ways in which the author uses sense imagery and the tools of writing.

2. Collect twelve objects with different and interesting shapes, such as shoes, boxes, cups, twigs and leaves, shells, pinecones, feathers, fruits, mirrors, jewelry, and old toys. Place them on a table along with a flashlight, an assortment of colored construction paper and tissue paper, and a set of architectural blocks.

3. Using a tape recorder, describe the objects *visually* with attention to shape, color, relative size, and texture. Move around the table and describe them from different angles and perspectives. Using the flashlight, describe the objects in terms of color and shade. Describe the architectural blocks in mathematical terms, using measurement as well as specific shape. Describe everything so accurately that someone else will be able to call up the image. Close your eyes and describe a scene from your memory. No one can see it but you, so you must describe it very vividly. Listen to the tape, and then write visual descriptions, adding imagery and using as many tools as you need.

Rationale

Initiates modes of observation and awareness.

Assists comprehension of visualization.

Illustrates descriptive techniques.

Sense-training can be integrated with other subjects and disciplines, such as French, social studies, science, and art. Sense-training for touch, for instance, is incorporated with other academic areas excerpted in the following (Harris, 1996):

1. Watch *Cyrano de Bergerac* with Gerard Depardieu (1990). Discuss the film with regard to color, sound (music), and texture (costumes and set), with special attention to the scenes of Paris. Explain the references to Les Precieux, Richelieu, and patronage. Describe the theater scene as if you were there, with concentration on textures of clothing, air temperature, and seating. Read *The Most Beautiful Villages of the Dordogne,* by James Bentley. Study the photographs with special attention to contrasts in textures.

2. Add to your previous collection of objects: cushions, fabrics, stones or pebbles, metal, glass, ice, and any other objects you can think of with interesting textures.

3. Touch each of the objects with your fingers, your toes, and with other parts of the body, especially lips and cheeks. Explore some of the objects quickly, and others slowly. Sit, lie down, or recline on the cushion in different positions. Tense and relax different parts of your body, concentrating on each part sepa-

rately. Feel the temperature of the room and of the objects you have collected. Feel your blood flow, your breathing, and your heartbeat after sitting, relaxing, and running. Do this exercise as many times as you need to and then describe the tactile sensations with touch descriptive phrases such as hot, cold, warm, soft, hard, prickly, light, heavy, fast, slow, up, down, backwards, forwards, tense, relaxed, supine, and so on. Write a description of touch, in English, in the style of Rimbaud's "Fleurs," describing the tactile experience of whatever is appropriate to the purpose of your description.

Sense-training is integrated with art and with music in the following exercises:

1. Study the painting, *L'Etoile,* by Edgar Degas.
2. Listen to the ballet music of *Swan Lake,* conducted by André Previn.
3. Relate the texture of the music to the textures in the painting. List touch words as you study the painting and then listen to the music separately and together, then writing as if you are there, with the girl in the painting, hearing the music. Make the reader *feel* the textures of the scene and the music.

The olfactory and gustatory senses can have similar workshops, also with application to academic areas:

1. Work with another person for this exercise. Collect spices, cookies, apples, bananas, carrots, salt, pepper, peppermint, cinnamon, parsley, bread, candy, lemon, and dry cereal.
2. With your eyes blindfolded, taste as your partner chooses, describe the taste, but do not name the object. Do the same for smell with suntan lotion, cold cream, potpourri, Caladryl®, perfume, mothballs, tea, mustard, onion, cherries, and five not mentioned. For each, ask the questions: Where am I? How can I describe these smells/tastes exactly? How do these smells/tastes make me feel?
3. Write two descriptions, one of smell and one of taste. Use setting and emotion for both your gustatory and olfactory descriptions (for example, hospital—smells, Thanksgiving—tastes).

All sense workshops have scientific applications that will assist the creative child to gain substance and insight in poems and in poetry writing. A model of the eye can be studied after a visual workshop and the physics of light introduced. The physiology of touch and motion can be integrated into touch workshops. Models of the tongue and taste buds can be studied in the taste workshop, along with terms such as acid, base, sucrose, and protein (Harris, 1985).

Integration of the tools of poetry can be incorporated into writing sessions following the sense-training workshops by reading and analysis sessions. Having the students read poems such as "Velvet Shoes" by Elinor Wylie, "Giraffes" by Sy Kahn, or "The Eve of St. Agnes" by John Keats and tell how the poet utilizes the tools of poetry will help them to understand their own process and aid in conscious application of literary terms. Walt Whitman is a great source for sense-directed reading and utilization of the tools of poetry for older students, whereas younger students will enjoy and understand collections by Dunning, Lueders, and Smith (1966) and Lueders and St. John (1976). Students of all ages will be attracted to the magnificent selections of art from the Metropolitan Museum of Art and the lovely selection of poems in the beautifully articulated volume by Koch and Farrell (1985). All teachers should read and understand the approaches of Koch (1970, 1974) as they explore and enjoy poetry writing with creative students.

Developmentally Appropriate Stimuli

Although sense-training and reading poetry aloud provide the foundation for stimulating creativity through poetry in children of all ages, there are some approaches that are better suited to the creative child at different stages of development. The following suggestions, therefore, can be modified and adapted for different grade levels and individual learning styles.

Grades K–3

Color poems will spark creativity at this grade level. Reading can include O'Neill and Weisgard (1961), which connects emotions with application of sense-aware writing and simple, direct illustrations through color. It is recommended that teachers simply extract examples accompanied by illustrations from this book and avoid the forced attempt at rhyme that mars many of the poems.

A good way to start off is to choose one color and write as many words as the class can think of associated with the color, turning the class ideas into a poem with the color written with a magic marker on a large pad for demonstration purposes. An example of the results of one such activity is:

> *ORANGE is Halloween and*
> *ORANGE is Thanksgiving*
> *ORANGE is a tangy smell*
> *ORANGE is a round howl, like a baby's O - O - O*
> *ORANGE is delicious and strange, and*
> *ORANGE peels its color into the rainbow*
> *ORANGE is almost an emergency*
> *ORANGE makes my nose fuzzy,*
> *ORANGE gives my eyes a surprise*
> *ORANGE in the afternoon makes me feel like starting a fight,*
> *ORANGE in the evening reminds me of a guitar,*
> *ORANGE is a warm color even when you hold a cold*
> > *ORANGE*

Other motivational activities include having children make lists of objects for a treasure hunt, with all of the objects on the lists the same color. The students form teams, pick the lists at random, and hold the treasure hunt, followed by writing sense-aware color poems. An additional motivational activity is making a room-sized "rainbow" with colored paper and staples. The children write names of objects or feelings associated with any rainbow color on index cards and hang the index cards on the rainbow, rearranging them to form poems.

One good poetry session with this age group revolved around flowers. After an introduction to unusual flowers like the sensitive plant and the Venus's-flytrap, Shelley's "Sensitive Plant" and Tennyson's "Flower in the Crannied Wall" were read aloud. The children were then given old flower catalogs and asked to cut out the pictures and rename the flowers. Then they chose a plant or flower from those they made up. They constructed the plant or flower out of crafts materials, put it in a container with green clay or tissue paper, and wrote a prestructured poem to go with the new, strange plant. This is to introduce the idea of structure in poetry, to differentiate it from prose, and to get the children away from forced rhyme.

Given the poem:

The Sailaway Plant
by
Carole Marks Schulkind

I found you
IN A DREAM BEACH
ON A PRETTY MORNING
Your colors are WHITE AND BRIGHT
Your petals look like sails.

Sailaway, you rock like a BOAT when the breeze blows,
And you smell like the salt sea.

followed by the structure:

The _____ Plant
           by _____
           Grade _____
I found you
IN _____
on _____
Your petals look like _____

_____

_____ plant,
You _____ like a _____
When the breeze blows
And you smell like _____

One boy produced:

GROUCHY,
I found you IN MY VEGETABLES

on a RAINY HOLIDAY
Your colors are GREEN and SOUR like a PICKLE
Your petals look like SKINNY BONES

GROUCHY,
You SHAKE like a STORM when the breeze blows
And you smell like a DIRTY SOCK.

The next part of the workshop was geared to higher thinking skills.

Imaginary Flowers.   It is easy to understand how some flowers got their names. Names like violet, rose, and marigold are like the color of the flower. Others, like the sunflower, the bleeding heart, and the silver dollar, look a little like their shape.

Draw a garden with at least five flowers that no one else but you has ever seen before. Give them good names that tell about the color, smell, size, or shape of the flower. As an example, I drew a cluster of flowers that looked like sailboats. The drawing activity was followed by poetry writing, and children were encouraged to draw pictures and write poems about at least one of the flowers they had drawn. They came up with the shyflower that blushed, the hamburger flower that cooked itself when the sun came out, and the noseflower that smelled you.

By this time, all of the children felt like poets. They were then encouraged to write poems about their special flowers and were introduced to different types of poems and concepts of rhythm, mood, and diction, so that the poems they wrote could match the unusual flowers they created.

Another good poetry session utilized sound and alliteration, coupling the poetry session with the study of animals. Reading from *Eric Carle's Animals* (Carle, 1989), with its broad collection of animal poems and charming illustrations by Laura Whipple, is a good place to start. Young children react well to playacting, and having them become the animals they want to write their poems about is a good way to get them into the total feeling following a sense workshop that concentrates on sound and touch. The teacher can start the children off with a poem, such as:

See me slither
Softly, slowly
Surely sliding,
Sneaking up into your shadow
Silent in my scaly skin

After the children read the poem, they can act like snakes, slide on the floor, weave, and so forth, followed by the writing activity. This can be done with any animal they choose and can be followed by a poetry session using alliteration and onomatopoeia, integrated with music and an introduction to the sounds made by musical instruments and their associated words.

Starting with sound-word pictures, such as hissy, slurry, sliding, slithering snake, and moving toward sound-image pictures made by listening to *Flight of the Bumblebee* by Rimsky-Korsakov in conjunction with buzzy, fuzzy sound thoughts, and pieces such as Saint-Saëns's *Carnival of the Animals,* Richard Strauss's *Merry Pranks of Till Eulenspiegel,* Edvard Grieg's *Peer Gynt Suites,* and Felix Mendelssohn's *Overture to a Midsummer Night's Dream,* creative children can make poems with freshness, originality, and style that emanate from their reactions to the music, incorporating the feelings evoked and the mind pictures they receive when they are listening (Schulkind, 1974). It is important to let them listen to the music as many times as they wish, and to give them the freedom to play back parts of the pieces so that they can reach for verbal articulation and accuracy in diction, mood, and tone of their poetry. Setting up listening centers for individual children would be helpful here. This activity also works well with grades 4–6. It can be applied with care to grades 7 and 8 in some cases, depending on the classroom atmosphere and attributes of the particular students. Students can be very self-conscious in early adolescence, however, and this may inhibit the result.

Grades 4–6

Shape poems—that is, poems that are typographically shaped to fit the subject, such as poems shaped like a particular animal or object—are very appealing to this age group. Outstanding examples of shape poems are "Crossing," by Philip Booth, in Dunning, Lueders, and Smith (1966, p. 43); "Swan and Shadow," by John Hollander, in Lueders and St. John (1976, p. 135); and "It's Raining," by Guillaume Apollinaire, in Koch and Farrell (1985, p. 99). Children can try making their own shape poems and should be encouraged to write anyplace on the page, using words that fit the word picture they are trying to make. Something that grows big and round, for instance, can start from the center, something that grows up can start from the bottom, and something that falls can start from the top of the page. Encourage experimentation, and let them use as many papers as they need to so that productivity is not inhibited.

A trip to a nature preserve, such as that described by Schulkind and Baskin (1973), can be the catalyst for some remarkable production. In this unit, the children were instructed to think about the things they observed with their senses in terms of:

above me

below me

in front of me

behind me

fifty yards to the east, west, north, south of me

many light-years away from me in space.

The students brought "memory boxes" on the outing and collected feathers, leaves, twigs, dead insects, and other objects, which they later used to make a collage and reconstruct the field experience, turning to group and individual writing and eventually publishing a book of poetry. Entitled *Around Me,* the book was bound, and in the process of publishing, the students learned editing, layout, dummying, and bookbinding.

Some excerpts from the poems produced in this unit included:

Above me
Two trees, Indian chiefs
spreading smoke signal clouds
In the council of the sky

Fifty yards to the south of me
The patch was desolate
Among the high and silent trees
And even I was not there

Many light years away
lightning, thunder
NEW WORLD COMING DOWN!!
BALLS OF FIRE TO KILL!!

Other poems in the book included poems by individual students and favorites chosen by students. The students also left blank pages at the end of the book and asked readers to copy their own favorites.

One of the most successful workshops I instituted as a poet in the schools and was to repeat in many schools with this age group was called *Shoebox Poetry* (Schulkind, 1975). When I arrived at the school, I asked the students to make informal lists of as many details of the room as they could. In a following discussion, we came to the conclusion that no two lists were alike even though they had many things in common. This was to assure the students of their uniqueness. The students then wrote about their perceptions of the room, expressing their feelings. One student wrote about temperature, another pride, another loneliness, and then read what they had written to the group. In the discussion that followed, we came to the conclusion that the individual's perception is valid and communicable through precision in language. They were now ready for shoebox poetry.

I had asked the students to bring shoeboxes, glue, paper, and odds and ends of material, shells, leaves, pebbles, styrofoam, and small found objects. I showed the children an "environment" I had created in a shoebox, with a triangle of aluminum foil pasted on a blue backdrop, and rows of acorns and styrofoam "pebbles" in the foreground. I then read a poem that had grown from my perceptions of the created "environment," in which the words NOW and AND were used to begin alternate lines describing sea, shore, and sky and to create a mood:

NOW the shore is made of pebbles
AND the sea is the kernel of a great acorn.

NOW *the light is sharp,*
AND *cuts my mind;*
NOW *a blue sound arcs overhead*
AND *the sky is its monotonous voice*
    Moaning.

Another "shoebox environment" made of overlapped, colored tissue paper, colored construction paper, markers, and glitter was shown to have inspired this poem:

NOW *the rose, the green*
AND *purple, melting.*
NOW *the pink-tinged fire,*
AND *green heart of the world;*
NOW *the white stars*
AND *the great glower;*
NOW *the orange: warm color, cold fruit,*
AND *the yellow stares, circling my green*
    Eye.

Having followed my example in constructing their own shoebox "environments," the students were able to follow the patterns of my poems and write their own. Environments created by the students were varied and highly creative. The concentration in the room was almost palpable. They were told they should write their poems whenever they were ready.

Cynthia Ferrara produced this serene poem:

NOW *the sun is shining in*
AND *the wind is blowing the leaves*
AND *then I stop and think,*
AND *where am I in this world of brown*
    and green?
NOW *the water goes gently past*
AND *the sun goes down.*
NOW *a new world of dark, yet light*
AND *down it comes to earth tonight.*

Charlie Mensching's poem held many facets of sense awareness:

NOW *the sky is dark purple*
AND *the sun is a guitar pick.*
NOW *my house is a fence top*
AND *my enjoyment is sliding down my*
    house.
NOW *my environment is different*
AND *my danger is prickly leaves.*

Susan Mangano's environment was romantic in mood, as was her poem:

NOW the wind is short
AND the day is long.
NOW I lay me down
AND sleep with all my treasures
   in the trees.

As a Poet-in-the-Schools, I was frequently asked where my ideas came from. I was usually unable to answer these queries, simply because it is difficult, if not impossible, to understand one's own creative process. I do know, however, that sometimes ideas for poetry sessions would come from unexpected events. Just after giving one of these workshops, for instance, I had been invited to be the guest of honor at a luncheon sponsored by the Parent-Teacher Association. They had gone to a great deal of trouble, with tablecloths, elegant settings, and specially prepared dishes, with the main luncheon course an asparagus casserole. Now, if there is anything I cannot abide, it is asparagus, but I managed to tackle the dish valiantly, with assumed gusto, and expressed appreciation for their efforts, which after all, were well deserved. A few days later, it occurred to me that food would make a good motivational vehicle for poetry writing, so I designed a workshop around sense-aware training devoted to taste, followed by writing on foods you absolutely *hate* and foods you absolutely *love* and later included it in the *Catch Me a Poem* project. I have reproduced one of the results here:

When I Eat Ice-Cream
by Blair Cohen

When I eat chocolate marshmallow ice-cream I like to
lick it slower than any living creature can move.
It tastes so rich, sweet, and delicious that
you have to lick it slowly. It tastes richer
sweeter, and more delicious than
marshmallows or chocolate
It has a smooth, and
creamy texture that
your tongue loves
to lick. I could
eat it all day
if it was
not so
cold.

Grades 7–8
Poetry for the student in grades 7 and 8 needs to begin with good reading, not only of good poetry, but reading that has richness of imagery, so that students can understand what poetic writing really means (Myers, 1997–1998). For this more mature group, selections such as D. H. Lawrence's "The Horse Dealer's Daugh-

ter," Robert Browning's "Porphyria's Lover," and T. S. Eliot's "The Love song of J. Alfred Prufrock" both stimulate literary discussion and provide pathways toward understanding the tools of a writer. Exercise of these tools requires discipline and meeting criteria. Discussion following the period of reading and analysis should give rise to criteria for excellence in poetic expression and should act as a firm, realistic guide encouraging writing discipline (Cobine, 1998; Schulkind, 1978b). Guidelines should include meter, artistic purpose, tone, sound and imagery, structure, mood, theme, and form, and should tell what each should do in order to achieve excellence in poetic expression.

Unusual objects can be a source of inspiration for students in this age group. Such an exercise was carried out over a period of time with pieces of olive wood. Students were given pieces of olive wood brought from Israel, shown some pictures of the trees growing, and asked to free-associate with the implications. They then wrote poems from the experience. The results were highly creative products. Students went back in time, felt the trees bend with the wind, saw scenes of what had happened under the trees, thought about harvests of olives, and included spiritual references in their poetry.

In another workshop, seventh and eighth grade students explored emotions through their senses, reaching inside their own feelings and relationships to gather material for their poetry writing. Some spoke of fairness, anger, anxiety, their feelings about growing up in a fast-moving world, of love, and of how they perceive and are perceived. Others wrote about the special beauty of the morning or a special person, and still others wrote of their feelings of trying to understand a world with poverty and war. For the most part, the creative students in this age group reflected highly sensitive natures and used poetry as the powerful tool for communication that it is. This workshop was later given to high school students in a creative writing class and appeared in student-written anthologies. Here are some of the examples of their work:

Sun Rise at the Bus Stop
by
Patrice L'Hommedieu

I saw the sunrise today,
*   A beautiful woman dancing seductively*
Swirling her silk dress in beautiful
*   clouds of gray, and pink, and blue.*
She danced and kissed the moon and stars
*   Goodbye.*

I walked to the bus stop and said
*   "The sunrise is beautiful."*
But Mary laughed and joked:
*   "I made it."*
So I looked out the window
*   of the dirty, yellow bus,*
But it was gone.

In the following poem, no punctuation was used. The student said that it would indicate a sense of no end, of timelessness.

עץ אה
by Tracey Stern

Beside your branches
  wars
Past your silver-green foliage
  ships
Beneath your lovely arches
  children
  lovers
Inside your massive body the wind howls
The ocean waves flow
Large ships haunt the long
  passages
Within your timeless bark

Celebrating Diversity in Poetry

Creative students of different backgrounds often bring a richness and experience to poetry writing that lends substance and special beauty to their work. Incorporating other languages, such as with the methods discussed by Koch (1970, 1974), produces exciting results. Multilingual children learn their deepest feelings in the first language, and thereafter must translate themselves, no matter how fluent they become in their second language. When other languages are spoken in the home, some concepts become untranslatable. Poetry allows the multilingual child to express true emotion through code-switching (Harris, 1991a). Writing, which often acts as the catalyst for creative expression, is sharpened and honed through the medium of poetry, where every word must count toward bringing about the entire aesthetic experience of the reader.

Children of diverse backgrounds should be encouraged to share both experience and culture through poetry writing (Felice, 1998). In Micronesia, where I spent many years, the children produced a book in Marshallese and English and incorporated both their legends and current events in both languages.

At the time, the Marshall Islands had just received independence, became a republic, and had their own flag for the first time ever. Here is what one trilingual child wrote (rendered in English here, but also written in Marshallese):

The Flag
by
Miles Ubedai

The flag was unwrapped inside a box
Three more days and it would
Be sky-high!

The first night the flag was washed by an unknown woman.
Being clean in an early dawn of the last day,
The flag awoke and smiled
The people saluted the FLAG
and awoke!

The author was age 8 at the time.

Another poem, written by a 14-year-old, tells a legend:

Bao Kirir Im Raj

The birds and the whale
Had a conversation
And the conversation turned
  into a
Quarrel, as some conversations do
Now the whale had a big mouth
  as most whales do
But the bird had flocks of friends
Too many for the whale.

And the birds came and drank up
The salt water
Taking it away
The whale spouted to put it back
But
As low tide came
Spouting was no use.
It never is.
Big mouths should know this
But they don't
So—
The birds won.

Conclusion

When all students, especially creative ones, are exposed to good poetry, to sense-training, and to expressing themselves through the medium of poetry, they find true creative expression of the self within a meaningful framework. Poetry encompasses the learning domains. It includes higher thinking skills along with critical judgement. It serves as a vehicle for precise expression through language while providing multiple pathways to introspection and self-knowledge even as it reaches outward, enhancing human connection and heightening awareness. The most intense and disciplined of the written arts, poetry allows the creative child to optimize verbal communication and serves as a catalyst to find the voice of the inner self, the voice that if suppressed, can be stilled forever:

He always wanted to explain things.
But no one cared.

He hated to hold the pencil and chalk,
With his arm still and his feet flat on
the floor,
Stiff,
With the teacher watching and watching.

And when he lay out alone looking at the sky,
It was big and blue and all of everything.
But he wasn't anymore.

He was square inside.
And Brown.
And his hands were stiff.
And he was like everyone else.
And the things inside him that needed saying
didn't need it anymore.
It had stopped pushing.
It was crushed.
Stiff.
Like everyone else.

Anonymous, excerpted from a longer poem
(Poetry Supplement, N/S-LTI-G/T Bulletin, 1978, unpaged)

The poem was written by a high school senior and given to his teacher. The teacher was surprised. It is not known today if the poem is actually the boy's work. He committed suicide.

As educators, we need to listen for and listen to young children and provide encouragement for creative expression through poetry while they are still young, before creative children become "like everyone else." There are things inside that need saying. Listen for the voices. Ask them to tell you so you can hear it.

Chapter 13

Teaching Creative Children with the Performing Arts Problem-Solving Pyramid

CAROLE RUTH HARRIS

The fusion of elements in the performing arts presents a complex challenge for creative children and provides a vehicle for problem solving. Tuned in to self-perception simultaneously with perceptions of the individual by both the working group and the target audience, the performing arts provide a vehicle for exercise of flexibility, strengthening the internal locus of control while demanding excellence of the participants. The performing arts can serve as a key to unlock creative potential, self-discovery, and productivity (Amabile, 1990; Wright, 1994) and provide both intrinsic and extrinsic motivation that do not cancel each other out (Perkins, 1995). The dynamic interrelationships and discipline generated by the performing arts can be clarified by conceptualizing the process as a pyramid, a concept that serves to define these attributes within a structure and dimension.

Performing arts take many forms, among which drama, music, and the dance make up the major categories, with each category supported by its own tangential, essential, and unique components and totality of artistic realization. Although the focus of this chapter will be on drama, the pyramid concept can be applied to other areas of performing arts.

In drama, costuming, lighting, directing, and scenery are as much a part of production as acting and interpretation of the script. The script, in fact, cannot reach its full dimension without performance. While the dramatic arts require discipline and practice and are achievable individually, the problem-solving attributes are optimized in a group setting that develops and maximizes effective problem-solving skills (Collins, 1991).

Application can be carried out in the classroom with a view to providing structure while maximizing creative potential (Montanaro & Montanaro, 1995; Ratliff, 1997). By giving the child a framework on which to build one creative idea upon another, the teacher fosters creativity through structure without stricture. The children build the pyramid; the teacher assists the children in the construction, facilitating and guiding each stage.

The construction of the pyramid includes components relating to critical and topical selection and methods of building goal-directed patterns. The process, which supports and strengthens the establishment of criteria for standards of excellence, culminates in an artistically appropriate aesthetic apex (Harris, 1990). Implementation of the pyramid construct is presented in a streamlined methodological approach that builds systems and management skills and incorporates performance evaluation. It concludes with flexible guidelines for successful adaptation to a variety of K–8 populations and settings.

The Pyramid Structure

Because the performing arts are realizable only in an end product, they depend for their fruition on a wide variety of skills, talents, and disciplines (Wilson, 1994). These combine logical, scientific problem approaches and intuitive, instinctive approaches to task involvement. In the pyramid, process and product are delineated as blocks. Broken into three basic components, these blocks include the *search* component, the *systems* component, and the *artistic* component. The performance itself, which is conceptualized as the apex of the pyramid, is reached only by correct structuring of the building blocks of the other components. Several steps are involved in the construction of the three-level pyramid, with each level made up of components or blocks that fit the overall pattern as well as serve a specific instructional purpose.

The baseline, or foundation, is the *search* component, which consists of establishing the purpose, exploring, and selecting. Although establishing the purpose is central to the baseline, exploration of appropriate subjects and critical and topical selection provide expansion of the central position of the baseline and give direction to the future shape of the pyramid (see Figure 13–1).

The second building level, or middle of the pyramid, is the *systems* component. Narrower in focus than the baseline, its purpose is the concentration of specific planning to suit the architectural purpose of the structure. The middle level depends for its support on the base but does not, of itself, provide the means to reach the higher goal of performance. The second level is conceptualized as blocks of the same size and importance. This level consists of goal-directed patterns and management and *systems* skills, as shown in Figure 13–1.

The apex is, of course, the point of the pyramid. The apex is the figurative conceptualization of performance: an aesthetic pinnacle of excellence subject to the discipline of *artistic* standards that now faces the moment of truth.

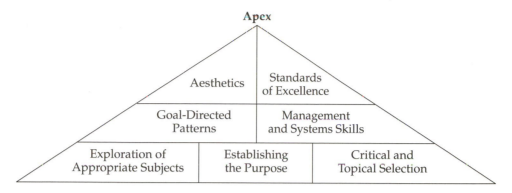

FIGURE 13–1

It is the completion that provides resolution and culmination of the aspects intrinsic to the realization of the various dimensions of creativity. Without all of the parts, the pyramid is either incomplete or at too low a level to attain distinction; thus, the construct requires a strong interdependent relationship for appropriate completion.

The initial step is the establishment of the purpose. This forms both the baseline and the central core of the pyramid. Coleridge (1849) defines the peak of excellence in *artistic* performance as a culmination of process, which has as its impetus a central purpose, or reasoning. He postulates that the product of the two separate, indestructible forces demanded by transcendental philosophy becomes a third force with a life of its own in the realm of aesthetic excellence, or what he terms as "the highest perfection of talent" (Coleridge, 1849, p. 96).

In order to reach this height, or peak, however, there must be a counteracting process at work. This process does not neutralize but results in a new creation that evolves from the notional, or idea, to the actual product. The new creation goes from intuition to reality powered by the artist through the *artistic* process (see no. 1 in Appendix to this chapter).

Coleridge is, of course, referring to poetry, but the process he outlines remains as the patterning process and *systems* that must precede the result. The process is an enabling process and serves as a vehicle, a means, or a series of steps to attainment of an ideal realizable only in its experientially tangible form—that is, the peak, or performance, at the moment it is received. The patterning of performance, therefore, must take into account that its durability is limited to the interactive experience of the moment, and that much depends on the audience.

This can perhaps best be understood by viewing the problem-solving relationship as the process that provides the means for reaching attainment. By further delineating the structure levels as *search* level=interactive process, *systems* level=step process, and *artistic* level=requirements for attainment process, we can see the *inner* workings of the three stages (Figure 13–2) or blocks. Examination of each process in Figure 13–2 shows how and why each level works, with the levels of the pyramid illustrating where each outer block goes, and in what order.

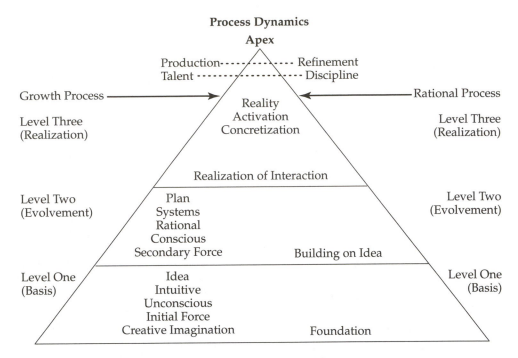

FIGURE 13–2   Process Dynamics of the Pyramid

The Search Level

In his *Biographia Literaria,* Coleridge (1849) speaks of the primary imagination as "repetition of the eternal act of creation" (p. 297) and secondary imagination as differing only in degree and in the "mode of its operation" (p. 297). Applied to the context of performance, this definition of the types of imagination leads to the creative, original idea as intuitive, or *search* level, seen by Coleridge as the primary level.

The *re-creation* of the original idea in its realizable form, at the secondary or *artistic* level, comes at the point when it is recognized and received by its audience. The point or peak is built, moreover, directly from the fact that the performance recipient is a judge or judgement-making body whose presence and influence must be established at the outset, and in the first stage of planning—that is, in the very essential *search* component, which serves as a foundation. In order to get from *search* level to *artistic* level, it is necessary to go through the *systems* level.

The Systems Level

When Coleridge (1849) delineates the characteristics of completeness of aesthetic expression, he tells us that each type of imagination has a distinct life and vitality in its own right. The types of imagination differ in the way in which they operate;

yet they interact with each other to re-create a kind of unification that is constantly becoming, growing, and gathering strength within its own creative force (see Appendix). These two forces create a third force.

As complex as this sounds, it is just what teachers do in the classroom when they encourage children to become more creative through performing arts, re-creating through two types of imagination operating on different levels and finally unifying. It *struggles* to unify, to idealize, to reach the pinnacle. The teacher helps the students through this struggle, this third force, by facilitating through the *systems* level. Realization of creativity through performing arts is not easy, but as children discover when they reach the successful apex, it is satisfying, rewarding, and true in the sense of being real accomplishment that both they and their audience understand.

Arieti (1976) connects the creative process with the creative product in a generative relationship differentiated by the quality of uniqueness. This takes expression in the end product or result of a process that culminates in the achievement of unity. Arieti makes a clear distinction between *spontaneity* and *creativity*, with the former characterized by *possibilities* and the latter realized by virtue of *patterned, controlled events* that culminate in actual production.

Production comes about only as a result of the degree of control over the process. In this respect, the problem-solving process is able to discipline and direct the generative, spontaneous idea, turning creative force to created product as it proceeds through the *systems* level. The realization is a direct outgrowth of a rational, conscious effort or system that is built upon the creative, intuitive idea level, allowing the unconscious initial force to evolve (see Figure 13–2) so that it can reach attainment and fulfillment at the next level.

The Artistic Level

It is appropriate and sensible to delineate the peak expression, or performance, in terms of what precedes the performance. The instructional empowerment comes about not as a result of what has already occurred, but what can occur if the process is structured so that a pinnacle is not only possible, but probable (Anarella, 1992; Baker, 1996).

Given that creative students possess the necessary attributes for reaching actualization of excellence in performing arts, the three-level, streamlined, methodological "pyramid" approach that brings this excellence about is closely aligned to educational goals shaped by maximization of creative potential, excellence, and the recognition of individual attributes.

Level One: Establishing the Purpose, Critical and Topical Selection, Exploration of Appropriate Subjects

Although establishing the purpose is central to this level, exploration of appropriate subjects for critical and topical selection provides subsidiary focal points where learning occurs (Osin & Lesgold, 1996). In this respect, level one of the pyramid is parallel to the initial step in Renzulli's (1977) triad, which has as its first step exploration of a general area or Type I enrichment. The purpose, however, differs from Type I in that it provides a strong, definite focus with parameters that will later assist in establishing the standard.

Consider first the purpose. At the outset, a decision must be made as to the purpose or purposes: to entertain, to instruct, to comment (such as political satire for high-level thinkers in upper grades, which does all of these), or to approach or renew the interpretation of an art form. The base structure must, of course, include consideration of genre, but although purpose and genre are strongly intertwined, care must be taken to ensure sufficient flexibility so that the genre is the tool of the performance and not the other way around (Ratliff, 1997). A premature freezing into genre can stifle creativity. Like trying to use multiple choice for creative writing, it forces ideas into a filing cabinet structure with limited drawer space.

In the Bread and Puppet theater, for instance, focus is on the visual experience rather than on the psychological, which, though central to modern theater, derives from classical tradition. According to Shank (1982), this experimental group thinks of "puppets and live performers as moving sculptures, and of the performance animated by movement" (p. 96). This medium, serving as a model for the K–4 grades, can go a long way to releasing creativity while providing a framework and modeling technique (Baker, 1996).

The performance focus may have as its purpose a number of things. Any performance, however, to have meaning, must have a real audience. Although Renzulli (1977) utilizes creative writing as an example, a parallel may be drawn to performance. The product was a book of poetry entitled *Catch me a Poem*, professionally printed, bound, and copyrighted, with a company that is organized like other commercial publishing houses in that it includes a board of directors, an editorial department, and various other departments such as advertising, budget, sales, layout, and distribution. Poets submitted their work to the editors, who reviewed it for excellence. The editors accepted some and rejected others, with the teacher sharing manuscript review and emphasizing self-evaluation (p. 55).

Similarly, if the performance is going to have limited exposure, then the level of performance will in all likelihood adjust to the audience. In a performance for parents only, for instance, qualitative differentiation can be weakened by bias and a diluted expectation. It matters more to the performer if the performance takes place in the real world. Every effort, therefore, should be made to give performance a wide exposure, increasing stringency of requirements and creating a stress level appropriate to apex potential, or what Coleman (1995) calls anticipatory anxiety. Videotaping is a particularly useful vehicle for stretching the creative student and promotes self-evaluation.

The receptivity of the audience is a strong consideration for students (York, 1997) and should be considered as part of level one. Exploration of appropriate subjects and critical and topical selection on this first level is essential for the strength and solidity of the structure (Rubin & Merrion, 1995). It is here, also, that the atmosphere for group interaction is established, and natural leadership and other important personality traits emerge. These have a strong influence on both the end product and on self-concept. Because the product is inextricably intertwined with self-concept, the entire learning process depends on group behavior (Bellman, 1974; Gilmore, 1973). This is consistently the case within both the interpersonal social structure of the group and the behavioral characteristics as a group.

When building the base, or formative structure, the greatest care must be taken to avoid the superimposition of teacher values. A teacher who is intrusive here will weaken the structure prematurely, perhaps even forcing out originality (Rogal, 1996; Sierra, 1997). Without the problem-solving attributes that maintain its qualitative differentiation for use with creative children, the structure lacks substance and cannot create or build that balanced support that allows that which is the student's own peak to come into being. At the same time, a completely "laissez-faire" teacher role can negate any progress with an absence of direction interpreted as indifference. This is strongly supported by Massey and Koziol (1978) in their review of research into the effects on performance in the academic disciplines. Their findings serve to emphasize that teacher guidance is an essential factor in maintaining a sense of order and purpose en route to the final product.

Bolton (1979), who takes the view that "the very notion of categorizing experience in this way even with its overtones of tension and implied values is still a barrier to the art form" (p. 124), advises the teacher to allow children of all ages to find their own reality and so avoid the barrier to creativity imposed by the inflexibility of a forced story line that comes before, not after, exploration. This indicates that level one must incorporate both experience and involvement both with the purpose of the topical selection and with the impetus provided by the energy and vitality of group dynamism. It is the group dynamism that establishes initial momentum and structures the parameters for validity within which any group problem solving must operate for successful closure and a rewarding result. Bolton (1979) reiterates the proposition that any action should not be viewed as an instance, but as that which "symbolizes something much bigger than itself" (p. 145) and that the teacher serves as a sharer, merely one who will "reflect back to them the levels of thought they [the students] are trying out" (p. 146).

Byers (1968) maintains that the role of the teacher is to provide encouragement. By recognition of student involvement and the total idea, perception growth as intrinsic to the dynamics of ideational fluency then evolves through process as sensitivity flow rather than process as fixed step. According to Byers (1968), focus should always be on the student, operating simultaneously with an awareness that takes into account the structure and its integration into the overall plan.

Exploration of appropriate subjects requires a far-ranging curiosity that operates in tandem with the performance purpose. The term, *appropriate*, in fact, implies an anchor and allows freedom of examination without the uncertainty of drift. At this stage, any idea is allowed, provided that it has some relation to the purpose.

An important part of the first stage, or pyramid base, is exposure to a variety of performances (Gordon, Derek, & Stoner, 1995). Performing arts do not operate in a vacuum, and the initial contributory ideas must come from an experiential base upon which the new structure is built, drawing ideas, readapting, changing, and creating new ideas, all incorporating expression (Swope, 1995).

In a society with a plethora of offerings, including video and the Internet, choice becomes a problematic situation with the problem largely devolving upon the instructor, who must provide guidance (AmRhein, 1997). Such choices were unavailable in primitive or unsophisticated cultures, eliminated problems of relevancy, and aesthetics and standards were built in. Performing arts in old Hawaii, for instance, were geared to the hula, with a natural selection process coupled with cultural inclusion not available to the young in today's sophisticated, technologically oriented, sometimes confusing milieu (Emerson, 1982).

Creative students do not today have the option of freedom *from* choice. Rather, their freedom *of* choice places a great burden on their unformed state and tends to dilute the focus so that the exploration itself becomes confusing. It is the job of the teacher or facilitator, therefore, to delimit, delineate, and provide guidance in a fluid manner, without stricture (Heathcote & Bolton, 1994). To stretch and reach, to explore and turn, is the essence of strong, flexible guidance.

Nunn (1983), in his essay, "Tails of Two Cities," which includes his commentary on the development of the musical *Cats,* and events related to its preparation, alludes to central purpose as the basic premise and the foundation of the musical's soaring success: "After the event we tend in the theater to take an Olympian view of our successes and failures, and looking back through diaries and notebooks, we find there was meaning and purpose" (p. 10). Later in the essay, Nunn (1983) alludes to "connecting the many collaborators together by attempting to describe the intention of the whole, and carrying the can" (p. 11). The "can" is the critical and topical selection or the *can it work* in relation to the purpose, the other side of the central block of the pyramid base (see Figure 13–1). How closely it is related to the central purpose is only part of this portion of the basis for building successful performance art, for it is here that leadership emerges, that responsibility becomes clear.

In an interview, Driver, characterized as a nonconformist dance choreographer by Brown (1984), maintains that the responsibility for audience perception lies with the performer and not with the audience: "It is essential for me to make work that is so immediate that it can be coped with and appreciated whether you know the system or not" (unpaged).

An awareness of the audience, or how a performance might be received, aids both the clarity of purpose and the selection of subject matter. A play performed for the school will have a vastly different kind of critical audience than a play performed at a community center, with different expected responses. At the same time, the awareness that the performance creates something new provides a reciprocal balance that ameliorates and changes the perceived role of the perceptor, or audience. The reciprocity creates an atmosphere open to freedom of experimentation, tempered by the self-regulatory aesthetic validity, becoming true *artistic* excellence. This requirement for validity holds true whether the performance is classical drama or guerrilla theater. If success is to be attained, then clarity must be present in the foundation of the structure, at the first level and at the youngest level. Children can tell when they are being hoodwinked, and expectations should be discussed at the outset or both performance and child will suffer.

Level Two: Goal-Directed Patterns, Management and Systems Skills

Goal-directed patterns combined with management and *systems* skills are essential to the success of the performance. These serve as the vehicle for reaching the apex. They are the "how" of the "what" and "why" established at level one. It is here that leadership skills, which became apparent at level one, are both strengthened and put to the test. The goals are known, and the date set. That which remains at this level is hard work, discipline, and a continuing sense of purpose (Haaga, 1995).

The most sensible way to approach level two is to create an atmosphere of teamwork and cooperative effort along with a sense of personal responsibility and involvement with plenty of room for creativity. At level two, it is imperative to provide stimuli so that the aesthetic ideal has an opportunity to develop fully. At this juncture, specific, strong direction by the teacher is required. Byers (1968) advocates ideation at this stage to facilitate growth and spontaneity and to encourage creative depth. Specific exercises provide continuity of the goal-directed patterns that build performance excellence through experience. Clarification of this stage is provided by Byers (1968), who advises that better results come with less restriction and greater freedom combined with teacher involvement of the type that includes dedication and true teacher-student connection.

Of course, the way a student saturates him- or herself depends on the stimulus and design of the exercise. Saturation in the stimulus should be spontaneous, without stricture or expectation. If students listen to two audiotapes with their eyes closed, for instance, ostensibly to stimulate visualization, but expect one to stimulate a character idea and the other a story idea, they operate under unnecessary restriction. Ideas have more room for growth if the teacher directs the student's attention toward specifics such as melody or rhythm in the music or cadence in the speech, rather than toward achievement of a specific result or reaction (Millward, 1996).

Some successful ideation exercises have required specific results, yet allowed freedom in the treatment of those results. For example, sixth grade students confronted a series of words designed to stimulate ideas for a story. The words were: gold, townspeople, daisies, villains, teardrops, gossip, and fortune-telling. The exercise led to creative thinking by forcing relationships among words to outline a story. Group ideation produced the best result, and both fantasy and melodrama were integral ingredients of the final story. The plot concerns a young girl who lives alone in a field of ten-foot daisies. She tells fortunes with teardrops, and afterwards the tears turn into gold. When the townspeople hear about the girl's strange powers, they gossip, but only the word "gold" reaches the eavesdropping villains. They begin to plot how to steal the money. The townspeople, the girl, and the villains are in for a surprise upon discovery that the golden teardrops possess a most peculiar characteristic that changes the outcome of events for everyone (Byers, 1968).

Byers (1968) cautions against premature decisions, and emphasizes the evaluation of the potential influence of an idea or system on the whole performance. According to Byers (1968), readiness of an idea to be incorporated into the whole structure is reached when the idea can "live and communicate on its own merit" (p. 70).

Establishment of an atmosphere of constructive criticism at this level assists both the group and the individual to attain objectivity (Byers, 1968) so that movement can be made toward a pinnacle, the perfection of expression of the idea in a specific sense—that is, an individual sense or idea that is successfully communicated. Winters (1957) reminds us that the idea of perfection obviates its individual existence; "If we were all perfect, we should all be precisely alike" (p. 143)—and that perfection is compartmentalized into talent areas so that it is the obligation of the artist "to arrive at a true judgment of his subject, whatever it may be" (p. 144). When that judgment is reached, a performance creates another judgment, a completion of truth for which the performer must be ready. It is arrival at the pinnacle, a single point, that tests the entire process by receiving, judging, and duplicating through connection and through true comprehension (Gardner, 1985a) to the point of completion.

Management and *systems* skills are an important component at this level because without their use, the project will not work; the apex will be beyond attainment, remaining an idea without subjecting it to evaluation. Gardner (1985a) deals with this concept when he discusses blends of intelligences in creative drama: "I said logical-mathematical intelligence wasn't important for an actor, but I think the producer had better have some; the finance manager better have some, and probably the author had better have some too" (p. 307). At this level, logic and planning become the servants of aesthetic effect, and whatever is possible and practical is done to achieve that effect.

Level Three: The Apex, Aesthetics, Standards of Excellence

When Reinert (1964) explains the characteristics of drama, he does so in terms of its art, which he defines as a "controlled elegance" (p. xxvi). Performance art, in order to maintain its life as aesthetic experience, must be controlled, sharpened, honed to a spare elegance that communicates and conveys with complete accuracy an uncompromising par, a pitch of absolute excellence, or it fails as art. The student with high creative potential, who is often characterized by perfectionism, (Gallagher, 1975; Maker, 1982; Tannenbaum, 1983), is a natural candidate for performing arts. In performing arts, however, specific aptitude areas can emerge without evidence of strong intellectual capability in other areas (Taylor, 1978). Performing arts can therefore serve as a vehicle of expression for a strong talent area, allowing creativity to emerge and to develop while simultaneously demanding the perfectionism that the creative child will come to understand and even crave.

According to Prakash and Waks (1985), excellence as self-actualization occurs when the individual has reached a state of integration of mental powers in the pursuit of authenticity. When the pinnacle or apex of performance is achieved, the authenticity or state of excellence is validated by the elegance or state of the aesthetic standard. To achieve this state, evaluation and critical analysis must take place. It completes and caps the effort and provides the final answer to the all-important aesthetic question that pervades every performance: Did it work?

The pyramid construct as methodology can be appropriately adapted to a variety of levels and a wide range of ethnic and cultural groups. Success, however, is built into the construct only as long as standards of aesthetic excellence in peak performance remain the only acceptable resolution, when completion of the concept is truly brought about: "When you have that feeling of rightness, then the something is just as it ought to be " (Perkins, 1981, p. 122).

The following guidelines provide a streamlined methodological approach for systematic application of problem solving in performance.

Architectural Guidelines for the Performance Pyramid

Level One: Search

1. Purpose should be clearly established.
2. The audience should be determined in as specific a way as possible as to level of sophistication, age, and expectations.
3. Continued exposure with several performances should be planned so that critical evaluation can take place and refinement made possible.
4. Exploratory activities should be delimited within boundaries that allow for flexibility of input, creativity, and originality.
5. Criteria of excellence should be established at the outset.
6. The relationship between self-discipline and excellence should be clarified.

Level Two: Systems

1. Allocation of responsibility should emerge from agreement among the group.
2. A time schedule should be set up that accommodates both small-group planning and large-group discussion.
3. Regular reiteration of goals should be interspersed with discussions in both small and large groups.
4. Evaluation of progress toward goals should be a part of daily activities.
5. A vehicle for anonymous informal commentary, such as a bulletin board or drop-in box, should be instituted.
6. Student leadership should be strongly encouraged.

Level Three: Artistic

1. Rehearsals should be regularly scheduled.
2. Perfection should be emphasized.
3. Hypothetical audience reaction should be gauged.
4. Playback using videotape or audiotape should be utilized when possible and studied for purposes of constructive criticism.
5. An outside judge should be called in to critique the rehearsals for the sake of objectivity and to provide critical expertise.
6. All environmental and physical details should be scrutinized prior to performance to obviate any mishaps or contingencies that could dilute the effort.

By using these guidelines, the pyramid can be adapted to accommodate any level and/or specialized population. In essence, the pyramid is a powerful tool for combining performing arts with problem solving for the creative child of any age and any type or combination of creativity that falls within the scope of the performing arts.

Appendix

1. "—from notional to actual, by contemplating intuitively this one power with its two inherent, indestructible, yet counteracting forces, and the results or generations to which their interpenetration gives existence, in the living principle, and in the process of our own self-consciousness. By what instrument this is possible, the solution itself will discover, at the same time that it will reveal to, and for whom, it is possible" (Coleridge, 1849, p. 96).

   "The counteraction, then, of the two assumed forces, does not depend on their meeting from opposite directions: the power which acts in them is indestructible; it is, therefore, inexhaustibly re-ebullient and as something must be the result of these two forces, both alike infinite, and both alike indestructible; and, as rest or neutralization cannot be this result, no other conception is possible, but that the product must be a *tertium aliguid* or finite generation. Consequently, this conception is necessary" (Coleridge, 1849, p. 296).

2. "The IMAGINATION, then, I consider either as primary or secondary. The primary IMAGINATION I hold to be the living Power and prime Agent of all human Perception, and as a repetition in the finite mind of the eternal act of creation in the infinite I AM. The secondary I consider as an echo of the former, co-existing with the conscious will, yet still as identical with the primary in the *kind* of its agency, and differing only in *degree,* and in the *mode* of its operation. It dissolves, diffuses, dissipates, in order to re-create or, where this process is rendered impossible, yet still, at all events, it struggles to idealize and to unify. It is essentially *vital,* even as all objects (as objects) are essentially fixed and dead" (Coleridge, 1849, p. 297).

Fostering Creativity in the Classroom through Music

LAURA M. SCHULKIND

Music is considered to be the first intelligence to present itself in the development of the human child (Gardner, 1983, p. 37). According to Gardner, there are three systems children develop that contribute to their aesthetic evolution: the making system, the perceiving system, and the feeling system. The *making system* is the development of purposeful actions or acts; the *perceiving system* is the development of discriminations or distinctions; and the *feeling system* is the development of the affective ability. It is during the initial developmental phase of the perceiving system that the human infant creates the connection between an object's characteristics and its permanence (Gardner, 1983, p. 90). This ability is the basis for object permanence, but more importantly, a sound-symbol relationship. It is this relationship that forms the basis for the human ability to use symbols; it is also this relationship that enables us to recognize musical meaning and feeling as well as the encryption of those sounds into a meaningful code, able to be reproduced by another human being. There is evidence of a "zone of proximal development" (Vygotsky, 1977) for children's musical ability: By approximately age 11, the actual neuronal circuits that permit all kinds of perceptual and sensory discrimination become closed off if they aren't subject to use. Use is necessary for a variety of central nervous system functions to develop, including the ability to discriminate pitch and rhythm—without use, development becomes forever impossible at the cellular level, at the level of development of the interneuronal synapses (Langstaff & Mayer, 1995).

As educators, it is therefore ethically imperative that we introduce children to the possibilities their own musical expression can provide. Creativity has been theorized to be the culmination of many divergent thoughts, possibilities, or facts.

The work of some of our most creative geniuses is the *result of*, not *because of*, their strong backgrounds (Csikszentmihalyi, 1996; Gardner, 1993b). According to Feldhusen, children should be presented with multiple options for experiential learning through which they can better understand their special "talents and increasingly commit themselves to the full development of their talents" (Feldhusen, 1997, p. 189). We do not all possess the ability of Isaac Stern to make the violin cry, or the beauty of Maria Callas' interpretation. This type of musical ability, while wonderful and an essential part of the beauty in our culture, is not all there is to being musical or enjoying music. As educators, we open the world to our students, and music is a powerful key to the doors of thinking and application. Music provides a scaffold for learning that is at once solid, but extremely flexible.

Many of us have had an experience in our respective pasts in which a peer or a teacher said to us something like: "Please don't sing so loudly—your voice doesn't blend with the rest of the group." This set up a series of emotional reactions, resulting in the belief that we could not sing (as in, "I can't carry a tune in a bucket"), or that we were in some way inherently nonmusical. Teachers can resolve that experience, understand how each of us is inherently musical, and use that musicality for the benefit of young learners.

Can you recite a poem? When you hear the music in the supermarket or in the elevator, do you find yourself walking in time to the music? Can you recall an advertising jingle from the television or radio? Has there been a time when a song "gets stuck" in your head? Do you and your significant other have a special song, or are there songs that transport you to another time in your life? These are all examples of *your* musical intelligence.

Using Music in the Classroom

Many teachers avoid the use of music in their classrooms because they do not feel adequately trained to use music, or they feel shy about singing or playing a musical instrument. While understandable, this places the emphasis on the teacher rather than on the children's participation in a musical activity (Isenberg & Jalongo, 1993, pp. 113–118). There are several ways to overcome this obstacle: use your voice, use recorded music, invite an instrumentalist into your classroom, and have an instrumentalist play the music so you can learn it first.

Use Your Voice

Most children's music has a very limited range: the pitch does not go up very high or down very low, and having a highly trained singing voice with children is *not* beneficial when trying to teach the children a concept or tune (Langstaff & Mayer, 1995). An operatic voice is a confusing element for a child to listen to, so your shower singing voice will be more than sufficient for children's songs.

Use Recorded Music

There are many resources for high-quality children's music on the market today. These range from the whole song being played to just the background chords for accompaniment purposes. Choose music you find interesting to listen to; if you think the music is boring or inane, chances are the students will also. A key element in choosing music is that you must convey your own enthusiasm and belief in the importance of the song (Langstaff, 1995).

Invite an Instrumentalist into Your Classroom

This is a very direct method for providing students with knowledge of how an instrument sounds. Also, each musician will bring his or her own background and musical agenda into your classroom, thus providing the students with different viewpoints of how music can be used for expressive purposes in the world beyond the classroom.

Have an Instrumentalist Play the Tune for You

If you do not read music and you have the printed music, have a musician play the piece for you. Make a tape so you can practice at home or in the car before you present the song to your class. If you happen to play a melody instrument; that is, a keyboard, recorder, flute, clarinet, and so on—use it to teach the melody after you have sung the song to the class. They will instantly begin to sing along with you, using whatever they remember from their brief exposure to the song. This will develop memory and attention span, especially if you tell them they will need to be able to sing this song with you.

Integrating Music into the Curriculum

The use of music as an aid to instruction is not limited to the accompaniment of poetry or language arts. Music can easily be integrated into all the content areas, providing a base for previous knowledge to build upon in addition to learning new concepts.

Science

Music is the result of organized sound. From this fact, we can plan many curriculum adventures: simple machines, properties of materials in sound, water exploration, and nature and sea life exploration will be explored here as models for creative applications with music.

Simple Machines

The exploration of friction is an essential component of the simple machines curriculum. Many musical instruments can be "invented" by the students in order to explore friction, most of which is accomplished by sandpaper. It is part of the exploratory process to try different mediums: try using different types of papers, stones to rub, metals to rub, and "orchestrate" the sounds to determine their effect. This type of hands-on work provides firsthand knowledge of friction. The interaction of these various elements introduces the students to different ways of working with common materials—an essential element of creativity.

Whereas most students will be able to understand and produce these creative applications, the creative child produces unusual applications. In one classroom activity, I had set up a variety of ramps with different grades of sandpaper, and the students were to test toy cars with varying weights on the ramps. One child in the class decided to attach the weights to the bottoms of the cars, and reported a difference in the sounds produced by the cars on the different grades of sandpapers, and with differing weights. It became an exploration of sounds as well as friction and ramps.

Another aspect of the simple machines curriculum is the use of levers. Many students will have, at one time or another, been exposed to a piano. In order to activate prior knowledge, the students can generate a list of how they think a piano works. At this point, it is a worthwhile and inexpensive field trip to either a piano store or a piano factory, depending on your location, in order to build background knowledge. Both Feldhusen and Renzulli support the value of field trips (Feldhusen, 1993; Renzulli, 1977). An alternative to this would be to have a piano technician visit the classroom, and have the expert display how the piano works within the school setting.

Gears are also an important simple machine. Although there are no orchestral instruments that require gears, clocks and windup metronomes are run by gears. By equating the rhythm of the music with the mechanical rhythms, students will have access to a third very important musical factor in simple machines.

At this point, the students would have developed a rudimentary working knowledge of several aspects of simple machines. If a local art museum has a Rube Goldberg machine in place, this would stimulate the creative juices of the students. If not, try to locate a film about the artist. As a cooperative effort, the students could invent their own Rube Goldberg machine, or invent new musical instruments utilizing the principles discovered in their scientific, musical explorations. A useful source is *The Best of Rube Goldberg* (Keller, 1944).

Properties of Materials in Sound Production

This would directly tie into the creation of a Rube Goldberg machine. The students would explore the combinations of different materials in order to produce a symphony of sounds. Gather containers made of different materials such as plastic, wood, glass, rubber, metal, or cardboard, and experiment with other materials to produce sounds. Some suggestions are: rubber balls, tennis balls, ball bearings, nuts, screws and bolts, leftover wood pieces of different types (mahogany, pine, oak, and so on), marbles, plastic toys, very gooey silly putty, dried beans, and old curlers. Just about anything can create a sound in combination with something else, so let you and your students' imaginations go with this exploration.

Water

The musical properties of water can be a very enjoyable method of exploring the water cycle. Water makes its own noises: dripping, splashing, sloshing, and of course, thunder and lightning noises, accompanied by rain and different types of rain: gentle, downpour, steady, and intermittent. When students add in the clinking of ice with its scraping, cracking qualities, they have made a very thorough investigation into water properties. Another aspect of the music-water connection would be to investigate what sounds travel through water, and how they change in water. This could provide many opportunities to hypothesize, chart and graph, and reach conclusions.

Filling glasses with water provides two more avenues for discovery: different water levels in the glasses or bottles will produce different tones when the water is blown or the glasses are tapped. The students could write some melodies, and a creative child could produce entire symphonies on these explorations.

Nature and Sea Life Exploration

In the many theories of how the human being developed music, birdsong is a consistent factor. Studying birds and introducing students to "birding" as a hobby will open a fascinating field to them. There are many symphonic pieces that utilize birdsong, and many solo pieces in individual instrumental literature. Flute and piccolo literature is full of examples: *Le Merle Noir* by Olivier Messiaen is a stunning piece in which Messiaen wrote down the actual songs of blackbirds and incorporated them into the music. Other suggestions include: *Firebird* by Igor Stravinsky, *Il Gardellino* (Concerto in D, Op. 10) by Vivaldi, *The Nightingale in Love* by François Couperin, *The March of the Bluebirds* by Leos Janácek, and *The Magic Flute* by W. A. Mozart: "Papageno's Aria."

There are so many sounds associated with the sounds of the sea that the difficult part is deciding what type of sounds to concentrate on, and what the students need to learn from them. Music is a form of communication, so investigating the communication techniques of various marine creatures and compiling the sounds into a tape recording is just one venue for exploration. Dolphins and whales are especially "vocal," and there are many resources that will provide information on their communication techniques such as the National Geographic Society or the Jacques Cousteau Society.

There are also many children's songs that introduce the sounds of seafaring culture, and songs about whales and other sea life. If you can think back to watching television as a child, you can probably remember the song that introduced your favorite show. In this same manner, songs about sea life will also stay with the students long after the unit is completed, and will provide a basis of knowledge they can draw on for more in-depth, factual, or hands-on study. In particular, I am thinking of Raffi's song and book *Baby Beluga* (*Learning with Raffi: Baby Beluga* by Sherrill B. Flora, 1997, Instructional Fair), and the musical *Sounds a Little Fishy to Me* by Donna Amorosia and Lori Weidemann (Hal Leonard Publishing Corporation, 1992). Use of these type of materials will spark an interest in children, and provide the basis for further exploration.

After the children have spent their time learning about sea life and water properties, it is time for them to act out their knowledge in a theatrical format, or create an artistic rendition of the information. This transfer of knowledge from one sense to the other will provide the teacher with a means of evaluation using concrete information as to what has been learned and retained by the students. Furthermore, bilingual and ESL students will have an equal chance to display their learning, leveling the playing field for them. Theatrical production would give ESL students a chance to practice language skills, utilizing the knowledge they have just acquired in a more kinesthetic fashion, and artistic production gives students a chance to synthesize and apply the information in a nonlanguage mode.

Mathematics

Many people have noted the connection between those who are strong in mathematics and those who have a natural ability in music. This is not always the case. However, many aspects of music are mathematically based, and the application of this fact to curriculum strengthens how children learn mathematical concepts.

There are two areas that naturally utilize mathematical principles: time and fractions. By using rhythmic principles to teach these concepts, the students gain a practical knowledge of these elements.

Metronomes are exquisite little instruments of torture for the developing musician. They are used to deliver a regular beat against which the musician strives to maintain his or her temper (pun intended). For curriculum purposes, though, they can be used to develop a sense of internal time for students. The setting on the metronome of quarter note equals sixty is the equivalent of one second on the clock. By using the metronome, the students can begin to feel how long a second, a minute, five minutes, and so on, actually *is*. By using body movements such as dancing, clapping, tongue clicking, or any other invention of movement correlated to the metronome beat, they will begin to internalize their sense of time. By splitting the beat in two, they begin to feel what a fraction *is*.

There are several musical pieces that would support the study of time: the song *My Grandfather's Clock* by H. C. Work (1875), *The Syncopated Clock* by Leroy Anderson (1951), *Twelve Pieces for the Musical Clock* by J. Haydn (1793), and the ballet *Cinderella* by S. Prokofiev (1944). Many ballet plots also deal with a spell running out at a particular time, or a spell becoming permanent at a particular time, such as *Giselle* by A. Adam, and these can be integrated into the curriculum as a fine arts or language arts component.

Social Studies

The social studies curriculum is greatly enhanced by the study of ethnomusicology, or music of other cultures. When the music of a culture is highlighted as a source of study, it honors that culture. By learning about the musical instruments used, and creating those instruments, the students will learn about the natural resources of the culture as well as how music is produced in a culture. This first-hand experiential learning stimulates the creative student to learn about the culture as a participant rather than an observer.

The study of Western European culture is also enhanced by learning about its music history. Oral communication and storytelling have been historically important forms of communication, and these can be taught to students as young as first grade. In my classroom, I first showed the students several examples of stories being told with songs. I used several different forms of presentation of these examples: I sang *Yankee Doodle* (Shackburg, Shackburg & Emberley, 1965) while holding up a printed book version of the song, I sang *Sarah the Whale* (Ives, 1950) to the children, they watched the rooster begin to tell the tale of Robin Hood (Disney, 1948, video), and they watched Danny Kaye sing the tale of *The Ugly Duckling* in the story of Hans Christian Anderson (Goldwyn, 1952, video). Their task was to write a poem that told a story.

Some stories became very long and involved, and some were simple but effective. Some of the examples of products by creative children are:

The Worm Who Could Not Squirm

There once was a worm who could not squirm.
Since that worm could not squirm he was not a worm,
'Cause a worm has to know how to squirm . . .
To be a worm.
And the moral of the story is:
Worms today, snakes tomorrow.
Ta-ta!
    by G., grade 3

SCARY

The wind,
The sun,
The police,
The zoo,
The van.
SCARY!
    by C., grade 1

Chocolate Honey

One day Pooh was making a new recipe:
Chocolate Honey!
OO, Yummy!

> *I wonder what it's going to taste like?*
> *Now he put in honey,*
> *Then he put in chocolate,*
> *Mix up, done!*
>   K., grade 2

Then, in the style of the troubadours and trouvères, I set each of their poems to music. I sat with each child, and clapped out the rhythms with the child. I would generate several melodies based on the rhythms, and the child and I would decide which one "sounded" most like the poem. I then wrote the ballad down on a sheet of music paper that had been dipped in tea to make it look "antiqued." This aspect of medieval/Renaissance culture then became "theirs," because they each had their own "ballad."

Language Arts

The use of music to teach language arts is a natural extension of both arts. The patterns of music repeat themselves in predictable rhythms, the fluency and phrasing of song and symphony mirror the same qualities in reading, and the combinations of sound create a basis for developing metacognitive strategies in developing readers and writers.

Children know immediately if something in the music has been changed or if something is "wrong." By presenting the creative child with a purposely altered musical version, he or she will be motivated to initiate critical thinking through systematic questioning and musical "play" to correct the material (see Lynch, Harris, & Williams chapter in this book). Changing the music or changing the words in a song by the children or the teacher will encourage and motivate the children to listen and think carefully. This aspect of musical memory, and the requirement for having the song "sound right," and to sing the "right words" will develop metacognitive skills in the emergent reader. This is the same skill music teachers work on with students as they are learning to play scales and other musical patterns. If the child can learn to attend to the patterns and how the music sounds in music or in reading, he or she will better understand the material, and develop the critical ear that is so crucial to success.

In utilizing the predictability of songs, children gain confidence in their ability with language. By using ballads, poetry set to music, jump rope rhymes, rap, songs written especially for children, folk songs, and so forth, the children have a handle to use to remember the language, and when they see the words in print will naturally interact with them. I use songs in my classroom all year, with different skills in mind, and follow the songs with a postreading type activity. One activity for first grade involved making small books on the computer of the song *BINGO*:

There was a farmer	*B - I - N - G - O,*
had a dog,	*B - I - N - G - O,*
And BINGO was his	*B - I - N - G - O,*
name-o.	*And BINGO was his*
	name-o.

A nonreading student finished her drawings on the accordion book (paper folded so it opens out like an accordion) without any print. It was clear she was able to create representational drawings, so I suggested she write the names of the people in the song on her book so we would all know about her fun with the *BINGO* song. She was able to go back to her mini-book, with the music tape, and label her own characters in her accordion book. This was the key that unlocked the reading doors for this highly creative nonreader because she was able to connect the song, her drawings, and the printed word.

The teacher can see a progression in the objectives for the students in the choice of music. I look for songs that are open-ended so that the children can add their own verses and create their own versions of the songs. At the beginning of the year, I chose songs such as *BINGO, Swing the Alphabet*, and *Apples and Bananas* to reinforce and extend beginning reading and phonics skills. We are now using songs with nonsense words such as *Foopa Woopa John* by Burl Ives (Ives, 1950), which will act as a further extension of their decoding abilities. The next set of songs can be folk songs, and the children will be able to illustrate books of the stories, act them out, and write their own verses.

A further extension of this idea would be to use music that tells a story without words as in ballet stories, or with words the children do not understand as in opera. The children would then be using the music to create their own stories.

In a creative writing lesson with a class of fifth graders, I first developed their background knowledge of music that tells a story by playing the flute solo from *Peter and the Wolf* (Prokofiev, 1936) for them, and reading them the story. They were able to relate this to their knowledge of Disney's *Fantasia*. I told them I was going to tell them a story, a story with my flute. I played *Syrinx* by Claude Debussy (1914), and the class brainstormed the images they saw and felt while I played for them. From these images, I formed the class into groups, and they wrote and illustrated stories based on the music. When the writing and illustrating were completed, the students presented their stories to each other. The stories ranged from giant beetles doing battle with giant spiders, to butterflies and rain that wiped out all the beautiful butterflies.

This lesson can also make use of the Baroque Era's use of affect in music. Each piece of music in the Baroque Era was said to have an affect—a specific emotion the composer intentionally wanted the listener to feel. This is a method for getting students to generate a very descriptive language of feeling words that will ultimately be reflected in their writing.

There are four categories of books that support music in a reading program: picture books of traditional folksongs, such as *Momma, Buy Me a China Doll* and *Row, Row Row Your Boat*; books about the stories behind the music, like Verdi's *Aïda* told by Leontyne Price, or ballet stories; books that are written with a patterned text such as the series by Creative Teaching Press; and books that put music into context, such as the *History of Ragtime*, or books about culturally diverse musical styles.

There are many curriculum books available to teachers that combine music with skills by using simplistic, cutesy music, or substitute words into familiar children's tunes. Although this approach is easily accessible to teachers if they are not comfortable learning new songs, it is not in the long-term best interests of their students because it does not provide the interest level for children and does nothing to stimulate their creativity. It is worth the time and effort to either use recordings for the children to hear a more complex song, or for the teacher to learn the song first in order to be comfortable teaching it to the class.

Conclusion

The extraordinary thing about using the arts as a means to express knowledge is that the arts act as metaphors. Dance and music are intangible expressions of an intangible reality, just like dreams. They can represent the feeling of the knowledge we have constructed, but just like the knowledge inside our own heads, can never be shared or perceived as exactly the same by any two people.

Music reaches into our souls at a deep and lasting level. It inspires us to do our best, and requires a high level of participation for everyone. Music can be a solitary activity in terms of practicing long hours, listening to the radio, or just singing by oneself, but ultimately it is in the community of music that we truly experience the joy. As educators, it is our privilege to build the citizens of the future. Music teaches us that it is by working together that we create a more beautiful world. By opening the door to the realization of potential in the creative child, we all benefit. For givers and receivers, creative endeavors enrich our society and enhance our lives through music.

I feel the music inside me. It says something more than just the notes, more than just the sounds. It is hearing with more than the ears.

Mila, from *The Music of Dolphins,* by Hesse (1996), p. 76

Art Talent Development, Creativity, and the Enrichment of Programs for Artistically Talented Students in Grades K–8

GILBERT A. CLARK   ENID ZIMMERMAN

Definitions and conceptions about relationships between giftedness, talent development, and creativity have been considered in the past five decades. Yet intellectual ability and academic aptitude still dominate identification procedures and the design of programs for students with high abilities in a variety of areas. Relationships between art talent, creativity, and giftedness in the arts need to be addressed so that conceptions about art talent development can be considered in identification procedures and programs for artistically talented students.

For educational interventions to have lasting effects, art curricula need to be developed for students with interests and abilities in the visual arts, and for students in academic gifted and talented programs where art is generally not included, as well as for all students (Clark & Zimmerman, in press). Rather than selecting only a special group of students to be singled out for special services, instructional programs need to be developed that emphasize the talents, strengths, and interests of all students (Treffinger et al., 1993). Attention should also be paid to developing the creative talents of high-ability students in the arts who have career-oriented aspirations (Feldhusen & Jarwan, 1993). In addition, there is a need for integration of art into general curricula because all artistically talented students may not pursue a career in the arts and should have opportunities to think creatively across the curriculum (Wakefield, 1992).

Definitions of Creativity

In respect to creativity, there is lack of consensus about what constitutes creativity itself; therefore, progress in developing operational definitions of the term *creativity* is hampered (Clark & Zimmerman, 1992; Hunsaker & Callahan, 1995). According to Treffinger, Sortore, and Cross (1993), "there has been no single universally-accepted definition or model, nor a unifying synthesis among models and definitions [of creativity]" (p. 555). They identified three recent eras relative to evolving conceptions of creativity: (1) the 1950s and 1960s, when creativity was viewed as diversity and creativity tests focused on divergent thinking; (2) the 1970s and 1980s, when packages of programs were developed that included creativity exercises and activities with emphases on complex skills, such as divergent and convergent thinking, problem solving, and decision making; and (3) the 1990s, when an ecological view dominated. This later view focuses on many characteristics, processes, contexts, and tasks that challenge traditional conceptions of intelligence as unidimensional and static and emphasize creativity and talents as influenced and enhanced in specific educational contexts.

Treffinger et al. (1993) advocated that "today's efforts to nurture creativity must take into account a variety of different personal, process, and situational factors" (p. 560). Administrators in most schools have adopted a definition of giftedness that includes creativity, but that term is not well defined. Often, the focus is on a single dimension, usually that of problem solving, however, and more research is needed about how to define and interpret data about creativity from multiple perspectives (Hunsaker & Callahan, 1995).

Although a number of scholars agree that creative achievement is reflected in production of useful, new ideas or products that call for finding a problem and solving it in a novel way (Hunsaker & Callahan, 1995; McPherson, 1997; Mumford, Connely, Baughman, & Marks, 1994; Wakefield, 1992), others distinguish between adult creative acts and those of students. Feldman (1982a) and Winner and Martino (1993) refer to creativity as inventiveness within a domain of knowledge, where a creative individual revolutionizes that domain. No talented children, they claim, have "effected reorganization of a domain of knowledge" (Winner & Martino, p. 253). According to Csikszentmihalyi (1988), emergence and recognition of creative activity in the visual arts is something that requires three elements: (1) participation of a specially endowed individual, (2) productivity within a domain of knowledge, and (3) confirmation and support of that individual's contribution by field experts. Applying these concepts of creativity to student acts, it would be rare that a student would create a work of art that is original, appropriate, and qualitatively different from creative products made by mature artists. Students, however, can create processes or make products that are novel to themselves and their previous work or that of others in their own peer group.

There are some traits associated with creativity that are related to mature artists' processes of conceiving ideas about and producing works of art that may have significance for educating artistically talented students in the elementary and middle schools in the United States. Problem finding, problem solving, divergent and convergent thinking, self-expression, and flexibility to adapt to new situations are traits commonly associated with creativity in educational literature (Mumford, Connely, Baughman, & Marks., 1994; Runco, 1993; Runco & Nemiro, 1993). We are not advocating that young students with special abilities and talents in the arts should be involved in activities identical to those of adult artists. Rather, certain processes used by professionals in the arts—such as art critics, art historians, aestheticians, and artists—can suggest educational interventions that may be successful in differentiated programs for artistically talented students.

Creativity, Giftedness, and Talent

With respect to creativity and its relationship to giftedness and talent, Hunsaker and Callahan (1995) describe three ways that this relationship can be formulated: (1) giftedness and talent can be viewed as separate intellectual abilities, with giftedness associated with high intelligence and creativity associated with novel or divergent thinking; (2) creativity can be seen as a fundamental concept of giftedness, as in Renzulli's (1978) three-ring model where there is interaction among constructs of above-average intelligence, creativity, and task commitment; and (3) creativity can be considered as a separate category or style of giftedness, as in the Marland Report (1972). In the Marland Report, creative and productive thinking, general intellectual ability, specific academic aptitude, visual and performing arts, leadership ability, and psychomotor ability were categories identified for creating differentiated programs for gifted and talented students in schools in the United States.

Conventional wisdom reflects the view that the term *gifted* is a fixed concept, not amenable to the influence of education, whereas talent and talent *development* imply more active concepts by which students can be nurtured to grow and develop special abilities in diverse pursuits and where educational intervention plays an important role (Feldhusen, 1994b). The conception of the term *talent*, recommended by Feldhusen (1994), and supported by contemporary research in the neurosciences, focuses on increasingly "specialized aptitudes or abilities that develop in youth as a function of general abilities . . . or intelligence and related educational experiences in home, school, and the broad community" (p. 13). He suggests five general domains (academic, intellectual, artistic, vocational-technical, and interpersonal-social) for developing talent in schools as correlates of subject matter areas. Feldhusen's *conception* of talent development is viewed in direct relation to academic school subjects that students will pursue in future careers as adults in our rapidly changing society.

Art Education and Creativity

Within the past decade, there has been a major shift in theory and practice in the field of visual arts education that had its beginnings more than thirty-five years ago. The present trend, popularly referred to as *discipline-based art* education, focuses on an orientation to art education that emphasizes art in the general education of all students, from kindergarten through high school. The term *discipline,* in this case, refers to fields of study, such as art history, art criticism, aesthetics, and art making, "marked by recognized communities of scholars or practitioners, established conceptual structures, and accepted methods of inquiry" (Clark, Day, & Greer, 1987, p. 131). Discipline-based art education (DBAE) differs *significantly* from *creative self-expression,* an approach to art education that had been dominant for more than four decades, prior to the emergence of DBAE. The core of creative self-expression was to develop each student's inherent creative and expressive abilities. Creativity was represented as being innate and developing naturally without imposing adult conceptions on a learner's creative development. Curricula usually were developed idiosyncratically, without articulation or sequencing through the grades. The teacher's role in creative self-expression, visual arts programs was to provide motivation, support, and resources and supplies, but not to interfere directly in any student's creative activities.

In discipline-based art education, creativity is viewed as *"unconventional behavior* that can occur as conventional art understandings are attained" (Clark, Day, & Greer, 1987, p. 134); untutored childhood expression is not necessarily regarded as creative. In a discipline-based approach to art education, students are taught directly through articulated and sequenced curricula in which art disciplines are emphasized and the work of adult art makers, from diverse cultural contexts, serve as motivators for students' creative development.

In visual arts education, before the late 1980s, directive teaching, ability testing, and evaluation of student artwork, though commonly practiced in other school subjects, were considered detrimental to highly valued creativity and unfettered self-expression. Creativity tests, such as those developed in the 1960s and 1970s by Guilford, were and still are focused on tasks related to divergent thinking. Creativity tests developed by Torrance, whose work is based on Guilford's work, were and still are common measures used to assess art talent (Clark & Zimmerman, 1984). In a survey reported in 1988 (Bachtel), 49 percent of programs for artistically talented students used results of creativity tests as selection criteria. In fact, high scores on creativity tests were the fourth most popular selection criteria chosen for identifying artistically talented students to be admitted into special programs.

Khatena (1982) and others have claimed that visual and performing arts abilities are closely associated with creativity as a measurable construct. Recently, Clark (1997) tested more than 1,200 third graders in four ethnically diverse communities in the United States. He found a strong correlation between *drawing ability* as measured by Clark's Drawing Abilities Test, *creativity* as determined by Torrance Tests of Creative Thinking, and statewide *achievement* tests. In the Clark's

Drawing Abilities Test, students were asked, in large, preprinted rectangles, to "Draw an interesting house as if looking at it from across the street," "Draw a person running very fast," "Draw a picture of you and your friends playing in the playground," and "Make a fantasy drawing from your imagination." In the abbreviated Torrance Tests of Creative Thinking used, students were asked to "List as many uses of junked automobiles as you can," "Make some pictures of the figures below" (from two rectangles with preprinted lines), and (on a page with twelve preprinted triangles) to "See how many objects or pictures you can make from the triangles below." Both tests use criteria that have proved to be valid and reliable. Clark concluded from his original variation of the Torrance Tests of Creative Thinking that his finding about correlation between the three measures indicates that performance on the drawing, creativity, and achievement tests may be affected by another factor, or set of factors, which may include intelligence and/or general problem-solving abilities.

Art Education and Talent in the Arts

Although it appears that art talent and creativity are related, *talent in the arts* does not have shared meaning in gifted and talented literature, because few researchers or educators agree about what constitutes high abilities in the visual and performing arts. One view is that good art students exhibit above-average abilities in a particular art form, such as drawing, and do not rely on formulas or direct copying from other sources. Another is that artistically talented students generate original ideas, inventions, or innovations in their artwork, but do not necessarily possess advanced skills of image-making. Others report a combination of art-making skill and high levels of motivation, perseverance, and problem solving. Except for superior art-making skills, most of the attributes of art talent just listed can also be viewed as indicators of talent in academic subjects and general intelligence. Creativity in the arts *may* at times take different forms from creativity in academic subjects, but it would be erroneous to draw the conclusion that student creativity, no matter how it is defined, would have a greater potency or impact in the arts than in other school subjects (Clark & Zimmerman, in press).

Characteristics of Artistically Talented Students

Common characteristics associated with artistically talented students in the United States are well-developed drawing skills, high cognitive abilities, interest, and motivation (Clark & Zimmerman, 1992). Other characteristics include intensity of application and early mastery of cultural forms typical of art exceptionality, production of a large volume of work over a sustained period of time, nurturance from family and teachers, and thematically specialized work (Pariser, 1997, p. 39). It has been suggested that artistically gifted and talented students manifest their talents along a number of trajectories, not just the single track of realistic drawing

(Wolf & Perry, 1988), and that people need to reconsider presentational skills and focus more on enthusiasm for visual ideas and the wide range of art talents and abilities within cultural traditions (Pariser, 1997).

We believe the ability to depict the world realistically should be considered only one among many indicators of talent in the visual arts. Contemporary art is not only graphic in nature, and depiction of abstract concepts often becomes more important than demonstration of realistic graphic skills based on perception. Some artistically talented young people concentrate on realistic depiction of objects and are influenced by Western spatial conventions. Others may concentrate on using art to depict visual narratives creatively, through the use of themes and variations, humor, paradoxes, puns, metaphors, and deep emotional involvement (Zimmerman, 1992b).

Peer pressure and adult intervention during early adolescent years probably push most talented young people toward creating realistic images. During these early adolescent years, problems being solved are usually spatial-perceptual, rather than abstract-conceptual ones that may focus on transformations, humor, analogies, puns, myths, rituals, symbols, games, or paradoxes. Popular culture and new conceptions of art talent development need to be addressed in programs for students with interest and abilities in the visual arts. Although skill with specific media may indicate precocious talent for some, it may not be a salient indicator for others because other factors, such as personality, home, and school environments, also play parts in determining what artistic skills are developed (Zimmerman, 1992b).

Educational Interventions, Creativity, and Art Talent Development

There is recent research that demonstrates that problem-finding and problem-solving skills can be taught, and students' abilities to be productive thinkers and creative problem-solvers can be nurtured (Treffinger et al., 1993). Talent development can be enhanced in a "supportive, flexible, but intellectually-demanding academic environment" (Mumford et al., 1994, p. 245) by encouraging students to work consistently and responsibly when confronted by frustration. According to Feldhusen (1992), students can be taught to find problems, clarify problems, and use certain skills when attempting to solve problems. They also can be taught to monitor their own teaming activities and seek and test alternative solutions.

Creativity also can be developed by adapting teaching strategies that balance student generation of new ideas, critical thinking abilities, and abilities to translate theory into practice (Sternberg & Williams, 1996). Feldman (1980) studied children who were prodigies in many different areas, including the arts, and was convinced that all progress in teaming is the result of intensive and prolonged instruction. Successful teachers of highly able students are knowledgeable about their subject matter, able to communicate instruction effectively, and select important teaming experiences that lead their students to attain challenging and advanced levels of achievement.

For more than a decade at Indiana University, we coordinated a summer institute for artistically talented upper elementary and junior high school students. At this institute, we conducted a number of studies about students and their teachers. One teacher had an objective for his students to learn about themselves and their artwork. His emphasis was on developing students' cognitive and affective skills (Zimmerman, 1991). He wanted his students to learn what it is like being an artist and believed that painting required skills that can be taught. He told his students not to worry about being creative, because they could not help being creative when finding solutions to problems, such as painting a self-portrait. Sometimes boredom and frustration prevented his students from progressing, and he was able to recognize this. He intervened when they were not performing adequately and helped them progress toward their goals and potential. He provided a powerful role model; his sense of humor and influence on his students' art-making skills were very positively cited in student interviews. He also was knowledgeable about subject matter, understood and communicated effectively with his students, and was deeply involved in teaching. His success was due to his directive teaching, individual attention to all students, positive feedback in private and public conversations, and ability to make classes challenging and interesting through humor and storytelling.

In another study, the teacher just described was compared with another teacher who taught at the institute the following year. This other teacher also met students' needs for developing skills and techniques. In addition to teaching skills and techniques, however, the teacher in the first study encouraged students to become engaged in art issues and think reflectively about the context in which they were creating art (Zimmerman, 1992a). It was suggested that teachers of artistically talented students go beyond acquisition of art skills and techniques and attempt to understand each student's sensibilities, teach proactively, instill feelings of competence, promote problem solving, encourage students' searches for novelty and complexity, and reflect critically about their teaching practices (Zimmerman, 1992a). To develop art talent and creativity, therefore, it is important that art teachers be sensitive to the needs of artistically talented students and go beyond simply teaching skills to encouraging independent thought, spontaneity, and originality. These are traits not typically encouraged in classrooms, although they often are evidenced in the behaviors of talented students.

A case study of Eric, a highly talented art student, from his preschool through high school years, demonstrates deferred benefits of accelerated and enriched art opportunities (Zimmerman, 1992b, 1995). Teacher encouragement and flexibility were relevant to Eric's feelings of being successful and challenged. Teachers he viewed positively possessed characteristics such as emphasizing developing students' art skills, possessing a general knowledge about art, empathizing with students, and having an ability to make classes challenging. Other teacher characteristics included readiness to help students become aware of contexts in which they make art and examine their reasons for creating art. Some of Eric's teachers in elementary and junior high school classes were flexible and taught theme-oriented classes, in which students could complete assignments according to their interests, in a variety of modes, and in combinations of verbal and visual problem finding and problem solving.

These kinds of enriched curricular adaptations permitted Eric to express his skills, values, and understandings creatively in a variety of discursive and nondiscursive educational projects. In his elementary school language arts classes, many options were presented to meet requirements for book reports. Eric often chose to do visual interpretations rather than verbal reports. In his fourth grade class, for example, he drew figures and backgrounds that illustrated a scene from each book in a five-book series. A book report, created in the fifth grade, took the form of a travel brochure that advertised life in a fantasy kingdom. In the sixth grade, a poster was Eric's form for reporting a book he had read. Visual interpretations of assignments were evident in other subjects as well. For a fourth grade social studies project, he created an illustrated time line about African American history. A "digestive game," in which the objective was to be ingested and later expelled, was created in lieu of an oral science report. For an eighth grade science project, rather than taking a test about a rat's body parts, Eric created a detailed drawing of a dissected rat with appropriately labeled parts.

Many themes and subject matters, such as games, visual narratives, self-portraits, and political cartoons, were evidenced in Eric's elementary and junior high projects. He described a number of transformational experiences that allowed him to view himself as a young artist achieving his own predetermined goals, rather than merely being a student creating art in isolation from the world of art. In accelerated and enriched programs, in elementary and junior high school, he had experiences of frustration that eventually led to illuminating insights and transformations from which he was able to grow intellectually and emotionally, and to express these experiences in his art making.

Technical challenges of making art often frustrated Eric. In the second grade, he was frustrated with drawing a tree and his inability to depict the complexity of interlocking branches and not knowing how to mix colors to represent the tree realistically. He grappled with these problems for several months until he realized artists abstract from reality, without rendering every detail. When he was in junior high school, he felt satisfied with his work and became angry when a teacher corrected one of his paintings. Later, he realized that as a young artist he should be able to listen to criticism and risk something he cherished, in order to try out new techniques and approaches to painting.

Curriculum Enrichment Activities for Developing Art Talent and Creativity

Educators have suggested a number of strategies for developing curricula that support creativity and talent development in many different subject areas. Some of these suggestions include having students: (1) practice problem-finding as well as problem-solving techniques; (2) use unfamiliar materials that elicit more original thinking and lead to new ideas and possibilities; (3) experience convergent (structured) and divergent (unstructured) tasks because students need knowledge and information for skill building and open-ended tasks for self-expression; (4) rely on both visual and verbal materials; (5) be exposed to curricula with open-ended outcomes that allow for unpredictable results a teacher may not foresee; (6) follow their own interests and work in groups, as well as independently; (7) choose environments that support their talents and creativity; and (8) encounter a wide range of tasks intended to encourage, reinforce, and enhance their emerging talents (Feldhusen, 1995; Mumford et al., 1994; Runco, 1993; Runco & Nemiro, 1993; Sternberg & Williams, 1996).

In 1978, we introduced a content model based on the premise that art education curriculum design should acknowledge entering-level art students as naive in their understandings and skills related to art. From naive beginnings, teacher interventions should play an important role in moving students through a series of levels in which they advance toward sophisticated attainment and participation in the visual arts. Consecutive, intervening levels in this content model were described as introductory, rudimentary, intermediate, advanced, and mastery levels. Content was suggested for teaching art at each level of the model, based on skills and understandings related to the work of adult professional roles of artists, art critics, art historians, and aestheticians. Different content strands, derived from analysis and adaptation of each of the four roles, such as media and skills, concepts and knowledge, and personal style, were included in this model (Clark & Zimmerman, 1978).

After developing this model, we wrote a textbook applying it to classroom practice at the middle school level (Clark & Zimmerman, 1978). In 1982, Feldman introduced a theoretical framework, the Universal to Unique Continuum, that focused on the importance of enriched educational opportunities and the influence of teaching strategies on talent development. This framework introduced the concepts that children's intellectual growth and talent development are: (1) found in specific domains of knowledge, (2) a direct result of educational intervention, and (3) controlled by the context in which they mature. Feldman also described cognitive development as a series of regions attained by increasingly smaller numbers of people. Feldman's Unique Region (the highest developmental level) was described as the only region where adult creativity may be attained and novel contributions made by a very small number of people. According to Feldman, student creativity should be viewed as an educational construct rather than an accomplishment at a mature level of development. Feldman also claimed that movement across his model is wholly dependent on prolonged and intensive instruction.

We recognized the power of Feldman's general education model and integrated our framework with Feldman's to provide an expanded model for art talent development for all students at all levels of achievement, and particularly for art talent development of highly able students (Clark & Zimmerman, 1986). In two programs, our Artistically Talented Program (ATP) and Project ARTS (Arts for

Rural Teachers and Students), we used this combined Clark and Zimmerman and Feldman framework to help teachers of artistically talented students develop curricula for their local teaching contexts.

The Schoolwide Enrichment Model, the Enrichment Triad Model, and the Revolving Door Identification Model often provided structures for the ATP and Project ARTS programs. The Schoolwide Enrichment Model is a product of fifteen years of research and field testing that combined Renzulli's previously developed Enrichment Triad Model and Revolving Door Identification Model (Renzulli & Reis, 1994). The Enrichment Triad Model offers three types of enrichment: *Type I*, explanatory experiences; *Type II*, instructional methods; and *Type III*, advanced levels of study. The Revolving Door Identification Model allows students to enter and exit talent-development programs according to their interests and abilities.

Both of these models often provided structures for ATP and Project ARTS teachers as they developed programs for artistically talented students in their home communities. Units of instruction focusing on particular themes with related art forms and art-making processes were developed as students were exposed to new concepts and interests. Some students went on to explore advanced levels of thinking and to use advanced research skills, and a few became engaged in in-depth inquiry and art production related to a specific theme.

Other conceptualizations also were introduced to the ATP and Project ARTS teachers, based in part on Maker's (1982) curriculum model for educating gifted and talented students, which emphasized: (1) controlling levels of content, process, product, and learning environments to make each more advanced than those in general art curricula; (2) modifying content to include differing degrees of abstractness, complexity, or organization and use of a wide variety of resource materials; (3) emphasizing study of the methods of art history, art criticism, art making, and aesthetics; (4) increasing group interactions, simulations, and learning through discovery, all proceeding at a faster and more varied pace than in regular classrooms; and (5) assuring that original products, based on real problems and addressing real audiences, were evaluated and displayed in public arenas. In addition, other suggestions from educators about developing talent and creativity were used to help ATP and Project ARTS teachers develop curriculum units that employed problem finding and problem solving and structured and unstructured tasks, a combination of discursive and nondiscursive tasks, independent units of study, integration of art with other subjects, and a wide range of tasks that challenged their artistically talented students.

Curricular Examples from the Artistically Talented Program

Each summer, from 1990 to 1994, we co-directed a two-week Artistically Talented Program (ATP) for in-service visual art teachers at Indiana University (Zimmerman, 1997a, 1997b). The ATP was designed to educate K–12 in-service teachers about artistically talented students. Emphasis was on developing understanding of problems, issues, and research related to identification, teaching methods and strategies, program policies, program evaluation, and resources designed to foster creativity and art talent development. This program emphasized processes of educating teachers about art and art teaching strategies, presenting their work in public forums, and assuming leadership roles in their schools and communities. All teachers attending ATP were required to write and implement curricula for identified artistically talented students in their schools, and publish their curricula in monographs to be disseminated throughout the state (Clark & Zimmerman, 1993; Zimmerman, 1994). Teachers were required to (1) stress thematic units of instruction that were intellectually challenging and based on socially relevant subject matter, (2) think broadly and question their assumptions, (3) examine their teaching strategies and interactions with artistically talented students, and (4) focus on developing problem-finding and problem-solving skills and ways to develop these skills in their students.

Some of the units of instruction that ATP teachers developed included themes such as *More Than Meets the Eye: Architectural Preservation Awareness,* a unit designed for fourth and fifth grade students that involved study of architecture in their local community. In this unit, students contrasted and compared buildings, and values and philosophies that shaped these buildings. These students investigated how space was used, value conflicts within their communities, and the importance of using aesthetic criteria to evaluate building design. Drawing skills were taught using a variety of drawing techniques. To develop understanding about the work of contemporary architects, after studying historically significant, local endangered buildings, students each chose one building and designed a new use for it, combining freehand drawings and computer-generated images.

Another unit, *How Impressionism Reflected Social Impact of the 1880s,* for fourth and fifth grade students, involved studying about the Impressionists and how they were impacted by social and historical concerns. Students critiqued works of art from this period, as well as created works of art that were socially and historically significant for them. Students also compared and contrasted styles, subjects, and expression in art in works created by the Impressionists with those of artwork created earlier. Students learned that artists in the late 1800s were affected by many changes happening in the world about them, and that these changes were reflected in their artwork. Students conducted research about how photography created new conditions, and how other inventions, like the collapsible paint tube, made it possible for artists to paint out of doors easily. Students then collected photographs related to a subject they intended to portray. Using these photographs, they did several sketches and created compositions that represented an impression of their subjects at a particular time of day.

Metamorphosis of the Portrait was a unit developed for fifth grade students. They studied portraits from a variety of cultures and media and participated in research activities, information sharing, studio lessons, and critique sessions. These students maintained process portfolios that included their artwork and research findings, reactions, comment sheets, preliminary sketches, and work in progress.

Other units of instruction were developed to be taught at the junior high school level. *Social Problems and Art: How Artists Use Their Talents to Help Their Communities* used the AIDS issue as an example. Students studied ways artists use their work to expose and confront social problems in their communities. This unit required problem solving, decision making, and looking, talking, and writing about art and artists in the students' local communities, art making, and marketing of artwork.

Another theme for middle school students was *Considerations of Geometric Proportions and Terrestrial Observations of the Serpent Mound*. The Serpent Mound, in Ohio, is a very large, prehistoric earth mound resembling the shape of a snake. In this unit, art students familiarized themselves with theories concerning construction of earthworks and then took a field trip to the Serpent Mound, where they calculated its proportions. Later, they studied contemporary earthworks that resulted in individual student interpretations of artifacts as symbols for social belief structures. For example, one student created an outdoor environment in clay and then recorded its demise, thus challenging Western culture's fascination with material objects and their permanence.

Boxes: Private/Public Spaces, created for junior high school students, focused on the study of "the box," from embryo to coffin, as a metaphor for life. Juxtaposition of themes of space, time, and energy directed new ways for students to create art. Students researched the psychology of space, explored construction techniques, and found solutions to atypical space and shape relationships. Students also investigated objects and their sources, analyzed integral features, and linked their own art making to personal experiences. As a result of the unit, one student designed a small, Japanese, meditative garden in a shadow box frame. She wrote that the experience of creating this garden helped her understand that visual experiences depend on the perspective of the viewer and that some artwork is constantly changing.

Curricular Development in Project ARTS

Another project we co-directed addressed the needs of elementary level, economically disadvantaged students from diverse cultural contexts in the United States, some of whom might in later years become practicing artists or leaders of the arts in their communities. Project ARTS (Arts for Rural Teachers and Students) was a three-year research and development project designed to serve students with high interest and abilities in the visual and performing arts in seven rural elementary schools in Indiana, New Mexico, and South Carolina (Clark, Marche, & Zimmerman, 1997; Clark & Zimmerman, 1997). Project ARTS' purposes were to identify underserved students in the third grade who had potential for high ability in the visual and performing arts, implement differentiated curricula in the fourth and fifth grades, and evaluate the successes of these efforts.

At each school, Project ARTS staffs built their art curricula around the theme of greater understanding of their local community. Emphases were placed on each community's people and their histories, local festivals and holiday celebrations, arts traditions, and other related subjects. Studying local arts and crafts, musical and oral traditions, skills of local artists and artisans, and other cultural aspects is an obvious vehicle that can become a conduit for later study of arts in other cultures.

The staff of Project ARTS emphasized a multiethnic approach to teaching students by helping them understand and appreciate a variety of art objects, such as those found in local crafts, folk arts, popular arts, women's arts, and vernacular art. Such studies helped students appreciate their own cultural traditions and those of their families. Teachers at each school were encouraged to form active parent and community-based advisory groups to help identify and bring local cultural resources into Project ARTS curricula.

Teacher-development workshops were provided at all sites throughout the course of the project. Along with work on inclusion of local cultural resources, areas of concern included differentiating curricula for artistically talented students and nonstudio approaches to art education. Although some teachers were reasonably familiar with some art-making processes, information about objectives, processes, and resources for doing art-related inquiry often were lacking. We offered curriculum workshops stressing the need for modification of art programs to feature resources, materials, and opportunities not generally offered in their schools. These workshops emphasized the use of locally created resources as a means for studying art history, art criticism, aesthetics, and art making. Suggestions were given for interviewing local artists, locating community resources, taking field trips to historical sites, conducting research about a community's art and culture, and creating opportunities for bringing local resources into classrooms.

During the second and third years of Project ARTS, teachers and parent-community groups created and implemented differentiated curricula and learning activities for identified high-ability visual and performing arts students. These programs emphasized having students study and record art activities in their local communities. Programs in all site schools featured exhibitions and performances of student work in a variety of public contexts. As curriculum writing and implementation progressed across the sites, numerous people came forward to offer their assistance, knowledge, and skills. These included local historians, artists, both amateur and professional craftspeople, parents and family members, as well as other interested community members. Through exhibits and performances, students were able to share their newfound awareness and appreciation of local history and culture with many who previously had been unconcerned about these issues. All site schools, students, and teachers experienced benefits of these new relationships with local institutions, and their communities profited as well. Parents and community members saw their history and culture validated, and they were encouraged by the excitement and interest shown by students.

In Project ARTS, students were encouraged to learn about and value art in their own cultures as a bridge to understanding art created in a variety of past and present Western and non-Western contexts. An exchange of student-produced videotapes from each school site provided avenues for understanding the history and culture of each community. Use of technology was very successful in Indiana schools. Video production became a focus, and students were actively involved in planning, filming, and editing school productions and other special events. Students studied filming techniques and learned to use video camcorders. They conducted research about their communities, then wrote scripts, created storyboards, and filmed segments about local cultural and seasonal events. They then reviewed, edited, and reshot film segments, resulting in videos that were shared with other Project ARTS classes in other states. Three-way video teleconferencing among Indiana, New Mexico, and South Carolina Project ARTS staff, selected students, and teachers helped establish a sense of community among the sites. Expecting to find each other strange and different, Project ARTS students from rural Indiana and Santo Domingo Pueblo were pleased to discover they shared many interests. In addition to participating in arts experiences, they also discovered that playing basketball and romping in the snow were pleasures they shared.

In Project ARTS, teachers and on-site staff were empowered to assess their own local situations, select their own directions, and plan their own means to achieve ends within the broad framework of the Project ARTS agenda. By stressing uniqueness of content or experiences across sites, project directors acknowledged local conditions, needs, and appropriate methods for meeting those needs. Educational accomplishments in the project were related to the approximately 200 students who were directly involved in special program opportunities, and the nature and degree of benefits they enjoyed. In South Carolina, for example, all of the schools chose to work on a common curriculum, based directly on Gullah life and culture. The sea islands community in South Carolina, since the earliest importation of African slaves into that state, has been home to African American people who created the Gullah language and culture. Study of a unit about Gullah work and leisure involved students in making games and toys, growing indigo plants to create dyes, and learning to make sweet grass baskets. In a unit about storytelling, students were made aware of the importance of storytelling in many cultures and studied the popular role of storytelling in their own Gullah culture. In another unit, about Gullah celebrations and rites of passage, students learned about marriage and death rituals, family reunions, and local heritage days. They then created story quilts, designed T-shirts, and made masks based on interpretations of these celebrations.

In all schools, students who did not participate in advanced levels of the program benefited from exposure to visiting artists, art displays, and performances, field trips, and other educational experiences supported by Project ARTS. Public presentations of student work, which took place at each site, enhanced student learning and provided a focus for each school's programs. Through participatory presentations, students and teachers shared benefits of each local project throughout their entire school population and made Project ARTS part of each school's arts program. At every site, there were connections to community arts and artists. In Indiana, students met dulcimer players and musical instrument makers, local architects, quilters, painters, authors, and historians, and visited a historic artist's studio. In South Carolina, several local artists and cultural sites were introduced to students and teachers both in their schools and on field trips.

At one of the schools in New Mexico, students became involved in the restoration of an old community church, including the painting of an interior mural by local artists. These students were able to walk to the church daily, and observe, videotape, and photograph the process of creating and completing the mural. They also conducted historical research and interviewed local artisans to discover how the church was originally constructed, what tools were used, and where the building materials originated. Students interviewed community members about their reminiscences of local architecture and developed their drawing skills by recording how buildings on the main street of their community changed over the passage of time. They also made sketches that emphasized observation of styles, materials, and decorations of local buildings. At each site, opportunities were created for parents and community members to become aware of and appreciate student accomplishments.

Conclusions and Recommendations

It has been established that there is a lack of consensus about definitions of creativity, giftedness, and talent, and their interrelationships. Our position is that it is most appropriate if talent development and aspects of creativity are defined in terms of educational practice and how they are responsive to educational interventions. In the field of visual art education, there has been a shift in emphasis from creative self-expression to discipline-based art education, in which creativity and talent development are related to the world of art and the work of artists. In addition, there is strong evidence that art talent development, creativity, and academic achievement are correlated.

The term *talent in the arts*, however, does not have an agreed-upon meaning in gifted and talented literature, and its usage in schools should be expanded to include indicators other than solely the ability to depict the world realistically through well-developed graphic skills. Evidence of art talent or potential for art talent—such as use of themes and variations, humor, puns, paradoxes, enthusiasm, deep emotional involvement, and production of a large volume of work over time—also should be considered as evidence of art talent. Productive and creative thinking in the visual arts also can be nurtured through enhancing students' problem-finding and problem-solving skills. Use of a variety of procedures is recommended for developing art talent and creativity through educational intervention that results in enriched educational experiences for K–8 students with high interest and abilities in the visual arts.

Teachers of artistically talented students can be powerful influences by being knowledgeable about subject matter, communicating effectively, guiding students using appropriately directive teaching methods, making classes interesting, giving challenging assignments, and helping students become aware of why they create art and of contexts in which they work. It is recommended that teachers go beyond teaching skills and encourage independent thought, spontaneity, and originality in their artistically talented students through differentiated and enriched curricula.

Frameworks for appropriate educational interventions—such as Clark and Zimmerman's Naive to Sophisticated Model, Feldman's Universal to Unique Continuum, Renzulli's Schoolwide Enrichment Model, and Maker's curriculum model—were suggested as having potential to help teachers develop differentiated and enriched curricula for students with high interest and ability in the visual arts. Theme-oriented units of instruction, based in part on these frameworks, can be developed that focus on student interests and having students set their own goals and objectives. It is recommended that open-ended assignments, which include a variety of tasks, be designed to emphasize both verbal and visual problem-finding and problem-solving skills, integrate art with other subjects, use socially relevant subject matter, and modify and differentiate art content to create enriched curricula for all K–8 students, including those with talent in academic areas as well as those with art talent.

In addition, it is recommended that enriched programs for artistically talented students include in their curricula arts from the communities in which students live. Parents as well as artists and other community members should be encouraged to be actively involved in educational interventions in schools in their communities. Through public presentations of their artwork, students can develop self-esteem and pride in their local communities and their own backgrounds that will help them better understand the contributions of other people creating art in different contexts.

The importance of developing enriched programs for artistically talented students cannot be underestimated. As we enter the twenty-first century, it is apparent that students need to be prepared for a new information age. Those students who will later become practicing artists should be prepared to think creatively and develop skills and abilities appropriate in a rapidly changing world. There also is a need to prepare appreciators and consumers of art who, as future leaders, will make decisions about the arts in their local communities and beyond. Educational interventions and accelerated and enriched programs, for kindergarten through junior high school students with interest and abilities in the arts, can foster leadership and creative thinking with the potential to generate solutions to real-life problems both now and in the future.

Chapter **16**

Teaching Mathematics to Young Children

The Math Circle

ROBERT KAPLAN

Why are most children bored by math—or worse, frightened of it—when its beauties are so many and its pleasures so great? Perhaps because it is often taught by people who fear it, and who therefore teach their fear.

To counter this, my wife Ellen (Chair of the Math Department at The New Jewish High School, Waltham, Massachusetts) and I began The Math Circle, a school for the enjoyment of pure mathematics, in September 1994. Our once-weekly meetings with twenty-nine students have grown now to five separate weekly sessions, meeting at Harvard and at Northeastern University, with seventy students. They range in age from 6 to 48, meeting in groups of no more than twelve—so that they can hear themselves and their colleagues think.

Our approach in The Math Circle is to pose questions and let congenial conversation take over. Conjectures emerge from a free-for-all, examples and counterexamples from the conjectures. Two steps forward are followed by a step back: What really is at issue here? How will we know when we've understood something? Is proving different from *seeing*? Where and with what should proofs begin, and how should we validate these beginnings? And if we get it, need we formalize it? Yes, following my old fencing master's adage about holding the foil like a bird—tightly enough not to let it get away, not so tightly as to crush it. We don't want a '60s feel-good sense of math as expressive handwaving. We explain that rigor without mortis consists of fluency at making a connected path back to foundations that will stand up to scrutiny. In our exchanges, the students are developing the knack of pushing insight adventurously ahead while protecting the supply lines that fuel it.

Here's an example of what happens, from the Wednesday afternoon sessions with 8- to 11-year-olds. I began by asking them each to give me very large numbers—and a rather conservative list of integers developed on the board (Littlewood calculated that the gigantic stretches of time in Indian mythology "only" amounted to 10^{35} years; for kids, however, 250 is way out there). Was there a last integer? Of course not, said 8-year-old Anna at once—if there were, just add one to it. I was struck by this instantaneous freeing of imagination with the passage to the general.

They all took easily to one-to-one correspondences, via the need to show Martians who count "1, 2, 3, many" that a heap of thirteen pencils contains a larger many than a pile of eight coins (some sorted by threes, some paired up, all relished the Martian astonishment that there were two sizes of "many"). By the end of the first hour, each was pairing up the naturals with the evens or the odds or multiples of 7 ("Let's walk through the numbers in seven-league boots!" said one) or the negatives and positives—or the integers (a puzzling moment, followed by a cry of "Shift!"). The children left that first session in two minds: they saw and could not but assent to the results of their work, but they "knew" it couldn't be right—there were clearly only half as many even numbers as naturals.

I was glad to see one boy return to the second session who had come to the first the way you go to a horror movie: frozen between fascination and flight. He had been brooding about the infinite, his mother told me, and found it terrifying, and had signed up for this class to overcome his fear. As you might expect, his were the most daring conjectures in what followed.

Could the positive rationals be counted? Passionate arguments raged about the lack of a starting place (the abyss of density opened, for the first time, for several there). I put the first few rows and columns on the board to claims ringing through the room that we could never get out of the row we once committed ourselves to—until a girl, quiet before this, asked if she could come up, and began spinning a drunken spider's web from the upper left-hand corner. Another girl suggested how we might regularize the pattern, and—despair turning to glee—each now constructed a bus route through these streets and avenues (to the accompaniment of popping insights and questions: "Look! Those diagonals are all repeats!" "But how can we tell ahead of time that the sixteenth stop will be 2/5?"). The diagonal proof belongs now to each of them, for as Locke pointed out, "Property is that with which one has commingled one's labor."

We headed toward Cantor's diagonal proof (that the real numbers *cannot* be counted!) through the largely unfamiliar territory of decimals, browsing among repeating and nonrepeating growths (much ingenuity here, on their part, in concocting and explaining). Then a long digression on what it would mean not to have a one-to-one correspondence between two sets, and on proof by contradiction (this pushes the limits of how much can equitably be held in mind)—heralding the metaphorical entrance of a figure modeled on the former Senator McCarthy, patting his jacket pocket: "I have here a list of all the card-carrying decimals between 0 and 1," each card bearing its ordinal. They followed the proof, complaining all the way, arguing with and explaining it to one another, ending up as flabbergasted as I am every time I think it through.

By the time I arrived for the next class, a girl with an uncannily precise mind was explaining Cantor's proof to a die-hard skeptic, countering his attempts to put "our decimal made up of 5s and 6s" "at the end of the list." Now the pace accelerated as we came back to the visual—they called the proof they devised of the one-to-one correspondence between points on closed segments of different lengths "the circus tent." Giving names, as Adam first knew, is a sign of confidence. Since I'd told them about $\aleph_0$, they christened our new cardinality "zigzag null."

And the open interval and the real line? This led to the greatest frustrations as well as ingenuity. At last, exhausted, with time running out and skepticism about everything creeping out of every corner, the boy who feared infinity had the saving insight. Tremendous relief, appreciation, exhilaration—but the last note was struck by the girl with the precise mind: "I see the proof and I accept it," she said, "and at the same time I don't. It doesn't tell us, does it, just *which* real number goes with the decimal we choose in (0, 1). That makes me uneasy." A good note to end—and begin afresh—on.

The topics we choose—but more particularly, the ways we work on them—are designed to avoid two things that tend to go wrong with accelerated or "enrichment" math courses. One is children being taught the punch lines without having worked their own way up to them ("I've already *had* Pascal's Triangle," says the child who knows neither its genesis nor implications). The second is teaching the magic that looks like math—Pavlovian training of 10-year-olds to push the right symbols for taking the derivatives of polynomials.

Why did we choose infinite sets for the youngest group? Because little kids love large numbers, the way they like elephants and dinosaurs—powerful friends in high places—but a liking tinged with titillating fear. Children have no reputations to protect—because they don't even know yet about reputation—so they are much better than older students at making and getting far-fetched ideas—not a card is held close to a chest. Unlike philosophy, math begins with awe and ends with wonder.

In another course, Ellen worked on polygon construction with the 8- to 11-year-olds. This meant using actual straight-edges and compasses; and while the hands were busy, a casual conversation about constructability steadily moved from the context to the content of the course. One student to another: "What do you mean, you can't trisect all angles? If you can trisect a 90° angle by copying 30° angles, can't you copy some angle twice to get any angle?" The crux of the matter is to seize on such assertions so as to let the students find out for themselves what's at stake (coming to grips with, among other things, the mysteries of quantification).

A generation brought up with calculators has difficulty manipulating fractions. Ellen led them to construct an equilateral triangle and a regular pentagon in the same circle, and to figure out how to construct a regular 15-gon—thus discovering that 1/3 minus 1/5 could be seen as the useful 2/15 rather than the unenlightening .13333. . . . The confidence that followed this self-won competence made them feel that this world was their oyster: They could construct whole series of regular polygons. Then why were the heptagon and the enneagon so resistant to their efforts? Fermat primes came up before the course ended; but as in all the best dramas, exeunt omnes in mysterium.

With the 11- to 14-year-olds, Ellen has run a course on polyhedra. Conversation accompanying scissors-and-paste constructions led very quickly to their discovery of the Euler characteristic. They tested it with Schlegel diagrams, studied and were convinced by Cauchy's proof, then read Lakatos' dialogue about the Euler characteristic, *Proofs and Refutations,* taking parts, and stepping out of character again and again to argue with the protagonists. They were startled to recognize in themselves the traits of monster-barrer and monster-adjustor, skeptic and omni-ameliorator. As in the dialogue, the semester ended with everything up in the air. Should things be neatly tied up?

With the same group, I worked one fall on number theory, beginning with this peculiarity: Why do the digits in half the period of the decimal expansion of 1/7 yield, when added to the other half, all 9s? (One 11-year-old immediately said: "You mean, one less than a power of 10!") And look, it's true of 1/13 too, and 1/101; but not of 1/2 or 1/5, much less 1/3 or 1/8. This took us on two long excursions into geometric series and, through the idea of congruence, to Fermat's Little Theorem (which again they came up with themselves, just by messin' around). The far-shining goal of our initial puzzle got us through difficult stretches. There is a push-me-pull-you rhythm to the best of these classes: Convictions put together the week before turn out to have been soldered, not welded, together, and come apart with flexing (how was it we got the sum of an infinite series?). We reconstruct them more solidly under the pressure of doubt.

The courses with the oldest students (14 on up) are the hardest fought. They want nothing told to them; all is to be invented. In a course on sequences and series, they came up with convergence criteria of their own (named after their new inventors), approximating ever more closely to the curve of the topic's history. By a judicious choice of examples and nudges at critical moments, I moved them, in another course on projective geometry, to where they could—and did—come up with Desargues' Theorem, followed by their vigorous, critical role as sous chefs in cooking up its proof. Because they were very puzzled by the maneuver of having to pass out of the plane and back to it, some doubting the validity of the proof, others the universality of the theorem, we had to digress to the free projective plane on four points—which they found startling and disturbing. They took an inventor's pride in coming up with a proof of the uniqueness of the fourth harmonic point, and that left us, at the end (ten sessions are too few), able to conjecture the Fundamental Theorem of Projective Geometry and prove its existence part. A real advantage of projective geometry for students whose graphing calculators usually do their visualizing for them is that their spatial imagination is awakened and exercised.

Our Sunday morning format consists of two one-hour classes (juice and cookies in between), followed by guest lecturers. A good high school mathematics course brings a student up to the eighteenth century. Here they can see contemporary mathematicians working on the frontier in the same manner that they had been developing for the last two hours.

Because our clientele is growing, we've taken on other hands—two third-year graduate students in math at Harvard. We would like to branch out to other cities. What may be hard to export is our style: We entertain all conjectures and questions with equal seriousness, letting them follow their conversational course and turning the current of that conversation into fruitful directions as unobtrusively as possible. If a line of inquiry hits a wall, we tend to let it lie and strike off in another direction, rather than throwing our students a sophisticated assortment of scaling ladders. What's left fallow one week tends to produce a flurry of ingenious growths by the next (and these dead-ends are the material of the week's homework). We do our best to hold off introducing a symbol until its abbreviator power is welcomed for packaging up what has become an unwieldy complex of relations. Best when the students come up with the symbol—and the need for it—themselves.

What we see in The Math Circle is the exhilarating rediscovery of our forgotten native language: that speech which names and sorts out abstract relations. Because it *is* our common language, all can rediscover it. The different paces we move at in this effort of recollection come from a huge array of frustrations and reinforcements each of us encounters when very young. Then how can people with radically different experiences paw at this elephant together and come up with shared insights? By conversation—by the mutual exchange of doubts, adjustments, guesses, and glimpses driven on by the sheer fun of the thing, and a losing of self in the common enterprise.

What have we learned from this? That the appetite for real math, done neither competitively nor scholastically but as the most exciting of the arts, is enormous. I see no limits to what children can learn, and am convinced that if you want to teach them A, and A implies B, work on B with them: A will be mastered en passant, painlessly, absorbed in the bones. I'm certain too that removing any pressure of time or achievement lets understanding blossom, as well as developing a delightfully collegial feeling in those involved, and a sense of the enterprise as contained within larger frameworks of question and significance. The students come away certain that math is mysterious, equally certain that its mysteries are accessible; unsure whether we discover or invent it; confident in their growing competence, and with that heightened threshold of frustration, that odd combination of watchfulness and willfulness, that characterizes the practitioners of our craft.

References

Adam, A. (1841). *Giselle*.

Adler, M. (1952). *The great ideas: A syntopticon of great books of the Western world*. Chicago, IL: Encyclopedia Britannica.

Amabile, T. M. (1982). Social psychology of creativity: A consensual assessment technique. *JPSP, 43*, 967–1013.

Amabile, T. M. (1983a). *The social psychology of creativity*. New York: Springer Verlag.

Amabile, T. (1983b). The social psychology of creativity: A componential conceptualization. *Journal of Personality and Social Psychology, 45*(2), 357–376.

Amabile, T. M. (1987). The motivation to be creative. In S. G. Isaken (Ed.), *Frontiers of creativity research* (pp. 223–254). Buffalo, NY: Brearly Limited.

Amabile, T. M. (1990). Within you, without you: The social psychology of creativity and beyond. In M. A. Runco & R. S. Albert (Eds.), *Theories of creativity* (pp. 61–69). Newbury Park, CA: Sage Publications.

Amabile, T. M., & Tighe, E. (1993). Questions of creativity. In J. Brockman (Ed.), *Creativity* (Ch. 1, pp. 7–27). New York: NY: Touchstone.

Amorosia, D., & Weidemann, L. (1992). *Sounds a little fishy to me: A musical introduction to the ocean*. Milwaukee, WI: Jenson Publications, Hal Leonard Publishing Corporation.

AmRhein, R. (1997). Internet references in the performing arts. *Reference Librarian*, (57), 139–146.

Anarella, L. A. (1992). Creative drama in the classroom. (ERIC Document Reproduction Service No. ED391206).

Anderson, J. R., Reder, L. M., & Simon, H. A. (1996). Situated learning and education. *Educational Researcher, 25*, 5–11.

Anderson, L. (1951). *The Syncopated Clock*.

Andreason, N. (1987). Creativity and mental illness: Prevalence rates in writers and their first-degree relatives. *American Journal of Psychiatry, 144*, 1288–1292.

Arieti, S. (1976). *Creativity: The magic synthesis*. New York: Basic Books.

Armstrong, T. (1994). *Multiple intelligences in the classroom*. Alexandria, VA: Association for Supervision and Curriculum Development.

Ashton-Warner, S. (1963). *Teacher*. New York: Simon and Schuster.

Bachtel, A. E. (1988). A study of current selection and identification procedures and schooling for K–12 artistically gifted and talented students. (Doctoral Dissertation, University of Southern California). *Dissertation Abstracts International, 49*, 12A, 3597.

Baer, J. (1993a). *Divergent thinking and creativity: A task-specific approach*. Hillsdale, NJ: Lawrence Erlbaum Associates.

Baer, J. (1993b, January–February). Why you shouldn't trust creativity tests. *Educational Leadership*, 80–83.

Baer, J. (1998). The case for domain specifity of creativity. *Creativity Research Journal*, *11*(2), 173–177.

Baker, B. R. (1996). Drama and young children. (ERIC Document Reproduction Service No. ED402637).

Baldwin, A. Y. (1985). Programs for the gifted and talented: Issues concerning minority populations. In F. Horowitz & M. O'Brien (Eds.), *The gifted and talented: Developmental perspectives* (pp. 223–249). Washington, DC: American Psychological Association.

Baldwin, A. Y. (1997). Is the 'bell curve' the whole story? In J. Chann, R. Li, & J. Spinks (Eds.), *Proceedings of the 11th World Conference on Gifted and Talented Children* (pp. 615–619). Hong Kong: University of Hong Kong Social Sciences Research Centre.

Bamberger, J. (1986). Cognitive issues in the development of musically gifted children. In R. Sternberg & J. Davidson (Eds.), *Conceptions of giftedness* (pp. 388–415). New York: Cambridge University Press.

Bandura, A. (1997). *Self-efficacy: The exercise of control*. New York: Freeman.

Banks, J. (1988). *Multiethnic education: Theory and practice* (2nd ed.). Boston, MA: Allyn & Bacon, 75.

Barman, C. R., & Kotar, M. (1989, April). The learning cycle. *Science and Children*, 30–32.

Barron, F. (1968). *Creativity and personal freedom*. New York: Van Nostrand.

Barron, F. (1969). *The creative person and the creative process*. New York: Holt, Rinehart, and Winston.

Barron, F. (1972). *Artists in the making*. New York: Seminar Press.

Barron, F. (1988). Putting creativity to work. In R. Sternberg (Ed.), *The nature of creativity* (Ch. 3, pp. 76–98). New York: Cambridge Press.

Barron, F. (1995). *No rootless flower: An ecology of creativity*. Cresskill, NJ: Hampton Press.

Barron, F., Montouri, A., & Brown, A. (1997). *Creators on creating: Awakening and cultivating the creative mind*. New York: Tarcher/Putnam.

Baum, S. M. (1988). An enrichment program for gifted learning disabled students. *Gifted Child Quarterly*, *32*(2), 226–230.

Baum, S. M., & Owen, S. V. (1988, Fall). High ability/learning disabled students: How are they different? *Gifted Child Quarterly*, *32*(3), 321–326.

Baum, S. M., Owen, S. V., & Dixon, J. (1991). *To be gifted and learning disabled: From identification to practical intervention strategies*. Mansfield Center, CT: Creative Learning Press.

Baum, S., Renzulli, J. S., & Gilbert, T. P. (1995). Reversing underachievement: Creative productivity as a systematic intervention. *Gifted Child Quarterly*, *39*(4), 224–235.

Bellman, W. (1974). The effects of creative dramatics activities on personality as shown in student self-concept. *Dissertation Abstracts International*, *35*, 5668A.

Bem, S. (1974). The measurement of psychological androgyny. *Journal of Consulting and Clinical Psychology*, *42*, 155–162.

Benjafield, J. G. (1997). *Cognition*. (2nd ed.). Upper Saddle River, NJ: Prentice Hall.

Benjamin, J., Li, L., Patterson, C., Greenberg, B. D., Murphy, D. L., & Hamer, D. H. (1996). Population and familial association between the D4 dopamine receptor gene and measures of novelty seeking. *Nature Genetics*, *12*, 81–84.

Bereiter, C., & Scardamalia, M. (1993). *Surpassing ourselves: An inquiry into the nature and implications of expertise*. Chicago, IL: Open Court.

Bermudez, A. B. (1993). Meeting the needs of the gifted and talented limited English proficient student: The UHCL proto. In L. M. Malave (Ed.), *Proceedings of the National Association for Bilingual Education Conferences*, 115–133.

Betts, G. T. (1986). Development of emotional and social needs of gifted individuals. *Journal of Counseling and Development*, *64*(9), 587–589.

Bloom, B. (1985). *The development of talent in young people*. New York, NY: Ballantine.

Bolton, G. A. (1979). *Towards a theory of drama in education*. London, England, United Kingdom: Longman Group Limited.

Boorstin, D. J. (1983). *The discoverers*. New York: Random House.

Brewer, C., & Campbell, D. (1991). *Rhythms of learning: Creative tools for developing lifelong skills*. Tucson, Arizona: Zephyr Press.

Brooks, J. G., & Brooks, M. G. (1993). *In search of understanding: The case for constructivist classrooms*. Alexandria, VA: Association for Supervision and Curriculum Development.

Brosterman, N. (1997). *Inventing kindergarten*. New York: Abrams.

Brown, A. M. (1984). Interview, Senta Driver, in *New Performance, XI*(1), unpaged.

Brown, J. S., Collins, A., & Duguid, P. (1989). Situated cognition and the culture of learning. *Educational Researcher, 18*(1), 32–42.

Brown, M. S. (1947). *Goodnight Moon*. New York: Harper & Row.

Bulosan, C. (1988). *America is in the heart*. Seattle: University of Washington Press. (Original work published 1943).

Burton, N. (1998). The effects of a refutational approach on the teaching of second grade reading. [Unpublished raw data.]

Byers, R. (1968). *Creating theater: The Paul Baker studies in theater, No. 2*. Austin, TX: Trinity University Press.

Campbell, D. (1992). *100 ways to improve teaching using your voice and music: Pathways to accelerate learning*. Tucson, Arizona: Zephyr Press.

Carle, E. Compiled by L. Whipple. (1989). *Eric Carle's animals*. New York: Philomel Books.

Carlyle, T. (1959). Reported by Hilgard in H. H. Anderson (Ed.), *Creativity and its cultivation* (p. 178). New York: Harper & Row.

Center for Educational Research and Innovation, CERI. (1987). *Immigrant children at school*. (Organization for Economic Cooperation and Development, OECD). Paris: Author.

Chall, J. S. (1983). *Learning to read: The great debate*. New York: McGraw-Hill.

Chislett, L. (1994). Integrating the CPS and school-wide enrichment models to enhance creative productivity. *Roeper Review, 17*(1), 4–7.

Clark, B. (1979). *Growing up gifted*. Columbus, OH: Charles E. Merrill.

Clark, B. R. (1985). Conclusions. In B. R. Clark (Ed.). *The school and the university: An educational perspective*. Berkely, CA: University of California Press, 290–325.

Clark, G. A. (1997). Identification. In G. A. Clark, T. Marche, & E. Zimmerman, *Project Arts: Programs for ethnically diverse, economically disadvantaged, high ability, visual arts students in rural communities* (pp. 17–87). U.S. Department of Education, Jacob Javits Gifted and Talented Discretionary Grant Program, #R206A30220.

Clark, G. A., Day, M. D., & Greer, W. D. (1987). Discipline based art education: Becoming students of art. In R. A. Smith (Ed.), *Discipline based art education: Origins, meaning, and development*. Urbana, IL: University of Illinois Press.

Clark, G. A., Marche, T., & Zimmerman, E. (1997). *Project Arts: Programs for ethnically diverse, economically disadvantaged, high ability, visual arts students in rural communities* (Handbook). U.S. Department of Education, Jacob Javits Gifted and Talented Discretionary Grant Program, #R206A30220.

Clark, G. A., & Zimmerman, E. (1978). A walk in the right direction: A model for visual arts education. *Studies in Art Education, 9*(2), 32–49.

Clark, G. A., & Zimmerman, E. (1984). *Educating artistically talented students*. Syracuse, NY: Syracuse University Press.

Clark, G. A., & Zimmerman, E. (1986). A framework for educating artistically talented students based on Feldman's and Clark and Zimmerman's models. *Studies in Art Education, 27*(2), 115–122.

Clark, G. A., & Zimmerman, E. (1992). *Issues and practices related to identification of gifted and talented students in the visual arts*. Storrs, CT: National Research Center on the Gifted and Talented.

Clark, G. A., & Zimmerman, E. (1993). *A community of teachers: Art curriculum units by teachers in the 1992 artistically talented program*. Bloomington, IN: Indiana University, School of Education and the Indiana Department of Education, Office of Gifted and Talented Education.

Clark, G. A., & Zimmerman, E. (1997). *Programs for ethnically diverse, economically disadvantaged, high ability, visual arts students in rural communities (Final report)*. U.S. Department of Education, Jacob Javits Gifted and Talented Discretionary Grant Program, #R206A30220.

Clark, G. A., & Zimmerman, E. (1998, Spring). Nurturing art talents in comprehensive programs for gifted and talented students. *Phi Delta Kappan, 79*(10), 747–751.

Clark, L. (1988, June). Early warning of refugee flows. Center for Policy Analysis and Research on Refugee Issues. (Available from Refugee Policy Group, 1424 16th Street, N.W. Suite 401, Washington, D.C. 20036).

Clark, L. (1988, October). Early warning of refugee flows. In *Research Seminar on International Migration,* presentation conducted at Massachusetts Institute of Technology, Cambridge, Massachusetts.

Clasen, D., Middleton, J., & Connell, T. (1994). Assessing artistic and problem-solving performance in minority and nonminority students using a nontraditional multidimensional approach. *Gifted Child Quarterly, 38*(1), 27–32.

Clay, M. (1990). *Observing young readers: Selected papers,* 15, Portsmouth, NH: Heinemann.

Cobine, G. R. (1998). Plying at poetic writing. *Viewpoints.* (ERIC Document Reproduction Service No. ED416493).

Cohen, M. (1988, April 21). Immigrant children need aid, study says. *The Boston Globe,* page 25.

Coleman, D. (1995). *Emotional intelligence.* New York: Bantam Books.

Coleridge, S. (1849). *Biographia literaria.* Philadelphia: Crissey & Markley.

Collin, J. (1997). What matters and 100 words: Two poetry writing ideas. *Teachers & Writers, 29*(1), 11–15.

Collins, C. (1991). Discovering hidden voices. *Bread Loaf News, 4*(3), 24–25.

Coopersmith, S. (1967). *The antecedents of self-esteem.* San Francisco: W. H. Freeman.

Csikszentmihalyi, M. (1988). Society, culture, and person: A systems view of creativity. In R. Sternberg (Ed.), *The nature of creativity: Contemporary psychological perspectives* (pp. 325–340). New York: Cambridge University Press.

Csikszentmihalyi, M. (1990a). *Flow.* New York: Cambridge.

Csikszentmihalyi, M. (1990b). *Flow: The psychology of optimal experience.* New York: Harper & Row.

Csikszentmihalyi, M. (1996). *Creativity: Flow and the psychology of discovery and invention,* New York: Harper Perennial.

Dai, D. Y., & Feldhusen, J. F. (1996). Goal orientations of gifted students. *Gifted and Talented International, 11*(2), 84–88.

Daniels, S. (1997). Creativity in the classroom: characteristics, climate, and curriculum. In N. Colangelo & G. Davis (Eds.), *Handbook of gifted education* (Ch. 24, pp. 292–307). Boston: Allyn & Bacon.

Dash, J. (1988). *A life of one's own: Three gifted women and the men they married.* New York: Paragon House.

Davis, G. A. (1971). *Creativity is forever.* Cross Plains, WI: University of Wisconsin.

Davis, G. A. (1973). *Creativity is forever.* (2nd ed.). Dubuque, IA: Kendall/Hunt.

Davis, G. A. (1992). *Creativity is forever.* (3rd ed.). Dubuque, IA: Kendall/Hunt.

Davis, G. A. (1997). Identifying creative students and measuring creativity. In N. Colangalo & G. Davis (Eds.), *Handbook of gifted education* (Ch. 22, pp. 269–281). Boston: Allyn & Bacon.

Davis, G. A. (1998). *Creativity is forever.* (4th ed.). Dubuque, IA: Kendall/Hunt.

Davis, G. A. (1999) [Review of unpublished manuscript of Creativity for Children, K–8: Fostering its Development through Theory and Practice].

Disney, W. (1948). *Robin Hood* (Video).

Duffy, T. M., Lowyck, J., Jonassen, D. H., with Welch, T. M. (Eds.). (1993). *Designing environments for constructive learning.* New York: Springer-Verlag.

du Maurier, D. (1938). *Rebecca.* Garden City, NY: Doubleday.

Dunn, R., Dunn, K., & Price, G. E. (1981). *Learning style inventory.* Lawrence, KS: Price Systems.

Dunning, S., Lueders, E., & Smith, H. (1966). *Reflections on a gift of watermelon pickle . . . And other modern verse.* Atlanta, GA: Scott, Foresman and Company.

Durham, J. (1997). On time and poetry. *Reading Teacher, 51*(1), 76–79.

Durrell, D. (1937). *Durrell analysis of reading difficulties.* New York: Harcourt Brace Jovanovitch.

Dweck, C. S. (1986). Motivational processes affecting learning. *American Psychologist, 41*(10), 1040–1048.

Dykstra, J., & Dykstra, F. E. (1997). Imagery and synectics for modeling poetry writing. In *VisionQuest: Journeys toward visual literacy. Selected readings from the annual conference of the International Visual Literacy Association.* (ERIC Document Reproduction Service No. ED408964).

Ebstein, R. P., Novick, O., Umansky, R., Priel, B., Osher, Y., Blaine, D., Bennett, E. R., Nemanov, L., Katz, M., & Belmaker, R. H. (1996). Dopamine D4 receptor (D4DR) exon III polymorphism associated with the human personality trait of novelty seeking. *Nature Genetics, 12,* 78–80.

Educational Products Information Exchange Institute. (1980–81). *Educational research and development report, 3,* 4.

Ellingson, M. K., Haeger, W. W., & Feldhusen, J. F. (1986). The Purdue Mentor Program: A university-based mentorship experience for gifted children. *The Gifted Child Today, 9*(2), 2–5.

Emerson, N. B. (1982). *Unwritten literature of Hawaii.* Rutland, VT: Charles E. Tuttle Company. (Original work published 1965).

Ephron, N. (1983). A few words about breasts. In M. Richler (Ed.), *The best of modern humor* (pp. 467–475). New York: Knopf.

Farley, F. (1971). Measures of individual differences in stimulation-seeking and the tendency toward variety. *Journal of Consulting and Clinical Psychology, 37,* 394–396.

Farley, F. (1974, August). A theoretical-predictive model of creativity. Paper presented at American Psychological Association Annual Meeting, New Orleans, LA.

Farley, F. (1985). Psychobiology and cognition: An individual differences model. In J. Strelau, F. Farley, & A. Gale (Eds.), *The biological bases of personality and behavior.* (Vol. 1). New York: Hemisphere/McGraw-Hill International.

Farley, F. (1986). The Big T in personality. *Psychology Today, 20,* 45–52.

Farley, F. (1991). The Type T personality. In L. Lipsitt and L. L. Mitnick (Eds.), *Self-regulatory behavior and risk-taking: Causes and consequences* (pp. 371–382). Norwood, NJ: Ablex.

Farley, F. (in press). Creativity's best shot. *Contemporary Psychology.*

Feinburg, S., & Mindess, M. (1994). *Eliciting children's full potential.* Pacific Grove, California: Brooks/Cole.

Feldhusen, J. F. (1991). Saturday and summer programs. In N. Colangelo & G. Davis (Eds.), *Handbook of gifted education* (pp. 197–208). Boston: Allyn & Bacon.

Feldhusen, J. F. (1992). *Talent Identification and Development in Education (TIDE).* Sarasota, FL: Center for Creative Learning.

Feldhusen, J. F. (1993). Talent Identification and Development in Education (TIDE). *Gifted Education International, 10,* 10–15.

Feldhusen, J. F. (1994a). A case for developing America's talent: How we went wrong and where we go now. *Roeper Review, 6*(4), 231–322.

Feldhusen, J. F. (1994b). Creativity: A knowledge base, metacognitive skills, and personality factors. *Journal of Creative Behavior, 29,* 255–268.

Feldhusen, J. F. (1994c). Creativity: Teaching and testing for. In T. Husen, & T. Neville (Eds.), *International Encyclopedia of Education* (pp. 1178–1183). New York: Pergamon Press.

Feldhusen, J. F. (1995). Talent development as the alternative in high school programs. *Understanding Our Gifted,* (4), 1, 11–14.

Feldhusen, J. F. (1995). *Talent Identification and Development in Education.* Sarasota, FL: Center for Creative Learning.

Feldhusen, J. (1996, February). How to identify and develop special talents. *Educational Leadership,* 66–69.

Feldhusen, J. F. (1997). Secondary services, opportunities and activities for talented youth. In N. Colangelo & G. A. Davis (Eds.), *Handbook of gifted and talented* (Ch. 15, pp. 189–197). Boston, MA: Allyn & Bacon.

Feldhusen, J. F., & Britton-Kolloff, P. (1986). The Purdue three-stage enrichment model for gifted education at the elementary level. In J. S. Renzulli (Ed.), *Systems and models for developing programs for the gifted and talented* (pp.

126–152). Mansfield Center, CT: Creative Learning Press.

Feldhusen, J. F., & Clinkenbeard, P. M. (1996). Creativity instructional material: A review of research. *Journal of Creative Behavior, 20*(3), 153–182.

Feldhusen, J. F., & Jarwan, F. A. (1993). Identification of gifted and talented youth for educational programs. In K. A. Heller, F. J. Monks, & A. H. Passow (Eds.), *International handbook of research and development of giftedness and talent* (pp. 233–251). New York: Pergamon.

Feldhusen, J. F., Treffinger, D. J., & Elias, R. M. (1970). Developing creative thinking: The Purdue creativity program. *Journal of Creative Behavior, 4*, 85–90.

Feldhusen, J. F., & Wood, B. K. (1997). Developing growth plans for gifted students. *Gifted Child Today, 20*(6), 24–26, 48–49.

Feldhusen, J. F., Wood, B. K., & Dai, D. Y. (1997). Gifted students' perceptions of their talents. *Gifted and Talented International, 12*(1), 42–45.

Feldman, D. H. (1980). *Beyond universals in cognitive development.* Norwood, NJ: Ablex.

Feldman, D. H. (1982a). *Developmental approaches to giftedness and creativity.* San Francisco: Jossey-Bass.

Feldman, D. H. (1982b). A developmental framework for research with gifted children. In D. Feldman (Ed.), *New directions for child development: Developmental approaches to giftedness and creativity* (Ch. 17, pp. 31–46). San Francisco: Jossey-Bass.

Feldman, D. H., Csikszentmihalyi, M., & Gardner, H. (1994). *Changing the world: A framework for the study of creativity.* Westport, CT: Praeger.

Feldman, D. H., & Goldsmith, L. (1986). *Nature's gambit: Child prodigies and the development of human potential.* New York: Basic Books.

Feldman, D. H., & Piirto, J. (1995). Parenting talented children. In M. Bornstein (Ed.), *Handbook of Parenting* (pp. 285–304). New York: Longman.

Felice, R. (1998). "Knoxville, Tennessee": Using Nikki Giovanni's Poem. *Teachers & Writers, 29*(3), 4–6.

Feng, J. (1997). *Yayi meiguo ertong: Jiaaoshi suo ying liaojie de (Asian American children: What teach-ers should know).* ERIC Digest. Champaign, IL: ERIC Clearinghouse on Elementary and Early Childhood Education. (ERIC Document Reproduction Service No. EDO-PS-97-1).

Flora, S. (1997). *Learning with Raffi: Baby Beluga.* Grand Rapids, MI: Instructional Fair, TS Denison.

Freihage, E., Murrell, P., & Phillips, A. (1995). *Final report of the elementary education committee.* Prepared for The Mayor's Blue Ribbon Commission for Community Learning Centers, City of Boston, MA.

Friedel, R., & Israel, P. (1986). *Edison's electric light: Biography of an invention.* New Brunswick, NJ: Rutgers University Press.

Friedrich, J. (1993). Primary error detection and minimization (PEDIM) strategies in social cognition: A reinterpretation of confirmation bias phenomena. *Psychological Review 100*(2), 298–319.

Fritz, P., and Weaver, R. (1986). Teaching critical thinking skills in the basic speaking course: A liberal arts perspective. *Communication Education, 35*(2), 174–182.

Fry, E., Polk, J., & Fountoukidis, D. L. (1984). *The reading teacher's book of lists.* Englewood Cliffs, NJ: Prentice-Hall.

Fuchs-Beauchamp, K., Karnes, M., & Johnson, L. (1993). Creativity and intelligence in preschoolers. *Gifted Child Quarterly, 37*(3), 113–117.

Gagne, F. (1997). Critique of Morelock's definition of giftedness and talent. *Roeper Review, 20*(2), 76–85.

Gallagher, J. J. (1975). *Teaching the gifted child* (2nd ed.). Boston, MA: Allyn & Bacon.

Gallagher, S. A., & Stepien, W. J. (1996). Content acquisition in problem-based learning: Depth versus breadth in American studies. *Journal for the Education of the Gifted, 19*, 257–275.

Gardner, H. (1973). *The arts and human development: A psychological study of the artistic process.* New York, NY: John Wiley and Sons.

Gardner, H. (1982). *Art, mind, and brain.* New York: Basic Books.

Gardner, H. (1983). *Frames of mind: The theory of multiple intelligences.* New York: Basic Books.

Gardner, H. (1985a). *Frames of mind* (2nd ed.). New York: Basic Books.

Gardner, H. (1985b). Towards a theory of dramatic intelligence. In J. Kase-Polisini, (Ed.), *Creative drama in a developmental context*. New York: University Press of America.

Gardner, H. (1993a). *Creating minds: An anatomy of creativity seen through the lives of Freud, Einstein, Picasso, Stavinsky, Eliot, Graham, and Gandhi*. New York: Basic Books.

Gardner, H. (1993b) *Multiple intelligences: The theory in practice*. New York: Harper Collins.

Gardner, H. (1993c). Seven creators of the modern era. In J. Brockman (Ed.), *Creativity* (Ch. 2, pp. 28–47). New York: Touchstone.

Gardner, H. (1998). "MI [Multiple Intelligence]: Intelligence, understanding, and the mind." (Video). Available from Into the Classroom Media, 10573 W. Pico Blvd. #162, Los Angeles, CA 90064.

Gehret, J. (1997a). Brilliant and out of step: The gifted child with learning disabilities. *The Journal of the Learning Disabilities Association of Massachusetts* (Part One), 7(3), 1–3.

Gehret, J. (1997b). Brilliant and out of step: The gifted child with learning disabilities. *The Journal of the Learning Disabilities Association of Massachusetts* (Part Two), 7(4), 1–4.

Gehring, W., Goss, B., Michael, G., Meyer, D., et al. (1993). A neural system for error detection and composition. *Psychological Science, 4*(6), 385–390.

Gentry, M. L. (1996). *Ability grouping: An investigation of student achievement, identification, and classroom practices*. Unpublished doctoral dissertation, University of Connecticut.

Getzels, J., & Csikszentmihalyi, M. (1976). *The creative vision: A longitudinal study of problem finding in art*. New York: Wiley.

Getzels, J. W., & Jackson, P. W. (1959). The highly intelligent and the highly creative adolescent: A summary of some research findings. In C. Taylor, *The third (1959) University of Utah research conference on the identification of creative scientific talent*. Salt Lake City, UT: University of Utah Press.

Getzels, J. W., & Jackson, P. W. (1962). *Creativity and intelligence*. New York: John Wiley.

Gilmore, S. (1973, February). Group processes in educational drama: Report of a pilot study. *Educational Review, 25*(2), 106–111.

Goffin, S. G. (1988). Putting our advocacy efforts into a new context. *The Journal of the National Association for the Education of Young Children,* March, 43(3), 52–56.

Goldberg, M. (1997). *Arts and learning: An integrated approach to teaching and learning in multicultural and multilingual settings*. New York: Addison-Wesley, Longman.

Goldberg, R., and Keller, C. (1979). *The Best of Rube Goldberg*. Englewood Cliffs, NJ: Prentice Hall.

Goldhaber, M. H. (1997, December). Attention shoppers: A radical theory of value. *Wired,* 182–190.

Goldstein, K. (1939). *The organism*. New York: American Book.

Goldwyn, S. (1952). *Hans Christian Andersen* (video). Written by M. Hart; words and music by F. Loesser.

Goodman, Y., & Burke, C. (1970). *Reading miscue inventory*. New York: Macmillan.

Gordon, D. E., Derek, E., & Stoner, S. D. (1995). Beyond enhancement: The Kennedy Center's commitment to education. *Arts Education Policy Review, 96*(4), 38–47.

Gordon, W. J. J. (1960). *Synectics*. New York: Harper & Row.

Gorman, M. E., & Plucker, J. (in press). Teaching invention as critical creative processes: A course on technoscientific creativity. In M. A. Runco (Ed.), *Critical creative processes*. Norwood, NJ: Ablex.

Gorman, M. E., Plucker, J., & Callahan, C. M. (1998). Turning students into inventors: Active learning modules for secondary students. *Phi Delta Kappan, 79*(7), 530–535.

Goulden, S. (1962). *The royal book of ballet*. Chicago: Follett.

Govindarajan, G., & Wright, E. (1994). Using minds on scientific discrepant events to motivate disinterested students worldwide. *Science Education International, 5*(2), 17–20.

Gratz, E., & Pulley, J. L. (1984). A gifted and talented program for migrant students. *Roeper Review, 6*(3), 147–149.

Gray, W. S. (1915). *Standard oral reading paragraphs*. Bloomington, IL: Public School Publishing Co.

Greenberg, M. (1979). *Your children need music*. Englewood Cliffs, NJ: Prentice-Hall.

Greenspan, S. I. (1995). *The challenging child: Understanding, raising, and enjoying the five "difficult" types of children*. Reading, MA: Addison Wesley.

Gresham, F., & Macmillan, D. (1997). Social competence and affective characteristics of students with mild disabilities. *Review of educational research, 67*(4), 377–415.

Gruber, H. E. (1982). On the hypothesized relation between giftedness and creativity. *New Directions for Child Development, 17*, 7–30.

Gruber, H. E. (1993). Aspects of scientific discovery: Aesthetics and cognition. In J. Brockman (Ed.), *Creativity* (Ch. 3, pp. 48–74). New York: Touchstone.

Gruber, H. E., & Davis, S. (1988). Inching our way up Mount Olympus: The evolving-systems approach to creative thinking. In R. Sternberg (Ed.), *The nature of creativity* (Ch. 10, pp. 243–270). New York: Cambridge University Press.

Guilford, J. P. (1950). Creativity. *American Psychologist, 5*, 444–454.

Guilford, J. P. (1956). Structure of the intellect. *Psychological Bulletin, 53*, 267–293.

Guilford, J. P. (1959). Traits of creativity. In H. H. Anderson (Ed.), *Creativity and its cultivation* (Ch. 10, pp. 142–161). New York: Harper & Row.

Guilford, J. P. (1967). *The nature of human intelligence*. New York: McGraw-Hill.

Guilford, J. P. (1986). *Creative talents: Their nature, uses and development*. Buffalo, NY: Bearly Limited.

Haaga, A. (1995). Winifred Ward: Voice of the future. *Stage of the Art, 7*(4), 21–24.

Haeger, W. W., & Feldhusen, J. F. (1989). *Developing a mentor program*. East Aurora, NY: DOK Publishers.

Haley, G. L. (1987). Creative response styles: The effects of socioeconomic status and problem-solving training. *Journal of Creative Behavior, 18*(1), 25–40.

Hamer, D. H. (1997). The search for personality genes: Adventures of a molecular biologist. *Current Directions in Psychological Science, 6*, 111–114.

Hamilton, E., & Cairns, H. (Eds.). (1996). (16th printing). Plato: The collected dialogues. Princeton, NJ: Princeton University Press.

Harris, C. R. (1985). A multidisciplinary approach to poetry for the gifted child in grades 4, 5, and 6. *G/C/T Magazine, 40*, 35–42.

Harris, C. R. (1988, April). *Cultural conflict and patterns of achievement in gifted Asian-Pacific children*. Paper presented at the meeting of the National Association for Asian and Pacific American Education.

Harris, C. R. (1990). The performing arts problem-solving pyramid. In S. Bailey, E. Bragett, & M. Robinson (Eds.), *The challenge of excellence: 'A vision splendid.'* Selected papers from the Eighth World Conference on Gifted and Talented Children (pp. 85–94). Melbourne, Australia: Barker & Co.

Harris, C. R. (1991a). Identifying and serving the gifted new immigrant: Problems, strategies, implications. *Teaching Exceptional Children, 23*(4), 16–30.

Harris, C. R. (1991b). Looking back, looking forward: Catch me a poem. *The Gifted Child Today, 14*(1), 2–5.

Harris, C. R. (1995a). Identifying and serving the gifted new immigrant: Problems, strategies. In K. M. Cauley, F. Linder, & J. H. McMillan (Eds.), *Educational Psychology, Annual Edition*. Guilford, CT: Dushkin Publishing Group, Inc. (Original work published 1991.)

Harris, C. R. (1995b, Fall). Developing creativity for third world gifted: A Head Start experiment. *Gifted and Talented International*. West Lafayette, IN.

Harris, C. R. (1996). Curriculum Unit I - Sense-Directed Writing. (Available from C. R. Harris, G.A.T.E.S. Research & Evaluation, 600 Main Street, Winchester, MA 01890).

Harris, C. R. (1997, March). *Identifying the gifted new Asian immigrant/refugee: problems, strategies, implications*. Paper presented at the Annual meeting of the National Association for Asian and Pacific American Education, Boston, MA.

Hausfather, S. J. (1992, November/December). It's time for a conceptual change: A flexible approach leads to understanding. *Science and Children,* 22–23.

Haydn, J. (1793). *Twelve Pieces for the Musical Clock.*

Heathcote, D., & Bolton, G. (1994). *Drama for learning: Dorothy Heathcote's mantle of the expert approach to education.* New York: McGraw-Hill.

Heinzen, T. (1989). On moderate challenge increasing ideational creativity. *Creativity Research Journal.*

Helson, R. (1983). Creative mathematicians. In R. Albert (Ed.), *Genius and eminence: The social psychology of creativity and exceptional achievement* (pp. 211–230). London: Pergamon Press.

Hennessey, B. A. (1997). Teaching for creative development: A social-psychological approach. In N. Colangelo & G. A. Davis (Eds.), *Handbook of gifted education* (Ch. 23, pp. 282–291). Boston: Allyn & Bacon.

Hennessey, B. A., & Amabile, T. M. (1988a). The conditions of creativity. In R. Sternberg (Ed.), *The nature of creativity* (Ch. 1, pp. 11–42). New York: Cambridge University Press.

Hennesssey, B. A. & Amabile, T. (1988b). Storytelling: A method for assessing children's creativity. *Journal of Creative Behavior, 22,* 235–246.

Hennessey, B. A. & Amabile, T. M. (1997). A social-psychological approach. In N. Colangelo & G. Davis (Eds.), *Handbook of Gifted Education* (2nd ed., pp. 282–291). Boston: Allyn & Bacon.

Herrnstein, R., & Murray, C. (1994). *The bell curve: Intelligence and class structure in American life.* New York: Free Press.

Hesse, K. (1996). *The music of dolphins.* New York: Scholastic Press.

Hilgard, E. R. (1959). Creativity and problem solving. In H. H. Anderson (Ed.), *Creativity and its cultivation* (Ch. 11, pp. 162–180). New York: Harper & Row.

Hillman, J. (1996). *The soul's code: In search of character and calling.* New York: Random House.

Hirshfield, J. (1997). *Nine gates: Entering the mind of poetry.* New York: HarperCollins.

Holt, J. (1964). *How children fail.* New York: Pitman.

Howe, F., & Lauter, P. (1972). How the school system is rigged for failure. In R. C. Edwards, M.

Reich, & T. E. Weisskopf (Eds.), *The Capitalist System.* Englewood Cliffs, NJ: Prentice Hall.

Hunsaker, S. L., & Callahan, C. (1995). Creativity and giftedness: Instrument uses and abuses. *Gifted Child Quarterly, 29*(2), 110–114.

Hurwitz, A., & Goddard, A. (1969). *Games to improve your child's English* (pp. 171–172). New York: Simon and Schuster.

Iran-Nejad, A. (1990). Active and dynamic self-regulation of learning process. *Review of Educational Research, 60*(4), 573–602.

Isaksen, S. G., Dorval, K. B., & Treffinger, D. J. (1991). *Creative approaches to problem solving.* Dubuque, IA: Kendall-Hunt.

Isaksen, S. G., & Treffinger, D. J. (1985). *Creative thinking and problem solving: The basic course.* Buffalo, NY: Bearly Limited.

Isenberg, J., & Jalongo, M. R. (1993). *Creative expression and play in the early childhood curriculum.* New York: Macmillan.

Ives, B. (1950). *Sarah the whale.* Columbia Records, NY.

Jamison, K. R. (1993). *Touched with fire: Manic depressive illness and the artistic temperament.* New York: Free Press.

Jamison, K. R. (1995). *An unquiet mind: A memoir of moods and madness.* New York: Vintage Books.

Jamison, K. R. (1995, February). Manic-depressive illness and creativity. *Scientific American,* 62–67.

Jung, C. G. (1965). *Memories, dreams, reflections.* New York: Vintage.

Jung, C. G. (1976). On the relation of analytical psychology to poetic art. In A. Rothenberg & C. Hausman (Eds.), *The creativity question* (pp. 120–126). Durham, NC: Duke University Press. (Original work published 1923.)

Keller, C. (1944). *The best of Rube Goldberg.* Englewood Cliffs, NJ: Prentice-Hall.

Khatena, J. (1982). *Educational psychology of the gifted.* New York: John Wiley & Sons.

Koch, K. (1970). *Wishes, lies and dreams.* New York: Vintage Books.

Koch, K. (1974). *Rose, where did you get that red?* New York: Random House.

Koch, K., & Farrell, K. (1985). *Talking to the sun: An illustrated anthology of poems for young people.* New York: Metropolitan Museum of Art; Holt, Rinehart and Winston.

Koestler, A. (1964). *The act of creation*. New York: Macmillan.

Kogan, J. (1987). *Nothing but the best: The struggle for perfection at the Juilliard School*. New York: Random House.

Kozol, J. (1967). *Death at an early age*. Boston: Houghton Mifflin.

Kuwuhara, Y. (1997, March). *Interactions of identity: Indochinese refugee youths, language use, and schooling*. Paper presented at the meeting of the American Educational Research Association, Chicago.

Langstaff, J., & Mayer, E. L. (1995). *Music makes a difference: Making music with children: Why it matters*. Berkeley, CA: Langstaff Video Project.

Laswell, H. (1959). The social setting of creativity. In H. H. Anderson (Ed.), *Creativity and its cultivation* (Ch. 13, pp. 203–221). New York, NY: Harper & Row.

Lave, J. (1988). *Cognition in practice*. New York: Cambridge University Press.

Leavitt, D. (1990). *A place I've never been*. New York: Viking.

Leavitt, D. (1997). *Arkansas: Three novellas*. Boston: Houghton Mifflin.

Lehmkuhl, D., & Cotter-Lamping, D. (1993). *Organizing for the creative person*. New York: Crown.

Levin, H. (1957). Understanding the reading process. *Report of the 31st educational conference* (pp. 127–133). New York: Educational Research Bureau.

Levin, J. (1993). Misery as a turning point for academic success. *Journal of Research in Education, 3*(1), 3–6.

Levin, J. (1996). *Sociological snapshots*. Thousand Oaks, CA: Pine Forge Press.

Levin, J., & Levin, W. C. (1991). Sociology of educational late blooming, *Sociological Forum, 6*(4), 661–680.

Loeb, K. (1975). Our women artist/teachers need our help: On changing language, finding cultural heritage, and building self image. *Art Education, 18*, 10.

Lueders, E., & St. John, P. (1976). *Zero makes me hungry: A collection of poems for today*. Glenview, IL: Scott, Foresman and Company.

Lynch, M. D. (1997). *The effects of creativity and gender on elementary grade level childrens' patterns of self-esteem, reactive curiosity, identification, empathy and anxiety*. Paper presented at the meeting of the Eastern Educational Research Association, Hilton Head, SC.

Lynch, M. D., & Edwards, T. (1974). The Miniscat: Its development and some evidence of its validity. *Educational & Psychological Measurement, 34*, 397–405.

Lynch, M. D., Harris, C. R., & Williams, E. (1997). *Stimulating performance of creatively gifted children through the use of refutational processes: Some preliminary thoughts*. Paper presented at the meeting of the National Association for Gifted Children, Little Rock, AR.

Lynch, M. D., & Kaufman, M. (1974). Creativeness: Its meaning and measurement. *J. of Reading Behavior, 12*(4), 375–394.

Lynch, M. D., & Lynch, C. L. (1996). Affective responses of seventh and eighth graders to homogeneous ability grouping. *J. of the Proceedings of the National Social Science Association, 8*(2), 114–129.

Lynch, M. D., & Nottingham, W. (1975). *Developmental differences in detail orientation of high as opposed to low creative children grades 1–8*. Paper presented at the meeting of the Eastern Educational Research Association, Hilton Head, SC.

Lynch, M. D., Scotti, R., & Rindler, S. (July, 1973). *Instructional modes and methods of testing creativity*. Presented at the meeting of the international symposium on testing. The Hague, Netherlands.

MacKinnon, D. W. (1961). Creativity in architects. In D. W. MacKinnon (Ed.), *The creative person* (pp. 291–320). Berkeley: University of California Press.

MacKinnon, D. W. (1962). The nature and nurture of creative talent. *American Psychologist, 17*, 484–495.

MacKinnon, D. W. (1968). Creativity and images of the self. In R. W. White (Ed.), *The study of lives* (Ch. 11, pp. 250–279). New York, NY: Atherton.

MacKinnon, D. W. (1975). IPAR's contribution to the conceptualization and study of creativity. In I. A. Taylor & J. W. Getzeks (Eds.). *Perspectives in Creativity*. Chicago, IL: Aldine Publishing Co. 60–79.

MacKinnon, D. W. (1978a). Educating for creativity: A modern myth? In G. A. Davis & J. A. Scott (Eds.), *Training creative thinking*. (pp. 194–207). Melbourne, FL: Krieger.

MacKinnon, D. W. (1978b). *In search of human effectiveness: Identifying and developing creativity*. Buffalo, NY: Bearly Limited.

Maker, C. J. (1982). *Curriculum development for the gifted*. Austin, TX: Pro-Ed.

Maltzman, I. (1960). On the meaning of originality. *Psychological Review, 4*(67), 229–242.

Maria, K., & Johnson, J. (1990). Correcting misconceptions: Effect of type of text. *National Reading Conference Yearbook, 39*, 329–337.

Maria, K., & MacGinitie, W. (1987). Learning from texts that refute the reader's prior knowledge. *Reading Research and Instruction, 26*(4), 222–238.

Marland, S. P. (1972). *Education of the gifted and talented: Vol. 1, Report to the Congress of the United States by the U.S. Commissioner of Education*. Washington, DC: U.S. Government Printing Office.

Martindale, C. (1989). Personality, situation and creativity. In J. A. Glover, R. R. Ronning, and C. R. Reynolds (Eds.), *Handbook of creativity* (pp. 211–232). New York: Plenum Press.

Maslow, A. H. (1954). *Motivation and personality*. New York: Harper & Row.

Maslow, A. H. (1959). Creativity in self-actualizing people. In H. H. Anderson (Ed.), *Creativity and its cultivation*. (Ch. 7, pp. 83–95). New York: Harper & Row.

Massey, J., & Koziol, S., Jr. (1978, February). Research on creative dramatics. *English Journal.*

Masson, M. (1990). Cognitive theories of skill acquisition. *Human Movement Science, 9*(3–5), 221–239.

Matlin, M. W. (1998). *Cognition* (4th ed.). Fort Worth, TX: Harcourt Brace.

May, R. (1959). The nature of creativity. In H. H. Anderson (Ed.), *Creativity and its cultivation* (Ch. 5, pp. 55–68). New York: Harper & Row.

McClelland, D. C. (1958). Risk taking in children with high and low need for achievement. In J. W. Atkinson (Ed.), *Motives in fantasy, action and society* (p. 154) Princeton, NJ: Van Nostrand.

McClelland, D. C., Atkinson, J. W., & Clark, R. A. (1953). *The achievement motive*. New York: Appleton Century Crofts.

McCue, F. (1997). *The poet in the warehouse. Creative writing as inquiry: Using imaginative writing to explore other disciplines*. Unpublished master's project, Columbia University.

McGuire, W. (1961). Resistance to persuasion conferred by active and passive prior refutation of the same and alternative counterarguments. *JASP, 63*(2), 326–332.

McGuire, W., & Papageorgis, D. (1961). The relative efficacy of various types of prior belief-defense in producing immunity against persuasion. *JASP, 62*(2), 327–337.

McNemar, Q. (1964). Lost: Our intelligence? Why? *American Psychologist*, 871–882.

McPherson, G. E. (1997). Giftedness and talent in music. *Journal of Aesthetic Education, 21*(4), 65–77.

McWilliams, C. (1973). In C. Bulosan, *America is in the heart*. Seattle: University of Washington Press, 1988.

Mednick, S. A. (1962). The associative basis of the creative process. *Psychological Review, 42*, 219–245.

Mednick, S. A., & Mednick, M. J. (1967). *Examiners manual: Remote Associates Test*. Boston: Houghton Mifflin.

Meeker, M. (1990). *The freedom of creativity: A handbook for stimulating creative thinking*. Vida, OR: SOI Systems.

Menlo, A. (1987). Everyday truths and effective school administration. *International Schools Journal, 14*, 23–31.

Miller, A. (1997). *Drama of the gifted child*. New York: Doubleday.

Millward, P. (1996). Children constructing dramatic contexts. *Current Issues in Language and Society, 3*(1), 65–81.

Moll, L. C. (Ed.). (1990). *Vygotsky and education: Instructional implications and applications of sociohistorical psychology*. New York: Cambridge University Press.

Montage, A. (1974). *Man's most dangerous myth: The fallacy of race* (5th ed.). New York: Oxford University Press.

Montanaro, T., & Montanaro, K. H. (1995). *Mime spoken here: The performer's portable workshop*. Gardiner, ME: Tilbury House.

Mosaic. South Boston High School Annual Journal of Student Writings.

Mumford, M. D., Connely, M. S., Baughman, W. A., & Marks, M. A. (1994). Creativity and problem solving: Cognition, adaptability, and wisdom. *Roeper Review, 16*(4), 241–246.

Myers, M. P. (1997–98, December/January). Passion for poetry. *Journal of Adolescent and Adult Literacy, 41*(4), 262–271.

National Coalition of Advocates for Students. (1988). *New Voices, immigrant voices in U.S. public schools*. (Research Rep. No 1988-1). Boston, MA: Author.

National Indochinese Clearinghouse, Center for Applied Linguistics, (1976). *A manual for Indochinese refugee education 1976–1977*. San Francisco: Author.

Navarre, J. Piirto. (1978). *A study of creativity in poets*. Paper presented at National Association for Gifted Children Conference, Houston, TX.

Neave, G. (1985). France. In B. R. Clark (Ed.). *The school and the university: An educational perspective*. Berkeley: University of California Press, 10–44.

Nevai, L. (1997). *Normal*. Chapel Hill, NC: Algonquin Books of Chapel Hill.

Nunn, T. (1983). Tales of two cities. In Nunn, T. (Ed.). *Cats, the book of the musical*. New York: Harcourt Brace Jovanovich.

Ogbu, J. (1994). Understanding cultural diversity and learning. *Journal for Education of the Gifted, 17*(4), 355–383.

Ogbu, K. I. (1978). *Minority education and caste: The American system in cross-cultural perspective*. New York: Academic Press.

Olenchak, F. R., & Renzulli, J. S. (1989). The effectiveness of the schoolwide enrichment model on selected aspects of elementary school change. *Gifted Child Quarterly, 33*(l), 36–46.

O'Neill, M., & Weisgard, L. (1961). *Hailstones and halibut bones*. Garden City, NY: Doubleday.

Osborn, A. F. (1957). *Applied imagination: Principals and procedures of creative thinking*. New York: Scribner.

Osin, L., & Lesgold, A. (1996). A proposal for reengineering of the educational system. *Review of Educational Research, 66*(4), 621–656.

Pappert, S. (1996). Private conversation at the meeting of the Eastern Educational Research Association, Cambridge, MA.

Pariser, D. (1997). Conceptions of children's artistic giftedness from modern and postmodern perspectives. *Journal of Aesthetic Education, 21*(4), 35–47.

Parnes, S. J. (1987). The creative studies project. In S. G. Isaksen (Ed.), *Frontiers of creative research* (pp. 156–188). Buffalo, NY: Bearly Limited.

Pearpoint, J., Forest, M., & O'Brien, J. (1996). MAPs, Circles of Friends, and PATH: Powerful tools to help build caring communities. In S. Stainback & W. Stainback (Eds.), *Inclusion: A guide for educators* (pp. 68–71). Baltimore: Paul H. Brookes.

Pellerite, J. J. (1978). *A handbook of literature for the flute*. Bloomington, IN: Zalo Publications.

Perkins, D. N. (1981). *The mind's best work*. Cambridge: Harvard University Press.

Perkins, D. N. (1995). *Smart schools*. New York: Free Press.

Philips, W. C. (1991). Earth science misconceptions: You must identify what they are before you can try to correct them. *The Science Teacher, 21*–23.

Phillips, A. (1995). *Inclusive autism support teams: Lessons for interprofessionals*. Roundtable for the annual meeting of the American Educational Research Association, San Francisco.

Phillips, A. (1997a). Developing partners to build urban community: An interprofessional undergraduate program for elementary and early childhood educators and social and health care workers. In P. Murrell (Chair), *The future of teacher preparation for culturally diverse urban schools and communities: Lessons from innovative programs*. Symposium conducted at the annual meeting of the American Educational Research Association, Chicago.

Phillips, A. (1997b). Unpublished results of poll of 18 college-educated adults, taken during October and November.

Piaget, J. (1948). *The moral judgment of the child*. New York: Free Press.

Piaget, J. (1952). *The origins of intelligence in children*. New York: International University Press.

Piirto, J. (1989a). Does writing prodigy exist? *Creativity Research Journal, 2,* 134–135.

Piirto, J. (1989b). Linguistic prodigy: Does it exist? *Gifted Children Monthly,* 1–2.

Piirto, J. (1990). Profiles of creative adolescents. *Understanding Our Gifted, 2*, 1.

Piirto, J. (1991a). Encouraging creativity and talent in adolescents. In M. Bireley & J. Genshaft (Eds.), *Gifted and talented adolescents* (pp. 104–122). New York: Teachers College Press.

Piirto, J. (1991b). Why are there so few? (Creative women: mathematicians, visual artists, musicians). *Roeper Review, 13*(3), 142–147.

Piirto, J. (1994). A few thoughts on actors. *Spotlight: Newsletter of the Visual and Performing Arts*. National Association for Gifted Children, 4(1), 2–5.

Piirto, J. (1995a). Deeper, wider, broader: The pyramid of talent development in the context of the giftedness construct. *Educational Forum, 59*(4), 363–371. Guest editor: J. Feldhusen.

Piirto, J. (1995b). Predictive behaviors and crystallizing experiences in male college student artists. *Spotlight: Newsletter of the NAGC Visual and Performing Arts SIG*.

Piirto, J. (1996). Why does a writer write? Because. *Advanced Development, 7*, 15–35.

Piirto, J. (1998a, March 9). *Feeling boys and thinking girls: The Myers-Briggs Type Indicator and talented adolescents*. Paper presented at the CAPT Conference, Orlando, FL.

Piirto, J. (1998b). A survey of psychological studies of creativity. In A. Fishkin & B. Cramond, Eds., *Research into children's creativity* (pp. 34–54). Cresskill, NJ: Hampton Press.

Piirto, J. (1998c). *Understanding those who create* (2nd ed.). Scottsdale, AZ: Gifted Psychology Press.

Piirto, J., Cassone, G., Ackerman, C., & Fraas, J. (1998d). (Revision submitted.) A study of intensity in artistically talented teenagers using the Overexcitability Questionnaire (OEQ). *Gifted Child Quarterly*.

Piirto, J., & Fraas, J. (1995). Androgyny in the personalities of talented teenagers. *Journal of Secondary Gifted Education, 1*(2), 93–102. Guest editor: F. Karnes.

Piirto, J. (1999). *Talented children and adults: Their development and education* (2nd ed.). Columbus, OH: Merrill/Prentice Hall.

Piirto, J. (in preparation.) *My teeming brain: Creativity in creative writers*. Cresskill, NJ: Hampton Press. Creativity series edited by M. Runco.

Piirto, J. (in press.) Themes in the lives of women creative writers at midlife. *Roeper Review* (Special issue on creativity).

Pleiss, M. K., & Feldhusen, J. F. (1995). Mentors role models, and heroes in the lives of gifted children. *Educational psychologist, 30*(3), 159–169.

Plucker, J. A. (1996). Gifted Asian-American students: Identification, curricular, and counseling concerns. *Journal for the Education of the Gifted, 19*(3), 315–343.

Plucker, J. A. (1998). Beware of simple conclusions: The case for content generality of creativity. *Creativity Research Journal, 11*, 179–182.

Plucker, J. A. (1999). Reanalyses of student responses to creativity checklists: Evidence of content generality. *Journal of Creative Behavior, 33*, 126–137.

Plucker, J., & Gorman, M. E. (1995). Group interaction during a summer course on invention and design for high ability secondary students. *The Journal of Secondary Gifted Education, 6*, 258–272.

Plucker, J., & Gorman, M. E. (1996). Teaching invention to gifted students. *Tempo: Journal of the Texas Association for the Gifted and Talented, 16*, 10–12.

Plucker, J., & Gorman, M. E. (1999). Invention is in the mind of the adolescent: Evaluation of a summer course one year later. *Creativity Research Journal, 12*, 141–150.

Plucker, J. A., & Runco, M. A. (1999). Enhancement of creativity. In M. A. Runco & S. Pritzker (Eds.), *Encyclopedia of creativity*. pp. 669–675. San Diego, CA: Academic Press.

Plumb, C., Butterfield, E., Hacker, D., & Dunlosky, J. (1994). Error correction in text: Testing the processing-deficit and knowledge-deficit hypotheses. *Reading and Writing, 6*(4), 347–360.

Poetry Supplement. (1978). *N/S-LTI-G/T Bulletin*, Ventura, CA, 1–2.

Pool, C. R. (1997). Brain-based learning and students. *Educational Leadership, 54*, 11–15.

Poplin, M. S., & Wright, P. (1983). The concept of cultural pluralism: Issues in special education. *Learning Disability Quarterly, 6*(4), 367–372.

Portes, A., McLeod, S. A., Jr., & Parker, R. N. (1978). Immigrant aspirations. *Sociology of Education, 51,* October, 241–260.

Prakash, M. S., & Waks, L. J. (1985). Four conceptions of excellence. *Teachers College Record, 87*(1).

Pressley, M., Borkowski, J. G., & Schneider, W. (1989). Good information processing: What it is and how education can promote it. *International Journal of Educational Research, 13,* 857–867.

Prokofiev, S. (1936). *Peter and the Wolf.*

Prokofiev, S. (1944). *Cinderella.*

Purkey, W. (1978). *Inviting school success: A self-concept approach to teaching and learning.* Belmont, CA: Wadsworth.

Ramirez, B. A. (1988). Culturally and linguistically diverse children. *Teaching Exceptional Children.* Summer, 45–51.

Ramirez, M. III, & Castenada, A. (1974). *Cultural democracy, bicognitive development, and education.* New York: Academic Press.

Ratliff, G. L. (1997). *Classroom "role-playing": A basic blueprint for performance.* Paper presented at the annual meeting of the National Communication Association, Chicago.

Reed, J. (1977). *The best little boy in the world.* NY: Ballantine Books.

Reinert, O. (1964). *Drama.* Boston: Little, Brown.

Reis, S. M., Bums, D. E., & Renzulli, J. S. (1992). *Curriculum compacting: The complete guide to modifying the regular curriculum for high ability students.* Mansfield Center, CT: Creative Learning Press.

Reis, S. M., Neu, T. W., & McGuire, J. M. (1995, January). *Talent in two places: Case studies of high ability students with learning disabilities who have achieved.* Storrs, CT: National Research Center on the Gifted and Talented, University of Connecticut.

Renzulli, J. S. (1976). The enrichment triad model: A guide for developing defensible programs for the gifted and talented. *Gifted Child Quarterly, 20,* 303–326.

Renzulli, J. S. (1977). *The enrichment triad model: A guide for developing defensible programs for the*
gifted and talented. Mansfield Center, CT: Creative Learning Press.

Renzulli, J. S. (1978). What makes giftedness? *Phi Delta Kappan, 60*(3), 180–184, 261.

Renzulli, J. S. (1986). The three ring conception of giftedness: A developmental model for creative productivity. In R. J. Sternberg & J. E. Davidson (Eds.), *Conceptions of giftedness* (pp. 53–92, 332–357). New York: Cambridge University Press.

Renzulli, J. S. (1994). *Schools for talent development: A practical plan for total school improvement.* Mansfield Center, CT: Creative Learning Press.

Renzulli, J. S. (1997). *The Enrichment Triad.* Mansfield, CT: Creative Learning Press.

Renzulli, J. S., & Reis, S. M. (1985). *The Schoolwide Enrichment Model: A comprehensive plan for educational excellence.* Mansfield Center, CT: Creative Learning Press.

Renzulli, J. S., & Reis, S. M. (1986). The enrichment triad/revolving door model: A schoolwide plan for the development of creative productivity. In J. S. Renzulli (Ed.), *Systems and models for developing programs for the gifted and talented* (pp. 216–266). Mansfield Center, CT: Creative Learning Press.

Renzulli, J. S., & Reis, S. M. (1991). The reform movement and the quiet crisis in gifted education. *Gifted Child Quarterly, 35*(1), 26–35.

Renzulli, J. S., & Reis, S. M. (1994). Research related to the Schoolwide Enrichment Model. *Gifted Child Quarterly, 38,* 2–14.

Renzulli J. S., & Reis, S. M. (1997). *The Schoolwide Enrichment Model: A how-to guide for educational excellence* (2nd ed.). Mansfield Center, CT: Creative Learning Press.

Renzulli, J. S., & Reis, S. M. (1997). The Schoolwide Enrichment Model: New directions for developing high-end learning. In N. Colangelo & G. A. Davis (Eds.), *Handbook of gifted education* (Ch. 11, pp. 136–154). Boston: Allyn & Bacon.

Renzulli, J. S., Reis, S. M., & Smith, L. H. (1981). *The revolving door identification model.* Mansfield Center, CT: Creative Learning Press.

Renzulli, J. S., & Smith, L. H. (1978). *The compactor.* Mansfield Center, CT: Creative Learning Press.

Resnick, L. B. (1987). *Education and learning to think*. Washington, DC: National Academy Press.

Reyes, L. (1988). The challenge. In *New voices, immigrant voices in U.S. public schools*. National Coalition of Advocates for Students. (Research Rep. No. 1988-1). Boston, MA.

Reynolds, F. C. (1990). Mentoring artistic adolescents through expressive therapy. *Clearing House, 64*, 83–86.

Reynolds, F. C. (1997, July 13). *Reifying creativity during the adolescent passage*. Paper presented at Ashland University Ohio Summer Institute.

Rimm, S. B. (1980). *GIFT, group inventory for finding creative talent*. Watertown, WI: Educational Assessment Service.

Rimm, S. B. (1981). *PRIDE, preschool interest descriptor*. Watertown, WI: Educational Assessment Service.

Rimm, S., & Culbertson, F. (1980). Validation of GIFT, an instrument for the identification of creativity. *Journal of Creative Behavior, 14*(4), 272–273.

Rimm, S. B., & Davis, G. A. (1976). GIFT: An instrument for the identification of creativity. *Journal of Creative Behavior, 10*(3), 178–182.

Rimm, S., & Davis, G. A. (1980). Five years of international research with GIFT: An instrument for the identification of creativity. *Journal of Creative Behavior, 14*(1), 35–46.

Rimm, S., & Davis, G. A. (1985). *Education of the gifted and talented*. Englewood Cliffs, NJ: Prentice-Hall.

Rimm, S. B., Davis, G. A., & Bien, Y. (1982). Identifying creativity: A characteristics approach. *Gifted Child Quarterly, 26*(4).

Rimsky-Korsakov. (1902) *Flight of the Bumblebee*.

Robertson, J. (1997, April). Poetry in science. *Voices from the Middle, 4*(2), 7–10.

Rogal, M. (1996). Grace under pressure: Student performers tackle tough issues. *Teaching Theatre, 7*(3), 1–2, 10–13.

Rogers, C. (1959). Toward a theory of creativity. In H. H. Anderson (Ed.). *Creativity and its cultivation* (Ch. 6, pp. 69–82). New York: Harper & Row.

Rosenthal, R., & Jacobsen, L. (1968). *Pygmalion in the classroom*. New York: Holt.

Rubin, J., & Merrion, M. (1995). *Drama and music: Creative activities for young children*. Atlanta: Humanics Learning.

Runco, M. (1993). *Creativity as an educational objective for disadvantaged students*. (No. 9306). Storrs, CT: National Research Center on the Gifted and Talented.

Runco, M., & Nemiro, J. (1993). Problem finding and problem solving. *Roeper Review, 6*(4), 235–241.

Runco, M. A., & Okuda, S. M. (1991). The instructional enhancement of the flexibility and originality scores of divergent thinking tests. *Applied Cognitive Psychology, 5*, 435–441.

Savoie, J. M., & Hughes, A. S. (1994). Problem-based learning as classroom solutions. *Educational Leadership, 52*(3), 54–57.

Savery, J. R., & Duffy, T. M. (1995). Problem-based learning: An instructional model and its constructivist framework. *Educational Technology, 35*(5), 31–38.

Schechner, R. (1977). *Essays on performance theory (1970–1976)*. New York: Drama Book Publishers.

Schulkind, C. M. (1972). *Around me*. Port Jefferson, NY: Poetry Mini-Unit, Scraggy Hill School.

Schulkind, C. M. (1974). Interdisciplinary approaches to teaching poetry to the elementary school child. *The English Record,* National Council of Teachers of English, 8–14.

Schulkind, C. M. (1975). Shoebox poetry. *Smithtown Arts Review, 9*, 16.

Schulkind, C. M. (1978a). Creative writing: Sound-sense training. In M. Landis (Ed.), *The class menagerie: A compilation of exciting activities for secondary school students* (p. 95). Lincoln, NE: Nebraska State Department of Education.

Schulkind, C. M. (1978b). Poetry is alive again. In poetry supplement, *N/S-LTI-G/T Bulletin*, Ventura, CA, 1–2.

Schulkind, C. M., & Baskin, B. (1973). Impaled on a wild entanglement of lace: Poetics for the young gifted child. *Elementary English, 50*(8) 1209–1214.

Schulkind, C. R. (Ed.). (1979). *Happy Days*. Washington, DC: U.S. Department of Education.

Schunk, D. H. (1991a). *Learning theories: An educational perspective*. New York: Macmillan.

Schunk, D. H. (1991b). Self-efficacy and academic motivation. *Educational Psychologist, 26,* 207–231.

Schunk, D. H. (1996). *Learning theories.* Englewood Cliffs, NJ: Merrill.

Selman, R. (1997, Fall). Let them eat poetry: Nourishing young poets. *Montessori Life, 9*(4), 38–39.

Shackburg, R., Shackburg, R., & Emberley, E. (1965). *Yankee Doodle.* New York: Simon and Schuster.

Shank, T. (1982). *American alternative theater.* New York: Grove Press.

Sheehy, G. (1986). *Spirit of Survival.* New York: Bantam Books.

Shekerjian, D. (1990). *Uncommon genius.* New York: Viking Press.

Sheridan, J. (Director). (1989). *My Left Foot.* [Film]. HBO Home Video.

Sierra, Z. (1997). *Children's voices through dramatic play.* Paper presented at the Annual Qualitative Analysis Conference, Toronto, Ontario, Canada, and at the annual convention of the American Psychological Association, Chicago.

Silberman, C. (1970). *Crisis in the classroom.* New York: Random House.

Silverman, L. K. (1989). Invisible gifts, invisible handicaps. *Roeper Review, 12*(1), 37–41.

Simonton, D. K. (1995). *Greatness: Who makes history and why.* New York: Guilford Press.

Slattery, P. (1995). *Curriculum development in the postmodern era.* New York: Garland.

Smith, I. C. (1976). Two girls singing. In Lueders, L., & St. John, P. *Zero makes me hungry.* Glenview, IL: Scott, Foresman.

Sperry, A. (1995). *Call it courage.* New York: Scholastic.

Starko, A. J. (1995). *Creativity in the classroom.* White Plains, NY: Longman.

Statman, M. (1998, January/February). *Teachers & Writers, 29*(3), 10–12.

Stephenson, W. (1967). *Creativity, intelligence and cleverness.* Unpublished paper, University of Missouri.

Sternberg, R. J. (1987). *Beyond IQ: A triarchic theory of human intelligence.* New York: Cambridge University Press.

Sternberg, R. J. (1988a). *The nature of creativity* (Ch. 5, pp. 125–147). New York: Cambridge University Press.

Sternberg, R. J. (1988b). A three facet model of creativity in R. J. Sternberg (Ed.), *The nature of creativity* (Ch. 12, pp. 181–202). New York: Harper & Row.

Sternberg, R. J. (1989). Domain-generality versus domain-specificity: The life and impending death of a false dichotomy. *Merrill-Palmer Quarterly, 35,* 115–130.

Sternberg, R. J. (1997). A triarchic view of giftedness: Theory and practice. In N. Colangelo and G. A. Davis (Eds.), *Handbook of gifted education* (Ch. 4, pp. 143–151). Boston: Allyn & Bacon.

Sternberg, R. J., & Williams, W. M. (1996). *How to develop student creativity.* Alexandria, VA: Association for Supervision and Curriculum Development.

Stoddard, G. (1959). Creativity in education. In H. H. Anderson (Ed.), *Creativity and its cultivation* (Ch. 12, pp. 181–202). New York: Harper & Row.

Sugai, G. & Maheady, L. (1988). Cultural diversity and individual assessment for behavior disorders. *Teaching Exceptional Children, 21*(1), 28–31.

Swan, W., & Hill, C. (1982). When our identities are mistaken: Reaffirming self-conceptions through social interaction. *JPSP, 43*(1), 59–66.

Swartz, R. J., & Perkins, D. M. (1989). *Teaching Thinking: Issues and approaches.* Pacific Grove, CA: Midwest Publications.

Swiniarski, L., & Halpern, P. A. (1998). *Teachers' use of poetry in the instruction of mathematics with various student populations as categorized by the theory of multiple intelligences.* Paper presented at the annual meeting of the Eastern Educational Research Association, Tampa, FL.

Swope, S. (1995). Changing shape and acting out. *Teachers & Writers, 27*(1), 8–11.

Szapocznik, J., Santisteban, D., Kurtines, W., Perez-Vidal, A., & Hervis, O. (1983). *Bicultural effectiveness training: A treatment intervention for enhancing intercultural adjustment in Cuban American families.* Paper presented at the Ethnicity, Acculturation and Mental Health

Among Hispanics conference. Albuquerque, New Mexico.

Tannenbaum, A. J. (1983). *Gifted children: Psychological and educational perspectives*. New York: Macmillan.

Tannenbaum, A. J., & Baldwin, L. J. (1983). Giftedness and learning disability: A paradoxical combination. In L. H. Fox, L. Brody, & D. Tobin (Eds.), *Learning disabled/gifted children: Identification and programming* (pp. 11–36). Baltimore, MD: University Park Press.

Taylor, C. W. (1978). *Teaching for talents and gifts, 1978 status*. Salt Lake City: Utah State Board of Education.

Taylor, C. W., & Barron, F. (Eds.). (1963). *Scientific creativity, its recognition and development: Selected papers from the proceedings of the first, second, and third University of Utah Conferences*. New York: John Wiley.

Taylor, C. W., Smith, W. R., & Ghiselin, B. (1963). The creative and other contributions of one sample of research scientists. In C. W. Taylor & F. Barron (Eds.), *Scientific creativity: Its recognition and development* (Ch. 5, pp. 53–76). New York: John Wiley.

Taylor, C. W., & Williams, F. E. (Eds.). (1966). *Instructional media and creativity*. New York: John Wiley.

Terman, L. M., & Merrill, M. A. (1937). *Measuring intelligence: A guide to the administration of the new Stanford Binet Tests of Intelligence*. Boston: Houghton Mifflin.

Terman, L. M., & Oden, M. H. (1947). *The gifted child grows up. Volume IV: Genetic studies of genius*. Stanford, CA: Stanford University Press.

Tingley, D. W. (1996). A dopamine receptor novelty gene. *Journal of NIH Research, 8,* 23–24.

Torrance, E. P. (1962). *Guiding creative talent*. Englewood Cliffs, NJ: Prentice Hall.

Torrance, E. P. (1966). *Torrance tests of creative thinking*. Bensonville, IL: Scholastic Testing Service.

Torrance, E. P. (1968). *Education and the creative potential*. Minneapolis: University of Minnesota Press.

Torrance, E. P. (1969). Prediction of adult creative achievement among high school seniors. *Gifted Child Quarterly, 13,* 223–229.

Torrance, E. P. (1971, April). *'I was a block and nobody builded me!'* Paper presented at the meeting of the Council on Exceptional Children, Miami Beach, FL.

Torrance, E. P. (1972). Can we teach children to think creatively? *Journal of Creative Behavior, 6,* 114–143.

Torrance, E. P. (1974). *Torrance tests of creative thinking. Norms. Technical Manual*. Bensonville, IL: Scholastic Testing Service.

Torrance, E. P. (1977). *Creativity in the classroom*. Paper presented at the meeting of the National Education Association, Washington, DC.

Torrance, E. P. (1984). The role of creativity in identification of the gifted and talented. *Gifted Child Quarterly, 28,* 153–156.

Torrance, E. P. (1987). Teaching for creativity. In S. G. Isaksen (Ed.), *Frontiers of creativity research* (pp. 189–215). Buffalo, NY: Bearly Limited.

Torrance, E. P. (1987). *The blazing drive*. Buffalo, NY: Bearly Limited.

Torrance, E. P. (1988). The nature of creativity as manifest in its testing. In R. W. Sternberg (Ed.), *The nature of creativity* (Ch. 2, pp. 43–75). New York: Cambridge University Press.

Torrance, E. P. (1990). *The Torrance tests of creative thinking: Norms. Technical manual*. Bensonville, IL. Scholastic Testing Service.

Torrance, E. P. (1997). *Torrance tests of creative thinking*. Bensonville, IL: Scholastic Testing Service.

Torrance, E. P., Goff, K., & Satterfield, N. B. (1998). *Multicultural mentoring of the gifted and talented*. Waco, TX: Prufrock Press.

Torrance, E. P., & Presbury, J. (1984). The criteria of success used in 242 recent experimental studies of creativity. *Creative Child & Adult Quarterly, 9,* 238–243.

Treffinger, D. J. (1993). Stimulating creativity: Issues and future directions. In S. G. Isaksen, M. C. Murdock, R. L. Firestein, & D. J. Treffinger (Eds.), *Nurturing and developing creativity: The emergence of a discipline* (pp. 8–27). Norwood, NJ: Ablex.

Treffinger, D. J. (1993). *International Handbook of research and development of giftedness and talent* (pp. 555–567). Oxford: Pergamon.

Treffinger, D. J., Feldhusen, J. F., & Isaksen, S. G. (1990). Organization and structure of productive thinking. *Creative Learning Today, 4*(2), 6–8.

Treffinger, D. J., Sortore, M. R., & Cross, J. A. (1993). Programs and strategies for nurturing creativity. In K. A. Heller, F. J. Monks, & A. H. Passow (Eds.), *International handbook of research and development of giftedness and talent*. Oxford: Pergamon.

Trueba, H. T. (1983). Adjustment problems of Mexican and Mexican-American students: An anthropological study. *Learning Disability Quarterly, 6*(4), 395–415.

Trueba, H. T. (1988). Culturally based explanations of minority students' academic achievement, *Anthropology & Education Quarterly, 19*, 270–287.

U.S. Bureau of the Census. (1995). *Statistical Abstract of the United States*. Washington, DC: U.S. Government Printing Office.

Van Der Veer, R., & Valsiner, J. (Eds.). (1994). *The Vygotsky reader*. Cambridge, MA: Blackwell.

Vasquez, J. A. (1988). Contexts of learning for minority students. *The Educational Forum, 6*(3), 243–253.

Vaughn, S. (1989). Gifted learning disabilities: Is it such a bright idea? *Learning Disabilities Focus, 4*(2), 123–126.

Verna, M. A. (1998, April). *The differential effects of family processes and SES on academic self-concepts and achievement of Asian American and gifted Caucasian high school students*. Paper presented at the meeting of the American Educational Research Association, San Diego, CA.

Vernon, P. E. (1970). *Creativity*. Hammondsworth, UK: Methuin.

Vernon, P. E. (1989). The nature–nurture problem in creativity. In J. Glover, R. Ronning, & C. R. Reynolds (Eds.), *Handbook of creativity* (pp. 93–110). New York: Plenum.

Vivas, E. (1955). *Creation and discovery: Essays in criticism and aesthetics*. New York: Noonday Press.

Voss, J., & Means, M. (1989). Toward a model of creativity based upon problem solving in the social sciences. In J. Glover, R. Ronning, & C. R. Reynolds (Eds), *Handbook of creativity* (pp. 399–410). New York: Plenum Press.

Vuong, V. (1988). Finding solutions. In *New voices, immigrant voices in U.S. public schools*. National Coalition of Advocates for Students. (Research Rep. No. 1988-1). Boston, MA.

Vygotsky, L. (1977). *Mind in society*. Cambridge, MA: Harvard University Press.

Vygotsky, L. (1978). *Mind in society: The development of higher mental processes*. Cambridge, MA: Harvard University Press.

Wachs, T. D. (1992). *The nature of nurturance*. Newbury Park, CA: Sage.

Wakefield, J. F. (1992). *Creative thinking: Problem solving skills and the arts orientation*. Norwood, NJ: Ablex.

Walczyk, J., & Hall, V. (1989). Is the failure to monitor comprehension an instance of cognitive impulsivity? *Journal of Educational Psychology, 81*(3), 294–298.

Wales, P. (1975, June). At sea in a circle of sound. *Sail Magazine*.

Wallach, M. A., & Kogan, N. (1965). *Modes of thinking in young children: A study of the creativity-intelligence distinction*. New York, NY: Holt.

Wallach, M. A., & Wing, C. W., Jr. (1969). *The talented student: A validation of the creativity-intelligence distinction*. New York: Holt, Rinehart and Winston.

Wei, T. (1983). The Vietnamese refugee child: Understanding cultural differences. In D. Omark & J. Erikson, (Eds.), *The Bilingual Exceptional Child*. San Diego: College Hill Press.

Wertheimer, M. (1945). *Productive thinking*. New York: Harper & Row.

White, R. W. (1959). Motivation reconsidered: The concept of competence. *Psychological Review, 66*(5), 297–333.

Wigginton, E. (1986). *Sometimes a shining moment: The Foxfire experience*. New York, NY: Doubleday.

Williams, D. (1996). *Autism: An inside-out approach*. London: Jessica Kingsley.

Wilson, E. (1994). *The theater experience* (6th ed.). New York: McGraw-Hill.

Winner, E. (1996). *Gifted children: Myths and realities*. New York: Basic Books.

Winner, E. (1997). Giftedness vs. creativity in the visual arts. *Gifted and Talented International, 12*(1), 18–26.

Winner, E., & Martino, G. (1993). Giftedness in the visual arts and music. In K. A. Heller, F. J. Monk, & A. H. Passow (Eds.), *International handbook of research and development of giftedness and talent* (pp. 253–281). New York: Pergamon.

Winters, Y. (1957). *The function of criticism.* Chicago: Swallow Press.

Wolf, D. P., & Perry, M. (1988). From endpoints to repertoires: New conclusions about drawing development. In H. Gardener & D. Perkins (Eds.), *Art, mind & education* (pp. 17–34). Urbana, IL: University of Illinois Press.

Work, Henry Clay. (1875). *Grandfather's Clock.*

Wright, C. H. (1994). The value of performing arts education in our schools. *NAASP Bulletin, 78*(561), 39–42.

Wright, E., & Govindarajan, G. (1994a). Stirring the biology pot with discrepant events. *American Biology Teacher, 54*(4), 205–210.

Wright, E., & Govindarajan, G. (1994b). *Teaching with scientific conceptual discrepancies.* Manhattan, KS: Kansas State University, College of Education.

Wright, E., & Govindarajan, G. (1995). Discrepant event demonstrations. *Science Teacher, 1,* 25–28.

York, J. (1997). Forging a partnership: Building a new generation of audiences. *Teaching Theatre, 8*(3), 1–2, 15–18, 21–22.

Zimmerman, E. (1991). Rembrandt to Rembrandt: A case study of a memorable painting teacher. *Roeper Review, 3*(2), 76–81.

Zimmerman, E. (1992a). A comparative study of two painting teachers of talented adolescents. *Studies in Art Education, 23*(2), 174–185.

Zimmerman, E. (1992b). Factors influencing the graphic development of a talented young artist. *Creativity Research Journal* (3), 295–311.

Zimmerman, E. (1994). *Making a difference: Differentiated curriculum units by teachers in the 1993 Artistically Talented Program.* Bloomington, IN: Indiana University School of Education, Art Education Program, and the Indiana Department of Education, Office of Gifted and Talented Programs.

Zimmerman, E. (1995). It was an incredible experience: The impact of educational opportunities on talented students' art development. In C. Golumb (Ed.), *The development of artistically talented children: Selected case studies* (pp. 135–170). Hillsdale, NJ: Lawrence Earlbaum.

Zimmerman, E. (1997a). Building leadership roles for teachers in art education. *Journal of Art and Design Education, 6*(3), 281–284.

Zimmerman, E. (1997b). I don't want to sit in the corner cutting out valentines: Leadership roles for teachers of talented art students. *Gifted Child Quarterly, 41*(1), 33–41.

Zuckerman, H. (1977). *The scientific elite.* New York: Free Press.

Zuckerman, M., Kolin, E. A., Price, L., & Zoob, I. (1964). Development of a sensation-seeking scale. *Journal of Consulting Psychology, 28,* 477–482.

Index